B&B

21st Edition 2009

The Australian
Bed & Breakfast
Book

Australia's Best Accommodation Guide

2009

Hundreds of Great Places to Stay . . .

"An amazing, relaxing experience. Never wanted to leave! Can't wait to get back."
Rebecca and Russell stayed at Lake Weyba Cottages, Peregian Beach, Qld.

"Hut on the Hill is the perfect escape! Astrid and David spared no expense in ensuring our time spent at the Hut was truly indulgent! Such beautiful views – especially at sunset."
Laura and Tom Whitehall stayed at Hut on the Hill, Heathcote, Vic.

"Good food, great people and the entertainment from the children was first class."
Drew Fairley stayed at Arrowee House, Gloucester, NSW.

"Toni and Richard have created a modern paradise, yet staying in the tune of Old Broome."
Kylie Grima stayed at BroomeTown B&B, Broome, WA.

THE AUSTRALIAN BED & BREAKFAST BOOK 2009
Australia's Best Accommodation Guide

Layout: Matt Thomas
Maps: Elizabeth Thomas
Editing and Spanish Translation: Ian Southern
Printing: Book Builders, Hong Kong
Paper: Printed on paper produced from Sustainable Growth Forest

Australia Distribution: Tower Books Frenchs Forest; Gordon and Gotch Frenchs Forest
UK and Europe Distribution: Vine House Distribution Ltd, Hampshire
New Zealand Distribution: Moonshine Press, Wellington
US Distribution: Pelican Publishing Company, Inc., Gretna, LA

Published October 2008
Editor Carl Southern

Inn Australia Pty Ltd
PO Box 330, Wahroonga, NSW 2076, Australia
Tel: +61 2 8208 5959 Fax: +61 2 9487 6650
Email: info@BBBook.com.au Web: www.BBBook.com.au

21st Edition
Copyright © October 2008 Inn Australia Pty Ltd

Includes Index
ISBN 978-0-9758040-4-9

We welcome your comments or suggestions

Cover Image:
Bowerbank Mill **by Peter Noel-Perkins**, Evansdale, Tasmania

Australia's Best Accommodation Guide

Accommodation with Outstanding Gardens
Pet Friendly Stays
Romantic Stays
Family Getaways
Accommodation with Easy Access
Breakaways with Wine Activities
Eco-Tourism
Self-Contained Cottages and Apartments
Bed & Breakfasts and Farmstays
Country Cabins and Beach Houses
Historic Inns
Guesthouses and Small Hotels

"We received the greatest hospitality, slept in the most wonderful bed and enjoyed the best breakfast in a long, long time. We will return!"
From one of our guests.

ACKNOWLEDGEMENTS

In this our 21st edition of The Bed & Breakfast Book we would like to thank the many thousands of B&B hosts across Australia who have brought the concept of Bed & Breakfast to millions of Australian and overseas guests for more than 20 years. This year we welcome more than 60 new properties to the B&B Book who join over 240 hosts from previous years in our 2009 edition.

Running a B&B is a rewarding experience. B&B hosts welcome strangers into their homes with little more than a phone call or email beforehand, but invariably guests leave as friends. Most hosts run their businesses as lifestyle options, a chance to meet people and share their home and town with others. Most B&Bs, whether traditional or self contained, are run by the owners themselves. They are your concierge, cook and cleaner. They meet and greet you, service your room and prepare your breakfast. Many extras are often included at no additional cost, a welcome drink on arrival, a bowl of fruit or fresh flowers in the room. The industry has grown through enterprise and personal investment, with little outside support and often idiosyncratic bureaucracy to say the least.

We used to be called the throw-away society with disposable this and that. But a book is one item of the household that we rarely discard. So I would like to thank all the hundreds of thousands of Australians and many thousands of overseas visitors who have used the Bed & Breakfast Book over the years to find their accommodation. To date over 400 000 copies have been printed. You might ask why a book is needed in the 21st century when we can look everything up today on the internet or mobile phone? Yes, we are on the internet too at www.BBBook.com.au but a book still feels good in the hands. It's quicker to flick through than search on net, it's easier to put in the glove box of the car, it doesn't require power to operate, it's the perfect gift, it's stylish, colourful and full of hundreds of getaway ideas. And at $19.95 it's great value, too.

I will here place an acknowledgement of thanks to all of you who use the book and a simple request. Please tell you host, "I found you in The B&B Book."

Thanks again to our in-house production team at Moonshine Press in New Zealand, particularly to Elizabeth Thomas who works tirelessly for The New Zealand Bed & Breakfast Book and to Matt Thomas who makes all the information hosts supply look so appealing in the book. Much appreciation to Ian Southern in Spain for his support in editing listing entries. To the team at Bookbuilders, Adam Crouch and Sarah Hilsden in Sydney and Kevin Kwan in Hong Kong We remain a small in-house publisher so many thanks to our many distributors around the world for their help in promoting Australian B&Bs: Tower Books, Gordon and Gotch and Australia Post in Australia, Vine House in the UK, Pelican Inc. in the US and Moonshine Press in New Zealand.

To all hosts and guests who regularly contact us with their comments, suggestions and valuable feedback on the properties included - your contributions are priceless. Last, but never least, we are indebted to you - the travelling public who use the Original Green Accommodation Guide to choose your next family getaway, romantic interlude or a stopover when travelling. We thank you for your ongoing support of our B&B hosts,

Carl Southern

Contents

THE AUSTRALIAN BED & BREAKFAST BOOK 2009
Australia's Best Accommodation Guide

B&B Hosts Treat You As Special Guests

If you take a look around Australia today you will find significant changes in the way we live to Australia of twenty or so years ago when we first published the Bed & Breakfast Book. The quarter acre block has disappeared and our homes are built closer than ever to our neighbour. The small hedgerows fronting our gardens have been replaced by walls and fences. We meet our neighbours only when we leave the garbage and recycling bins by the kerbside or when we pick up the mail. Walking your dog is still a good excuse to meet your neighbours, somehow the family pet identifies us a friendly person.

Whilst we live closer than ever to one another in our increasing congested cities, it seems our lifestyle options are taking us further than ever from the community in which we live. But there are many who still love their community and want to share it with others. They are the B&B hosts of the 21st century.

B&B Book hosts treat you as a special guest from the moment you arrive until the moment you leave.

If, after staying at a B&B you arrive home and realise you have left something you will probably find it's not too long before your host calls and offers to forward your belongings to you. If you are unwell, they'll call the doctor or even drive you to the surgery. Some hosts will pick up at the airport or rail station, others will provide for special diets, many will offer you welcome drinks on arrival and suggest local restaurants or even cook you a meal for a small additional charge.

So what are the differences between B&Bs of the 1980's and the B&Bs of today? Whether you choose a traditional homestay B&B or the purpose built self contained cottage, you will find It's easier to consider what is unchanged.

B&B Book hosts still offer Great Accommodation, Good Value and Generous Hospitality.

If you want to be spoilt or pampered choose a traditional B&B, if you want some private time choose the self contained. But in all the properties you choose from the B&B Book you will find that spirit of community is still there for you to enjoy and take home with you after you leave.

Australian B&Bs now cover all styles with many shades in between. To be included in the B&B Book hosts guarantee to meet a set of standards - our Quality Assurance, which covers housekeeping, facilities and hospitality. Put simply it means no unpleasant surprises after you arrive.

If you are new to the B&B Book or to staying in one of the properties included, we suggest you take a few minutes and read our Quick Guide. Then check out the hundreds of properties included in the book. Most properties now have their own websites which we gladly include within each listing to assist you find further information before making your booking.

Please tell your hosts, *"I found you in The B&B Book."*

© Carl Southern 2008

A QUICK GUIDE

Properties included in The Bed & Breakfast Book offer wonderful accommodation, fantastic breakfasts and outstanding value. They are the ideal way to appreciate genuine Australian Hospitality. B&B hosts can suggest wonderful places to visit, recommend the best restaurants or even prepare a wonderful meal. Above all they promise superior hospitality and are committed to ensuring your stay is both enjoyable and memorable.

Each entry in the guide has been written by the hosts themselves and you will discover the special features of the accommodation through their eyes, and their warmth and personality through their writing.

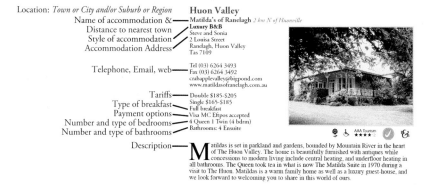

Location: *Town or City and/or Suburb or Region*
Name of accommodation &
Distance to nearest town
Style of accommodation
Accommodation Address

Telephone, Email, web

Tariffs
Type of breakfast
Payment options
Number and type of bedrooms
Number and type of bathrooms

Description

Huon Valley

Matilda's of Ranelagh *2 km N of Huonville*
Luxury B&B
Steve and Sonia
2 Louisa Street
Ranelagh, Huon Valley
Tas 7109

Tel (03) 6264 3493
Fax (03) 6264 3492
crabapplevalley@bigpond.com
www.matildasofranelagh.com.au

Double $185-$205
Single $165-$185
Full breakfast
Visa MC Eftpos accepted
4 Queen 1 Twin (4 bdrm)
Bathrooms: 4 Ensuite

Matildas is set in parkland and gardens, bounded by Mountain River in the heart of The Huon Valley. The home is beautifully furnished with antiques while concessions to modern living include central heating, and underfloor heating in all bathrooms. The Queen took tea in what is now The Matilda Suite in 1970 during a visit to The Huon. Matildas is a warm family home as well as a luxury guest-house, and we look forward to welcoming you to share in this world of ours.

Accommodation

Accommodation included in the B&B Book covers a range of styles, each with uniquely different characteristics. Some properties offer simple and homely B&B accommodation, others offer grand suites or luxurious self contained facilities.

You will have your own comfortable and private bedroom*, usually with a private or ensuite bathroom. Breakfast+ is usually included in your room rate.

* Some accommodation, for example in ski regions offer share accommodation.
+ Some properties usually self contained offer accommodation only or offer breakfast for a small additional charge.

Styles

Homestay: Private bedrooms. Guests share living or dining rooms with hosts.
B&B: Private bedrooms. Guests share living and dining rooms with other guests.
Separate Suite: Private accommodation, usually includes dining and living areas.
Self-Contained: Separate accommodation with kitchen, living and dining areas.
Farmstay: Accommodation on a working farm with farm activities.
Guesthouse or Hotel: Larger style accommodation, often with a restaurant but retaining the warm hospitality found in B&Bs.
Luxury: Higher quality accommodation, often including quality furnishings, bed linen and toiletries.

Accommodation Description

Each listing entry and photograph in the guide has been provided by the hosts themselves through which you will discover the uniqueness of the accommodation. Entries are arranged alphabetically by states, then city or region.

Icons

- **Swimming Pool** – great for a cool swim on a hot day
- **Accommodation with Outstanding Gardens or Unique Location** – great if you are a garden lover
- **Winery or Wine Activities** – Accommodation at a vineyard or where wine activities are possible
- **Restaurant** – Accommodation next to or with a restaurant as part of the facilities
- **Eco Tourism** – Accommodation complying with or supporting Eco tourism
- **Accommodation with Onsite Activities** – maybe horse riding, farm activities or tennis
- **Easy Access** – suitable for less able or non ambulant guests
- **Children Welcome** – contact hosts first. Some hosts have facilities for babies only, others for older children
- **Accommodation for Adults/Romantic Getaways** - Some accommodation is designed for romantic getaways, other properties might have unfenced water such as dams making it unsuitable for children
- **Pets Welcome** – contact hosts first to check on facilities available
- **No Smoking on Property** – just fresh air
- **Member of State B&B Association or approved by the B&B Book**
- **AAA Tourism Assessed** – the stars!
- **Tourism Accredited** – the green tick issued by Australian Tourism Accreditation Association

Breakfast

After a good night's rest, breakfast is the meal that 'breaks' our 'fast' between night and day. Too often today, it is a meal that is neglected at worst or rushed at best. But to a B&B host a good breakfast is the most important meal of the day. Whether it is a traditional country breakfast of well cured bacon and farm fresh eggs or a platter of seasonal fruits, home made bread and preserves, it will be generous and is one of the pleasures of a good B&B. Your breakfast is included unless otherwise indicated.

Some B&Bs request an additional charge for a cooked breakfast. Some hosts also cater for special diets.

Continental or Light: Usually includes cereals, bread or toast, fruit or fruit juice, tea or coffee.

Full: A light breakfast plus a cooked course.

Breakfast Provisions: Breakfast supplies or Welcome Basket provided. ie Supplies sufficient for a Continental Breakfast, Full Breakfast or sufficient for the first night only.

Accommodation Only: Some Self Contained Accommodation does not provide breakfast or offers breakfast for a small addition charge.

Special: Ask your host for details. Some hosts offer gourmet breakfast. Some hosts offer varied options for B&B or Self Contained Accommodation.

Additional Meals

Some B&Bs, farmstays, rural B&Bs or guesthouses offer additional meals. Others offer barbecue packages or picnic hampers. You may need to request meals in advance or by arrangement (B/A).

Beds and Bedrooms

Entries show the number and size of beds, bedrooms and guests that can stay.
Beds for 1 person:
Single (1 bed)
Twin (2 single beds)
King twin (2 large single beds)
Beds for 2 persons:
Double (small)
Queen (large)
King (very large)

Bathrooms

Most accommodation provides ensuite or private bathrooms for your exclusive use. Older or historic B&Bs may offer private bathrooms for your exclusive use but off the hallway. Some B&Bs offer luxurious bathrooms - some with spas.
Ensuite: Exclusive use from your bedroom
Private: Exclusive use, usually off the hallway
Shared: Shared with other guests.

Reservations

We recommend that you book well in advance to confirm your accommodation. Book directly with your host by email or telephone. Advise dates of arrival and departure, time of arrival, the room/s you require, how many guests in your party, if you are travelling with children or pets or any special requirements. Some B&Bs have minimum stays during peak periods. You may need to pay a deposit in advance. Ask how much is due, when full payment is required and the cancellation policy. Most hosts accept credit cards.

Tariffs

B&Bs offer great value accommodation, particularly as your breakfast is included. Rates shown include GST and are valid for the current year but are subject to change. They are for two persons (double) or 1 person (single) and vary according to the quality of the accommodation, the location, the facilities offered and seasonal variations. Low season or midweek bookings can offer good value particularly in popular tourism destinations. Confirm rates when booking. Some hosts offer discounts for extended stays. Some can put another bed in the room, for an extra person for a small additional charge.

Check-In

Hosts are often flexible with check-in and check-out times. Check-in times are usually from 1.00 -3.00 in the afternoon with check-out 10.00-12.00 in the morning.

Conditions of Stay

Hosts welcoming guests to stay at their accommodation aim to provide not only you but subsequent guests similar experiences of wonderful accommodation and great hospitality. Most hosts keep their terms and conditions to a minimum; some may invite you to 'sign-in' on arrival and agree to their 'Conditions of Stay'. This could cover you as well as the host in case of an unforseen incident. Moreover it guarantees all guests that the accommodation will always offer the finest standards.

B&B Gift Vouchers

B&B Book Vouchers are a great Way to Travel. Purchase before you travel and use them in exchange for staying at accommodation included in The Bed & Breakfast Book. They are also the perfect Gift for birthdays, anniversaries, or Corporate Gifts. You may purchase Bed & Breakfast Book Vouchers to any value. Each Voucher comes with a copy of The Australian Bed & Breakfast Book (worth $19.95). There is a small handling charge.

B&B Book Orders

Order a copy of The Australian Bed & Breakfast Book or The New Zealand Bed & Breakfast Book as a gift for a friend or relative. Books are only $19.95 each plus postage and handling: $4.95 Australia, $15 international airmail.
Or mention this ad in the 2009 B&B Book and receive your book postage free.

Order Gift Vouchers or Books directly from:

The Bed & Breakfast Book
PO Box 330
Wahroonga
NSW 2076
info@BBBook.com.au
(02) 8208 5959

The Website - www.BBBook.com.au

Some guests prefer books – some the web. We like books but acknowledge the role of the web, which is why you can find all entries included in The Bed & Breakfast book on our comprehensive website at www.BBBook.com.au You will find more information on each property, more photographs and direct links to each B&B hosts own website.

Tell Your Hosts, "I Found You In The B&B Book!"

Accommodation

www.bbbook.com.au/index.html *Browse By Maps*
www.bbbook.com.au/search.html *Search for a B&B*

More Information

www.bbbook.com.au/about_the_book.html *About the Book*
www.bbbook.com.au/faq.html *FAQs*
www.bbbook.com.au/buy_the_book.html *Buy the Book*
www.bbbook.com.au/contact.html *Contact Us*

Joining the Book

www.bbbook.com.au/newlisting.html *Registration Form*
www.bbbook.com.au/about_joining.html *Become a Member*
www.bbbook.com.au/services_hosts.html *Benefits for Members*

Other Countries

www.bnb.co.nz *New Zealand*

Members Only

www.bbbook.com.au/members.html *Members' Login*

B&Bs For Sale

Are you looking to buy a B&B or even to sell your existing property?

Visit **www.Inn.com.au** and click on B&Bs For Sale.

Quality Assurance

Properties included in The Australian Bed & Breakfast Book offer a Commitment to Generous Hospitality and guarantee to offer the following standards

Housekeeping
The Property is well maintained internally and externally
Absolute cleanliness in all guest areas
Absolute cleanliness in the kitchen, refrigerator and food storage areas
All inside rooms are non-smoking unless indicated in the text

Hospitality
Hosts present to welcome and farewell guests (unless advised in self-contained accommodation)
Guests treated with courtesy and respect
Guests have contact details if hosts leave the premises
Room rates, booking and cancellation policy advised to guests
Local tourism and transport information available.

Bedrooms
Bedrooms solely dedicated to guests with -
bedroom heating and cooling appropriate to the climate
fans and heating (alternatively reverse cycle air-conditioning)
quality mattresses in sound condition on a sound base
clean bedding appropriate to the climate, with extra available
clean pillows with extra available
bedside lighting for each guest
blinds or curtains on all windows where appropriate
night light or torch in case of power failures
wardrobe space with selection of hangers
adequate storage space
good quality floor coverings in good condition
adequate sized mirror
power point
alarm clock
waste bin
drinking glasses

Bathrooms
Sufficient bathroom and toilet facilities for all guests -
bath or shower
hand basin and mirror
waste bin in bathroom
extra toilet roll
privacy lock on bathroom and toilet doors
power point
soap, towels, bathmat, facecloths, for each guest
towels changed or dried daily for guests staying more than one night
Towel rail/hook per guest in the bathroom or bedroom

Meals
Drinks: water, tea and coffee offered or available
Breakfast: A generous breakfast is provided (unless advised otherwise in self-contained accommodation)
Breakfast: Self Contained Accommodation indicates if Hamper/Breakfast provisions are provided or Accommodation Only

General
Roadside identification of property
An honest and accurate description of listing details and facilities
Hosts accept responsibility to comply with government regulations
Description includes if hosts' pets and young children are sharing a common area with guests
Operational Smoke Alarms
Adequate Public and Product Liability under a B&B Insurance Policy

Optional extras
Lock on guest rooms or secure storage facilities available
Air-conditioning, particularly in hotter areas
Laundry facilities for guests
Bathroom/toilet - air freshener, tissues
Television, radio, fresh flowers, magazines, books, fresh fruit
Membership of State B&B Association
Accredited Tourism Business (Green Tick)
Independently inspected B&B (eg, by AAA Tourism or B&B Association)

Tell hosts you found them in the Bed & Breakfast Book

☛ PETS WELCOME

These properties welcome guests travelling with pets. Some welcome small 'house dogs' inside, other may have a run or enclosure for larger animals. Do contact hosts beforehand to ask what facilities are available.

ACT:
Canberra - Hall: Surveyor's Hill Winery and B&B
Canberra - MacGregor: Grevillea Lodge

NSW:
Armidale: Poppys Cottage
Bega Valley - Bemboka: Giba Gunyah
Bellingen: Bellingen Heritage Cottages
Berry - Kangaroo Valley: Barefoot Springs
Berry - Kangaroo Valley: Wombat Hill B&B
Candelo - Bega Valley: Bumblebrook Farm
Central Coast - Tuggerah: Greenacres B&B
Coffs Harbour Hinterland - Dorrigo: Fernbrook Lodge
Dubbo - Central West: Walls Court B&B
Dunedoo - Central West: Redbank Gums B&B
Glen Innes - Ben Lomond: Silent Grove
Grafton - Seelands: Seeview Farm
Hunter Valley - Aberdeen: Craigmhor Mountain Retreat
Hunter Valley - Lochinvar: Lochinvar House
Hunter Valley - Pokolbin: Catersfield House
Narooma - Tilba: Pub Hill Farm
Newcastle - Hamilton: Hamilton Heritage
Parkes: The Old Parkes Convent
Port Macquarie - Camden Haven: Benbellen Country Retreat
Port Macquarie - Camden Haven: Penlan Cottage
Port Macquarie - Camden Haven: Cherry Tree Cottage
Springwood - Faulconbridge: Mountain Jewel
Sydney: Bed & Breakfast Sydney Central
Sydney - Balmain: An Oasis In The City
Sydney - Forestville: Jan's Forestville B&B
Sydney - Paddington: Paddington B&B
Taree - Wingham: Tallowood Ridge
Taree - Wingham: The Bank Guesthouse
Thredbo - Jindabyne - Snowy Mountains: Bimblegumbie
Ulladulla: Ulladulla Guest House
Yass: Kerrowgair
Young - Cootamundra: Old Nubba Schoolhouse

NT:
Alice Springs: Kathy's Place Bed & Breakfast
Alice Springs: The Hideaway

QLD:
Cairns - Holloways Beach: Billabong B&B
Cairns - Stratford: Lilybank
Cairns Hinterland - Kuranda: Koah B&B
Gold Coast Hinterland - Nerang: Riviera B&B
Hervey Bay - Howard: Montrave House
Stanthorpe: Jireh

SA:
Adelaide - North Adelaide: Cornwall Park
Adelaide - Seacliff Park - Brighton: Homestay Brighton
Adelaide - Somerton Park: Forstens B&B
Barossa Valley - Lyndoch: Bellescapes
Strathalbyn - Fleurieu Peninsula: Watervilla

TAS:
Launceston: Alice's Cottages and Spa
Port Arthur - Taranna: Norfolk Bay Convict Station

VIC:
Alexandra: Idlewild Park Farm Accommodation
Bairnsdale: Tara House
Cudgewa - Corryong: Elmstead Cottages
Dandenong Ranges: Candlelight Cottages
Dandenong Ranges - Mount Dandenong: Observatory Cottages
Heathcote - Goldfields: Emeu Inn Bed & Breakfast, Restaurant and Wine Centre
Horsham: Orange Grove B&B
Melbourne - Fairfield: Fairfield Guest House
Rutherglen: Mount Ophir Estate
Swan Hill - Lake Boga: Burrabliss Farms
Wangaratta: The Pelican
Warrnambool - Allansford: Burnbrow
Gingin - Muckenburra: Amirage

♔ CHILDREN WELCOME

There area whole variety of properties that welcome families travelling with children. Some have cots available, others are more suitable for older children. Do contact hosts beforehand to ask what facilities are available.

ACT:
Canberra - Hall: Surveyor's Hill Winery and B&B
Canberra - MacGregor: Grevillea Lodge
NSW:
Adaminaby - Snowy Mountains: Reynella
Albury: Elizabeth's Manor
Alstonville - Ballina: Hume's Hovell
Armidale: Poppys Cottage
Armidale - Uralla: Cruickshanks Farmstay B&B
Batemans Bay: Chalet Swisse Spa
Bawley Point: Interludes at Bawley
Bega Valley - Bemboka: Giba Gunyah
Bellingen: Bellingen Heritage Cottages
Berry - Kangaroo Valley: Wombat Hill B&B
Blue Mountains - Blackheath: Amani B&B
Blue Mountains - Hampton - Jenolan Caves: Hampton Homestead
Blue Mountains - Lithgow: Majic Views B&B
Blue Mountains - Wentworth Falls: Blue Mountains Lakeside
Blue Mountains - Woodford: Braeside
Candelo - Bega Valley: Bumblebrook Farm
Central Coast - Tuggerah: Greenacres B&B
Coffs Harbour Hinterland - Dorrigo: Fernbrook Lodge
Crookwell: Markdale Homestead
Dubbo - Central West: Walls Court B&B
Dunedoo - Central West: Redbank Gums B&B
Gerringong - Gerroa: Tumblegum Inn
Glen Innes: Halloran House
Glen Innes - Ben Lomond: Silent Grove B&B
Gloucester - Barrington Tops: Arrowee House

Grafton - Seelands: Seeview Farm
Hunter Valley - Aberdeen - Scone: Craigmhor Mountain Retreat
Hunter Valley - Broke: Ferguson's Hunter Valley Getaway
Hunter Valley - Lochinvar:; Lochinvar House
Hunter Valley - Lovedale - Pokolbin: Hill Top Country Guest House
Hunter Valley - Pokolbin: Catersfield House
Hunter Valley - Pokolbin: Elfin Hill
Hunter Valley - Pokolbin: Holman Estate
Hunter Valley - Wollombi: Capers
Jervis Bay - Vincentia: Nelson Beach Lodge
Jindabyne - Snowy Mountains: Troldhaugen
Kiama: Kiama Bed & Breakfast
Kiama: Seashells Kiama
Merimbula: Robyn's Nest Guest House
Milton - Mollymook - Ulladulla: Meadowlake Lodge
Nambucca Heads - Macksville: Jacaranda
Narooma - Tilba: Pub Hill Farm
Narromine: Camerons Farmstay
Newcastle: Newcomen B&B
Newcastle - Hamilton: Hamilton Heritage
Newcastle - Merewether: Merewether Beach B&B
Parkes: Kadina B&B
Parkes: The Old Parkes Convent
Port Macquarie - Camden Haven: Benbellen
Port Macquarie - Camden Haven: Penlan Cottage
Port Macquarie - Camden Haven: Cherry Tree Cottage
Springwood - Faulconbridge: Mountain Jewel

Sydney: Bed & Breakfast Sydney Central
Sydney: Manor House Boutique Hotel
Sydney - Chatswood: The Charrington of Chatswood
Sydney - Engadine: Engadine B&B
Sydney - Forestville - Manly: Jan's Forestville B&B
Sydney - Glebe: Cathie Lesslie B&B
Sydney - Hunters Hill: Magnolia House B&B
Sydney - Marrickville: Michaela's Place
Sydney - Newtown: Golden Grove B&B
Sydney - Northern Beaches Peninsula: The Pittwater Bed & Breakfast
Sydney - Paddington: Paddington B&B
Sydney - Parramatta: Harborne B&B
Sydney - Potts Point: Simpsons of Potts Point Boutique Hotel
Sydney - Rose Bay: Syl's Sydney Homestay
Sydney - Scotland Island: Scotland Island Lodge
Taree - Wingham: Tallowood Ridge
Taree - Wingham: The Bank Guesthouse
The Entrance - Blue Bay: Talinga
Thredbo   Candlelight Lodge
Thredbo - Jindabyne - Snowy Mountains: Bimblegumbie
Tilba Tilba - Narooma: Green Gables
Ulladulla   Ulladulla Guest House
Wagga Wagga: Dunn's B&B
Wellington: Carinya B&B
Yass: Kerrowgair
Yass - Rye Park: The Old School
Young - Cootamundra: Old Nubba Schoolhouse

NT:
Alice Springs: Kathy's Place Bed & Breakfast
Alice Springs: The Hideaway
Darwin - Fogg Dam - Humpty Doo: Eden at Fogg Dam
Darwin - Malak: Beale's Bedfish & Breakfast

QLD:
Airlie Beach - Whitsunday: Whitsunday Moorings B&B
Airlie Beach - Whitsundays: Whitsunday Heritage Cane Cutters Cottage
Brisbane - Birkdale: Birkdale B&B
Brisbane - Paddington: Fern Cottage B&B
Brisbane - Shorncliffe: Naracoopa B&B
Brisbane - West End: Eskdale B&B
Cairns - Edge Hill: Galvin's Edge Hill B&B
Cairns - Lake Tinaroo: Tinaroo Haven
Cairns Hinterland - Kuranda: Koah B&B
Daintree - Cape Tribulation: Cape Trib Exotic Fruit Farm
Daintree - Cow Bay: Cow Bay Homestay
Eumundi: Eumundi Rise B&B
Gold Coast Hinterland - Nerang: Riviera B&B
Hervey Bay - Howard: Montrave House
Kingaroy: Rock-Al-Roy B&B
Noosa - Lake Weyba: Eumarella Shores
Noosa Hinterland - Cooroy: Cudgerie Homestead B&B
Rainbow Beach: Rainbow Ocean Palms
Rockhampton - Capricorn Coast: Brae Bothy
Stanthorpe: Jireh
Sunshine Coast Hinterland - Maleny: Maleny Country Cottages

SA:

Adelaide - Burnside - St Georges: Kirkendale
Adelaide - Glenelg: Water Bay Villa B&B
Adelaide - Largs Bay: Seapod B&B
Adelaide - North Adelaide: Cornwall Park Heritage Accommodation
Adelaide - Seacliff Park - Brighton: Homestay Brighton
Adelaide - Somerton Park: Forstens B&B
Adelaide Hills - Mt Pleasant: Saunders Gorge Sanctuary
Barossa Valley - Lyndoch: Bellescapes
Barossa Valley - Tanunda: Goat Square Cottages
Kangaroo Island - Emu Bay: Seascape on Emu Bay
Limestone Coast - Beachport: Bompas
Naracoorte: Willowbrook Cottages B&B's
Strathalbyn - Fleurieu Peninsula: Watervilla

TAS:

Deloraine: Bowerbank Mill B&B
Derwent Bridge: Derwent Bridge Chalets & Studios
Hobart - Battery Point - Sandy Bay: Grande Vue & Star Apartments
Hobart - Lindisfarne: Orana House
Launceston: Trevallyn House B&B
Launceston: Alice's Cottages and Spa
Port Arthur - Taranna: Norfolk Bay Convict Station
Richmond: Mulberry Cottage B&B
Richmond: Mrs Curries Bed and Breakfast
Swansea: Schouten House

VIC:

Alexandra: Idlewild Park Farm
Apollo Bay: Arcady Homestead
Bairnsdale: Tara House
Cudgewa - Corryong: Elmstead Cottages
Dandenong Ranges: Candlelight Cottages
Dandenong Ranges - Sassafras: Clarendon Cottages
Geelong: Ardara House
Grampians - Wartook: Wartook Gardens
Grampians - Wartook Valley: The Grelco Run
Heathcote - Goldfields: Emeu Inn Bed & Breakfast, Restaurant and Wine Centre
Heathcote - Goldfields: Hut on the Hill
Horsham Orange Grove B&B
Macedon Ranges - Sunbury: Rupertswood
Melbourne - Camberwell: Springfields
Melbourne - Fairfield: Fairfield Guest House
Melbourne - Richmond: Rotherwood
Melbourne - St Kilda: Alrae Bed & Breakfast
Princetown - Twelve Apostles: Arabella
Rutherglen: Mount Ophir Estate
Sarsfield - Bairnsdale: Stringybark Cottages B&B
Swan Hill - Lake Boga: Burrabliss Farms B&B
Torquay - Surf Coast: Ocean Manor B&B
Wangaratta: The Pelican
Warrnambool: Manor Gums
Warrnambool: Quamby Homestead
Warrnambool - Allansford: Burnbrow
Wilsons Promontory - Waratah North: Bayview House

WA:

Bunbury: Colomberie B&B
Dongara - Geraldton: Gracelyn B&B
Fremantle Terrace Central B&B
Gingin - Muckenburra: Amirage
Mandurah - Peel Region: Port Mandurah Canal B&B
Margaret River: The Noble Grape
Perth: Pension of Perth

♿ ACCOMMODATION WITH EASY ACCESS

Some accommodation have facilities for less ambulant guests that are fully accredited, others may have a step or a bathroom slightly too small to be fully accredited but nonetheless may be suitable for less ambulant guests. Do contact hosts beforehand to ask what facilities are available.

ACT:
Canberra - Hall: Surveyor's Hill Winery and B&B
NSW:
Alstonville - Ballina: Hume's Hovell
Bega Valley - Bemboka: Giba Gunyah
Blue Mountains - Hampton - Jenolan Caves: Hampton Homestead
Blue Mountains - Lithgow: Majic Views B&B
Byron Bay: Victoria's Byron Bay
Candelo - Bega Valley: Bumblebrook Farm
Central Coast - Tuggerah: Greenacres B&B
Crookwell: Markdale Homestead
Dorrigo: Lisnagarvey Cottage
Glen Innes: Halloran House
Glen Innes - Ben Lomond: Silent Grove
Gloucester - Barrington Tops: Arrowee House
Hunter Valley - Aberdeen - Scone: Craigmhor Mountain Retreat
Hunter Valley - Broke: Ferguson's Getaway
Hunter Valley - Lochinvar: Lochinvar House
Hunter Valley - Lovedale - Pokolbin: Hill Top Country Guest House
Hunter Valley - Pokolbin: Catersfield House
Hunter Valley - Pokolbin: Elfin Hill
Jervis Bay - Huskisson: Sandholme
Merimbula: Robyn's Nest Guest House
Nambucca Heads - Macksville: Jacaranda Country Lodge
Newcastle - Hamilton: Hamilton Heritage
Pacific Palms - Coomba: Whitby on Wallis
Sydney - Hawkesbury - Colo: Ossian Hall
Sydney - Marrickville: Michaela's Place
Taree - Wingham: The Bank Guesthouse
Ulladulla: Ulladulla Guest House
Urunga: Aquarelle Bed & Breakfast
Wollongong - Mount Pleasant: Above Wollongong at Pleasant Heights B&B
Yass: Kerrowgair

NT:
Darwin - Malak: Beale's Bedfish & Breakfast
QLD:
Cairns - Lake Tinaroo: Tinaroo Haven Holiday Lodge
Cairns - Stratford: Lilybank
Cairns Hinterland - Kuranda: Koah B&B
Eumundi: Eumundi Rise B&B
Gold Coast Hinterland - Nerang: Riviera B&B
Noosa - Peregian: Lake Weyba Cottages
Rockhampton - Capricorn Coast: Brae Bothy
Sunshine Coast Hinterland - Maleny: Maleny Country Cottages
Yeppoon - Capricorn Coast: While Away B&B
SA:
Adelaide - North Adelaide: Cornwall Park
Kangaroo Island - Emu Bay: Seascape on Emu Bay
Strathalbyn - Fleurieu Peninsula: Watervilla
Beauty Point: Pomona Spa Cottages
Derwent Bridge: Derwent Bridge Chalets & Studios
Hobart - Lindisfarne: Orana House
Huon Valley: Matilda's of Ranelagh
Richmond: Mrs Curries Bed and Breakfast
VIC:
Apollo Bay: Arcady Homestead
Grampians - Halls Gap: Mountain Grand
Heathcote - Goldfields: Hut on the Hill
Macedon Ranges - Sunbury: Rupertswood
Melbourne - Fairfield: Fairfield Guest House
Rutherglen: Mount Ophir Estate
Sarsfield - Bairnsdale: Stringybark Cottages B&B
Warrnambool: Quamby Homestead
WA:
Margaret River: The Noble Grape
Pinjarra - Peel Region: Lazy River B&B

❀ OUTSTANDING GARDENS OR UNIQUE LOCATION

Australians have a love affair with gardens! Whilst the drought may cause a problem for you at home, many hosts are able to show creative ways to use water wisely and still have a beautiful garden. Others are fortunate and live in parts of the country where droughts are not so much of a problem or just have a unique location.

NSW:

Alstonville - Ballina: Hume's Hovell
Armidale - Uralla: Cruickshanks Farmstay
Batemans Bay: Chalet Swisse Spa
Bawley Point: Interludes at Bawley
Bega Valley - Bemboka: Giba Gunyah
Bellingen: Bellingen Heritage Cottages
Berry - Kangaroo Valley: Barefoot Springs
Berry - Kangaroo Valley: Wombat Hill B&B
Blue Mountains - Blackheath: Amani B&B
Blue Mountains - Hampton - Jenolan Caves: Hampton Homestead
Blue Mountains - Leura: Broomelea
Blue Mountains - Leura: Bethany Manor
Blue Mountains - Leura: Magical Manderley
Byron Bay: Victoria's Byron Bay
Byron Bay Hinterland: Green Mango Hideaway
Central Coast - Terrigal: AnDaCer B&B
Central Coast - Tuggerah: Greenacres B&B
Coffs Harbour Hinterland - Dorrigo: Fernbrook Lodge
Crookwell: Markdale Homestead
Hunter Valley - Aberdeen - Scone: Craigmhor Mountain Retreat
Hunter Valley - Lochinvar: Lochinvar House
Hunter Valley - Morpeth: Morpeth Convent
Hunter Valley - Pokolbin: Catersfield House
Hunter Valley - Pokolbin: Elfin Hill
Hunter Valley - Pokolbin: Holman Estate
Hunter Valley - Wollombi: Capers
Jervis Bay - Huskisson: Dolphin Sands
Jervis Bay - Huskisson: Sandholme Guesthouse
Jervis Bay - Vincentia: Nelson Beach Lodge
Kiama: Kiama Bed & Breakfast
Kiama: Bed and Views Kiama
Merimbula: Robyn's Nest Guest House
Milton - Ulladulla: Meadowlake Lodge
Nambucca Heads - Macksville: Jacaranda
Narromine: Camerons Farmstay
Newcastle: Newcomen B&B
Newcastle - Hamilton: Hamilton Heritage
Port Macquarie: Woodlands B&B
Port Macquarie - Camden Haven: Benbellen Country Retreat
Port Macquarie - Camden Haven: Penlan Cottage
Port Macquarie - Camden Haven: Cherry Tree Cottage
Southern Highlands - Bowral: Chorleywood
Springwood - Faulconbridge: Mountain Jewel
Sydney - Engadine: Engadine B&B
Sydney - Glebe: Tricketts
Sydney - Hawkesbury - Colo: Ossian Hall
Sydney - Manly: Pepper Tree B&B
Sydney - Paddington: Paddington B&B
Tamworth: Jacaranda Cottage B&B
Taree - Wingham   Tallowood Ridge
Thredbo - Jindabyne - Snowy Mountains: Bimblegumbie
Tilba Tilba - Narooma: Green Gables
Ulladulla: Ulladulla Guest House
Wellington: Carinya B&B
Wollongong - Corrimal: Corrimal Beach B&B
Wollongong - Mount Pleasant: Above Wollongong at Pleasant Heights B&B
Yass: Kerrowgair

NT:

Alice Springs: Nthaba Cottage B&B
Alice Springs: Kathy's Place Bed & Breakfast
Darwin - Fogg Dam : Eden at Fogg Dam

QLD:

Airlie Beach - Whitsunday: Whitsunday Moorings B&B
Airlie Beach - Whitsunday: Whitsunday Heritage Cane Cutters Cottage
Brisbane - Birkdale: Birkdale B&B
Brisbane - Paddington - Rosalie: Fern Cottage
Bundaberg: Inglebrae
Cairns - Edge Hill: Galvin's Edge Hill B&B
Cairns - Holloways Beach: Billabong B&B
Cairns - Stratford: Lilybank
Daintree - Cow Bay: Cow Bay Homestay
Eumundi: Eumundi Rise B&B
Gold Coast Hinterland - Nerang: Riviera B&B
Hervey Bay: The Chamomile B&B
Hervey Bay: Alexander Lakeside B&B
Hervey Bay - Howard: Montrave House
Noosa - Noosa Valley: Noosa Valley Manor
Noosa - Peregian: Lake Weyba Cottages
Rockhampton - Capricorn Coast: Brae Bothy
Sunshine Coast Hinterland - Glasshouse Mountains: Glass on Glasshouse
Sunshine Coast Hinterland - Montville: Secrets on the Lake
Sunshine Coast Hinterland - Mooloolah Valley: Mooloolah Valley Holidays

SA:

Adelaide - Burnside - St Georges: Kirkendale
Adelaide - College Park: Possums Rest B&B
Adelaide - Glenelg: Water Bay Villa B&B
Adelaide - North Adelaide: Cornwall Park
Adelaide Hills - Stirling: The Retreat
Barossa Valley - Tanunda: Goat Square Cottages
Goolwa: Vue de M B&B

Kangaroo Island - Emu Bay: Seascape on Emu Bay
McLaren Vale: Willunga House
Naracoorte: Willowbrook Cottages B&B's
Strathalbyn - Fleurieu Peninsula: Watervilla
TAS:
Beauty Point: Pomona Spa Cottages
Deloraine: Bowerbank Mill B&B
Devonport - Port Sorell: Tranquilles
Hobart - Lindisfarne: Orana House
Hobart - Rose Bay: Roseneath B&B
Huon Valley: Matilda's of Ranelagh
Richmond: Mrs Curries Bed and Breakfast
VIC:
Alexandra: Idlewild Park Farm
Apollo Bay: Paradise Gardens
Apollo Bay: Point of View
Apollo Bay - Gt. Ocean Road: Glenoe Cottages
Bairnsdale: Tara House
Beechworth: Kinross Guest House
Beechworth: Foxgloves
Castlemaine: Clevedon Manor
Cudgewa - Corryong: Elmstead Cottages
Dandenong Ranges: Candlelight Cottages
Dandenong Ranges - Gembrook: Cherry Garden Cottages
Dandenong Ranges - Mount Dandenong: Observatory Cottages
Dandenong Ranges - Sassafras: Clarendon Cottages
Dandenong Ranges - Yarra Ranges: The Villa Renaissance

Gippsland - Nilma North: Springbank B&B
Grampians - Wartook: Wartook Gardens
Heathcote - Goldfields: Emeu Inn Bed & Breakfast, Restaurant and Wine Centre
Horsham: Orange Grove B&B
Lorne - Otway Ranges: Elliminook
Melbourne - Brighton: Waratah B&B
Mildura: Mildura's Linsley House
Mornington - Mount Eliza: Sartain's
Phillip Island - Cowes: Genesta House
Phillip Island - Cowes: Glen Isla House
Princetown - Twelve Apostles: Arabella
Sarsfield - Bairnsdale: Stringybark Cottages
Sorrento - Mornington Peninsula: Tamasha House
Swan Hill - Lake Boga: Burrabliss Farms B&B
Warrnambool: Merton Manor
Warrnambool: Quamby Homestead
Wilsons Promontory: Bayview House
Yarra Valley - Dandenong Ranges: Holly Gate House Bed and Breakfast
WA:
Brigadoon - Perth Hills: Stocks
Gingin - Muckenburra: Amirage
Mandurah - North Yunderup: Nautica Lodge
Margaret River; The Noble Grape
Margaret River: Rosewood Guesthouse
Perth - Mt Lawley: Durack House B&B
Perth - Nedlands: Caesia House Nedlands
Pinjarra - Peel Region: Lazy River B&B

🍇 Winery or Wine Activities

Some properties are not only located in wine areas but in the vineyard itself. Choose one of the properties below if it is your dream to wake up in the morning surrounded by vines. Some properties also offer wine tasting or other related activities.

ACT:
Canberra - Hall: Surveyor's Hill Winery and B&B
NSW:
Armidale: Poppys Cottage
Bawley Point: Interludes at Bawley
Hunter Valley - Broke: Ferguson's Hunter Valley Getaway
Hunter Valley - Lochinvar: Lochinvar House
Hunter Valley - Pokolbin: Elfin Hill
Hunter Valley - Wine Country - Wollombi: Capers Guest House and Cottage
Kiama: Seashells Kiama
SA:
Barossa Valley - Tanunda: Goat Square Cottages
McLaren Vale: Willunga House

TAS:
Devonport - Port Sorell: Tranquilles
Launceston: Alice's Cottages and Spa
Richmond: Mulberry Cottage B&B
VIC:
Dandenong Ranges - Gembrook: Cherry Garden Cottages
Dandenong Ranges - Sassafras: Clarendon Cottages
Grampians - Halls Gap: Mountain Grand
Heathcote - Goldfields: Emeu Inn Bed & Breakfast, Restaurant and Wine Centre
Heathcote - Goldfields: Hut on the Hill
Rutherglen: Mount Ophir Estate
WA:
Ferguson Valley - Bunbury: Peppermint Lane Lodge
Mandurah - North Yunderup: Nautica Lodge

☯ Eco Tourism

Eco tourism is not all hard work. More and more Australians are looking to live sustainable lives and in harmony with nature. Some properties are fully 'green' accredited. Some offer Eco tourism activities, whilst others use organic foods and environmentally balanced products in their accommodation.

NSW:
Adaminaby - Snowy Mountains: Reynella
Alstonville - Ballina: Hume's Hovell
Batemans Bay: Chalet Swisse Spa
Bega Valley - Bemboka: Giba Gunyah
Berry - Kangaroo Valley: Barefoot Springs
Gloucester - Barrington Tops: Arrowee House
Hunter Valley - Aberdeen - Scone: Craigmhor Mountain Retreat
Hunter Valley - Lovedale - Pokolbin: Hill Top Country Guest House
Port Macquarie - Camden Haven: Benbellen Country Retreat
Port Macquarie - Camden Haven: Penlan Cottage
Port Macquarie - Camden Haven: Cherry Tree Cottage
Sydney - Engadine: Engadine B&B
Thredbo - Jindabyne - Snowy Mountains: Bimblegumbie

QLD:
Airlie Beach - Whitsundays: Whitsunday Heritage Cane Cutters Cottage
Cairns - Lake Tinaroo: Tinaroo Haven Holiday Lodge
Daintree - Cape Tribulation: Cape Trib Exotic Fruit Farm
Noosa - Lake Weyba: Eumarella Shores Lake Retreat
Rainbow Beach: Rainbow Ocean Palms
Sunshine Coast Hinterland - Montville: Secrets on the Lake

SA:
Adelaide Hills - Mt Pleasant: Saunders Gorge Sanctuary
Kangaroo Island - Emu Bay: Seascape on Emu Bay

TAS:
Derwent Bridge: Derwent Bridge Chalets & Studios
Devonport - Port Sorell: Tranquilles
Port Arthur - Taranna: Norfolk Bay Convict Station

VIC:
Bright - Myrtleford: The Buckland
Cudgewa - Corryong: Elmstead Cottages
Dandenong Ranges - Gembrook: Cherry Garden Cottages
Gippsland - Nilma North: Springbank B&B
Heathcote - Goldfields: Hut on the Hill
Princetown - Twelve Apostles: Arabella Country House
Rutherglen: Mount Ophir Estate
Sarsfield - Bairnsdale: Stringybark Cottages B&B

SA:
Kalbarri: Gecko Lodge
Mandurah - North Yunderup: Nautica Lodge
Pinjarra - Peel Region: Lazy River B&B

⚕ ACCOMMODATION WITH ONSITE ACTIVITIES

More are more properties are now offering onsite activities. It may be horse riding or canoeing down the river or farm activities for the children. Some are spas offering full spa treatment facilities for you are your partner.

NSW:
Adaminaby - Snowy Mountains: Reynella
Alstonville - Ballina: Hume's Hovell
Armidale: Poppys Cottage
Batemans Bay: Chalet Swisse Spa
Blue Mountains - Leura: Bethany Manor B&B
Blue Mountains - Wentworth Falls: Blue Mountains Lakeside
Byron Bay: Victoria's Byron Bay
Crookwell: Markdale Homestead
Grafton - Seelands: Seeview Farm
Hunter Valley - Pokolbin: Hill Top
Hunter Valley - Pokolbin: Catersfield House
Jervis Bay - Huskisson: Sandholme
Merimbula: Robyn's Nest Guest House
Milton - Ulladulla: Meadowlake Lodge
Nambucca Heads - Macksville: Jacaranda
Narromine: Camerons Farmstay
Port Macquarie - Camden Haven: Benbellen
Port Macquarie - Camden Haven: Cherry Tree Cottage
Sydney - Hawkesbury - Colo: Ossian Hall
Sydney-Scotland Island: Scotland Island Lodge
Thredbo: Candlelight Lodge

NT:
Darwin - Fogg Dam - Humpty Doo: Eden at Fogg Dam

QLD:
Daintree - Cape Tribulation: Cape Trib Exotic Fruit Farm
Gold Coast Hinterland - Nerang: Riviera B&B
Noosa - Lake Weyba: Eumarella Shores
Noosa - Peregian: Lake Weyba Cottages
Sunshine Coast Hinterland - Montville: Secrets on the Lake
Sunshine Coast Hinterland - Mooloolah Valley: Mooloolah Valley Holidays

TAS:
Kangaroo Island - Emu Bay: Seascape on Emu Bay
Port Arthur - Taranna: Norfolk Bay Convict Station
Richmond: Mulberry Cottage B&B

VIC:
Bright - Myrtleford: The Buckland
Dandenong Ranges - Gembrook: Cherry Garden Cottages
Dandenong Ranges - Yarra Ranges: The Villa Renaissance
Gippsland - Nilma North: Springbank B&B
Grampians - Wartook Valley: The Grelco Run
Mornington - Mount Eliza: Sartain's
Wangaratta: The Pelican
Warrnambool: Quamby Homestead

WA:
Brigadoon-Perth Hills: Stocks Country Retreat
Ferguson Valley - Bunbury: Peppermint Lane Lodge
Mandurah - North Yunderup: Nautica Lodge
Pinjarra - Peel Region: Lazy River B&B

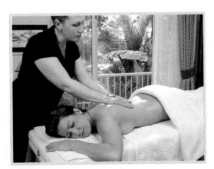

⊕ ACCOMMODATION FOR ADULTS/ROMANTIC GETAWAYS

Many properties in The B&B book are the 'Getaway-from-it-all' option just for you and your partner. So leave the kids at home and be indulged. Other properties might have unfenced water such as dams or creeks making it unsuitable for children.

NSW:

Bellingen: Rivendell
Blue Mountains - Katoomba: Melba House
Blue Mountains - Leura: Bethany Manor B&B
Blue Mountains - Leura: Magical Manderley
Blue Mountains - Leura: Argyll House
Blue Mountains - Mount Tomah - Bells Line of Road: Tomah Mountain Lodge
Byron Bay: Victoria's Byron Bay
Byron Bay Hinterland: Green Mango
Central Coast - Terrigal: AnDaCer B&B
Coffs Harbour - Woolgoolga: Solitary Islands Lodge
Coffs Harbour - Northern Beaches: Headlands Beach Guest House
Eden: Crown & Anchor Inn B&B
Hunter Valley - East Maitland: The Old George and Dragon Guesthouse
Hunter Valley - Morpeth: Bronte Guesthouse
Hunter Valley - Morpeth: Morpeth Convent
Jervis Bay - Huskisson: Dolphin Sands
Jervis Bay - Huskisson: Sandholme
Kiama: Bed and Views Kiama
Murwillumbah - Crystal Creek Hillcrest Mountain View Retreat
Pacific Palms - Coomba: Whitby on Wallis
Port Macquarie   Woodlands B&B
Port Stephens - Shoal Bay: Shoal Bay B&B
Southern Highlands - Bowral: Chorleywood
Southern Highlands - Bowral: Chelsea Park
Sydney - Glebe: Bellevue Terrace
Sydney - Glebe: Pompei Bed and Breakfast
Sydney - Hawkesbury - Colo: Ossian Hall
Sydney - Manly: Pepper Tree B&B
Sydney - Paddington: Harts
Urunga: Aquarelle Bed & Breakfast
Wollongong - Corrimal: Corrimal Beach B&B

NT:

Alice Springs: Nthaba Cottage B&B

QLD:

Bundaberg: Inglebrae
Hervey Bay: The Chamomile B&B
Hervey Bay: Alexander Lakeside B&B
Sunshine Coast - Ninderry: Ninderry House
Sunshine Coast Hinterland - Glasshouse Mountains: Glass on Glasshouse
Sunshine Coast Hinterland - Montville: Secrets on the Lake
Yeppoon - Capricorn Coast: While Away B&B

SA:

Adelaide - College Park: Possums Rest B&B
Goolwa: Vue de M B&B

TAS:

Beauty Point: Pomona Spa Cottages
Devonport - Port Sorell: Tranquilles
Hobart - Rose Bay Roseneath B&B
Huon Valley: Matilda's of Ranelagh

VIC:

Apollo Bay: Paradise Gardens
Apollo Bay: Point of View
Apollo Bay - Gt. Ocean Road: Glenoe Cottages
Beechworth: Kinross Guest House
Beechworth: Freeman on Ford
Beechworth: Foxgloves
Bright - Myrtleford: The Buckland
Dandenong Ranges - Gembrook: Cherry Garden Cottages
Dandenong Ranges - Mount Dandenong: Observatory Cottages
Dandenong Ranges - Yarra Ranges: The Villa Renaissance
Gippsland - Nilma North: Springbank B&B
Grampians - Halls Gap: Mountain Grand
Lorne: La Perouse B&B
Lorne - Aireys Inlet: Lorneview B&B
Lorne - Otway Ranges: Elliminook
Melbourne: Villa Donati
Melbourne - Brighton: Waratah Boutique B&B
Melbourne - Williamstown: Captains Retreat
Mildura Mildura's Linsley House
Mornington - Mount Eliza: Sartain's
Phillip Island - Cowes: Abaleigh
Phillip Island - Cowes: Genesta House
Phillip Island - Cowes: Glen Isla House
Rutherglen: Ready Cottage
Sorrento-Mornington Peninsula: Tamasha House
Warrnambool: Merton Manor Exclusive B&B
Yarra Valley - Dandenong Ranges: Holly Gate House Bed and Breakfast
Yarra Valley - Healesville: Myers Creek Cascades
Yarra Valley - Yarra Glen: The Gatehouse at Villa Raedward

WA:

Albany: Albany View St Lodge B&B
Brigadoon-Perth Hills: Stocks
Broome: BroomeTown B&B
Ferguson Valley - Bunbury: Peppermint Lane Lodge
Kalbarri: Gecko Lodge
Margaret River: Rosewood Guesthouse
Perth - Mt Lawley: Durack House B&B
Perth - Nedlands   Caesia House Nedlands
Pinjarra - Peel Region: Lazy River B&B
Toodyay: Pecan Hill B&B

INTRODUCTION

Bienvenue sur le site du livre Bed & Breakfast, le guide du logement en chambres d'hôte le plus populaire en Australie. Première édition: 1989.

Les chambres d'hôtes (ou B&Bs) offrent une valeur exceptionnelle et sont une manière idéale d'apprécier la véritable hospitalité australienne. Les gîtes touristiques se sont investis pour vous assurer un agréable et mémorable séjour et pour vous proposer une hospitalité supérieure, que vous restiez une nuit ou une semaine. Ils offrent un accueil chaleureux, un excellent logement et des petits déjeuners succulents. Ils peuvent suggérer de magnifiques endroits locaux à visiter, recommander les meilleurs restaurants ou même préparer des recettes maison.

Les chambres d'hôtes comprennent une gamme de styles, chacune avec des caractéristiques exclusivement différentes. Certaines sont simples et confortables, d'autres sont grandes et luxueuses. Votre chambre à coucher sera confortable, généralement avec salle de bains attenante ou privée et le petit déjeuner est habituellement compris dans le tarif de votre chambre.

Hébergement chez l'habitant : Partage du salon et de la salle à manger avec l'hôte.
Chambres d'hôte : Partage du salon et de la salle à manger avec d'autres invités.
Séjour à la ferme : Hébergement dans une ferme en exploitation avec des activités de la ferme.
Indépendant: Hébergement privé avec cuisine, salon et salle à manger.
Suite séparée : Hébergement privé. Sans cuisine.
Maison d'hôte ou hôtel : Un style d'hébergement plus grand, souvent avec un restaurant.
Luxe: Un hébergement de plus haute qualité.

Descriptions des hébergements
Les descriptions sont écrites par les hôtes eux-mêmes. Classées par ordre alphabétique par état, puis par ville ou par région.

Petit déjeuner
Continental ou léger : Comprend habituellement des céréales, du pain ou des toasts, des fruits ou des jus de fruit, du thé ou du café.
Complet: Petit déjeuner léger plus un plat cuisiné.
Spécial : Petit déjeuner exceptionnel souvent avec plusieurs plats.
Provisions : Eléments du petit déjeuner fournis

Repas additionnels
Certains B&Bs prépareront des repas du soir sur arrangement (B/A).

Lits et chambres à coucher
Les données décrivent le nombre et la taille des lits, des chambres à coucher et le nombre d'invités qui peuvent séjourner.
Lits pour 1 personne: Simple (1 lit). Twin (2 lits simples). King twin (2 grands lits simples).
Lits pour 2 personnes: Double (petits). Queen (grands). King (très grands).

Salles de bain
Ensuite: Utilisation exclusive de votre chambre.
Privées: Utilisation exclusive dans le couloir.
Partagées: Partagées avec d'autres visiteurs.

Logos

⋐	Piscine
❀	Jardin magnifique
⚘	Vignoble ou activités vinicoles
🍴	Restaurant
☺	Eco tourisme
🏃	Activités sur site
♿	Accès chaise roulante
👫	Accueil enfant ou sur arrangement
🐕	Animaux domestiques bienvenus
🚭	Non fumeur
B&B	Association B&B
AAA Tourism ★★★★★	Tourisme évalué AAA
✔	Tourisme accrédité

Réservations
Les tarifs sont en dollars australiens pour deux personnes (double) ou 1 personne (simple) et comprennent le petit déjeuner, sauf indication contraire. Frais additionnels pour des personnes supplémentaires dans la chambre. Les tarifs varient selon la qualité, l'endroit, les équipements ou la saison et devraient être confirmés lors de la réservation. Réservez à l'avance par courrier, par e-mail ou par téléphone.

"La différence entre un hôtel et un B&B est que vous ne serrerez pas dans vos bras le personnel d'hôtel quand vous partez."

www.BBBook.com.au

EINLEITUNG

Willkommen bei unserem Bed & Breakfast Buch, der beliebteste B&B-Führer Australiens, der 1989 das erste Mal erschienen ist.

Bed and Breakfasts (oder B&Bs) sind eine fantastische Unterbringungsmöglichkeit, die Ihnen die Gelegenheit bietet, die Gastfreundschaft Australiens wirklich zu genießen. Die B&B-Gastgeber sorgen dafür, dass Sie Ihren Aufenthalt genießen und viele schöne Erinnerungen mit nach Hause nehmen können. Außerdem verspricht ein B&B, außerordentliche Gastfreundschaft, ob für eine Nacht oder eine ganze Woche. Unsere B&B-Gastgeber begrüßen Sie mit ausgezeichneten Unterkünften und fantastischem Frühstück. Durch ihre Ortskenntnis können sie Ihnen hiesige Orte sowie die besten Restaurants empfehlen oder Ihnen sogar hausgemachte Speisen zubereiten.

B&Bs sind vielfältig und jedes hat seine eigene, einzigartige Atmosphäre. Einige sind einfach und heimelig, andere elegant und luxuriös. Ihr Schlafzimmer ist bequem und hat üblicherweise ein eigenes Badezimmer oder ein Badezimmer auf dem Flur, während das Frühstück üblicherweise in unseren Zimmerpreisen enthalten ist.

Privatunterkunft (Homestay): Gemeinsame Nutzung der Wohn- und Esszimmer mit dem Gastgeber.
Bed & Breakfast: Gemeinsame Nutzung der Wohn- und Esszimmer mit anderen Gästen.
Ferien auf dem Bauernhof (Farmstay): Unterkunft auf einem Bauernhof mit Aktivitäten.
Selbstversorger (Self-Contained): Private Unterkunft mit Küche, Wohn- und Esszimmer.
Separate Suite: Private Unterkunft. Keine Küche
Gästehaus oder Hotel: Größere Unterkunft, oft mit Restaurant.
Luxus: Qualitativ hochwertige Unterkunft.

Beschreibungen der Unterkünfte
Einträge werden von den Gastgebern selbst verfasst. Alphabetisch sortiert nach Staaten, dann Stadt oder Region.

Frühstück
Kontinental oder Leicht: Umfasst üblicherweise Cornflakes, Brot oder Toast, Früchte oder Fruchtsaft, Tee oder Kaffee.
Voll: Leichtes Frühstück plus gekochter Gang.
Special: Außerordentliches Frühstück, oft mit mehreren Gängen.
Lebensmittel: Frühstücksutensilien werden zur Verfügung gestellt.

Zusätzliche Mahlzeiten
Einige B&Bs bereiten nach Absprache Abendessen zu (B/A).

Betten und Schlafzimmer
Einträge zeigen die Anzahl und Größe der Betten, Schlafzimmer und Gäste, die übernachten können.
Betten für 1 Person: Einzelbett (1 Bett) Zwei Betten (2 einzelne Betten). Zwei Betten (2 große einzelne Betten).
Betten für 2 Person: Doppelbett (klein) Queen (groß). King (sehr groß).

Badezimmer
Im Zimmer: Ausschließliche Nutzung in Ihrem Schlafzimmer
Privat: Ausschließliche Nutzung eines Badezimmers im Flur.
Gemeinsame Nutzung: Gemeinsame Nutzung mit anderen Gästen.

Logos

- Swimmingpool
- Fantastischer Garten
- Weinbau oder Aktivitäten rund um den Weinbau
- Restaurant
- Öko-Tourismus
- Aktivitäten auf dem Gelände
- Rollstuhlgerecht
- Kinder willkommen oder nach Absprache
- Haustiere willkommen
- Nichtraucher
- B&B Verband
- Geprüft durch AAA Tourism
- Zertifiziert durch Tourism

Reservierungen
Preise sind in australischen Dollar für zwei Personen (Doppel) oder 1 Person (Einzel) und enthalten Frühstück, außer anderweitig angegeben. Zusätzliche Gebühr für zusätzliche Person im Zimmer. Preise variieren je nach Qualität, Standort, Anlage oder Jahreszeit und sollte bei Buchung bestätigt werden. Buchen Sie im Voraus per Post, E-Mail oder Telefon.

„Der Unterschied zwischen einem Hotel und einem B&B ist, dass man das Hotelpersonal bei der Abfahrt nicht umarmt.

www.BBBook.com.au

はじめに

オーストラリアで最も人気のあるB&B宿泊施設(一泊朝食付旅館)ガイドブック、ベッド・アンド・ブレックファスト・ブック(Bed & Breakfast Book)へようこそ。1989年初刊。

ベッド・アンド・ブレックファスト(B&B)は 優れた価値を提供しており、本当の意味でのオーストラリアの温かいもてなしをよく理解するには理想的な宿泊施設です。B&Bのホストは、あなたの滞在が楽しく印象に残るものであるように最大の努力を払っており、あなたの滞在期間にかかわらず上等なもてなしをお約束します。温かい歓迎、すてきな宿泊施設、素晴らしい朝食でもてなしてくれます。地元の観光スポットを提供したり、一流レストランの推薦あるいはホームメードの食事を準備してくれます。

B&B宿泊施設にはさまざまなスタイルがあり、それぞれ異なった独自の特徴があります。シンプルで家庭的なものから大きく贅沢なものまで多様です。快適なベッドルームには、通常、専用バスルームあるいはバスルームと一続きのベッドルームが付いており、宿泊料金には朝食も含まれています。

ホームステイ:ホストとリビングルームあるいはダイニングルームの共有。
ベッド・アンド・ブレックファスト:他のゲストとリビングルームやダイニングルームの共有。
ファームステイ: 家畜を飼育する労働農場での宿泊施設。
セルフコンテイン:キッチン、リビングルーム、ダイニングルーム付き専用宿泊施設。
セパレートスイート:専用宿泊施設。キッチン無。
ゲストハウスあるいはホテル:大抵、レストラン付き大型宿泊施設。
ラグジュアリー: 高級宿泊施設。

宿泊施設詳細
宿泊施設の詳細はホスト自身が記述しています。各州ごとに、市あるいは地域のアルファベット順に記載されています。

ブレックファスト
コンチネンタルあるいは軽い朝食:通常、シリアル、パンあるいはトースト、フルーツあるいはジュース、紅茶あるいはコーヒーなど。
フルブレックファスト:軽い朝食と調理したお食事コース。
スペシャル:大抵、数種類のコースが付いた特別な朝食。
食料提供:朝食の食料提供。

追加の食事
手配いただければ、夕食を提供するB&Bもあります(B/A)。

ベッドおよびベッドルーム
詳細にはベッドの数と大きさ、滞在できるベッドルーム数とゲスト数が表示されています。
一人用ベッド:シングルベッド(1ベッド)。ツインベッド(シングルベッド2台)。大型ツインベッド(大型シングルベッド2台)。
二人用ベッド:ダブルベッド(小型)。クイーンベッド(大型)。キングベッド(特大型)。

Tell hosts you found them in the Bed & Breakfast Book

バスルーム
一続き：ご利用のベッドルームから専用で使用。
私用：廊下から専用で使用。
共有： 他のゲストと共有。

ロゴ

🏊 スイミングプール

✿ 素晴らしい庭

🍇 ぶどう酒醸造場あるいはワイン造り

🍴 レストラン

🌍 エコツーリズム

🧍 現地活動

♿ 車椅子乗車可

👫 子供可あるいは要手配

🐕 ペット可

🚭 禁煙

℗ B&B協会

AAA Tourism
★★★★★ AAAツーリズム評価

✓ ツーリズム基準品質保証

予約
二人用（ダブル）あるいは一人用（シングル）の料金はオーストラリアドルで表示されており、特に記載がない限りは朝食も含まれています。各お部屋の定員以上のゲストがご使用になる場合は、割増料金をいただきます。料金はB&Bの質、場所、施設あるいは季節によって異なりますので、ご予約の際にご確認ください。郵便、Eメールあるいは電話で事前にご予約ください。

「ホテルとB&Bの違いは、ホテルではご帰宅の際にスタッフを抱きしめることはしません。」

www.BBBook.com.au

소개

호주 1989년 첫 발간을 시작으로 한 인기 절정의 Bed & Breakfast
(아침식사를 제공하는 민박집) 숙식 가이드에 어서 오십시오.

Bed and Breakfasts (B&Bs)를 통해 극진한 서비스의 진정한 호주
인들의 삶의 모습을 바탕으로 친절한 대접 형태를 받게 된다. 하룻밤을
묵어도 상관이 없으며 주인네들의 진정어린 환대로 추억에 남는 여정으
로 남게 될 베드 앤 브랙퍼스트는 집에서 정성이 담긴 아침식사 (이외
식사도 개별 스케줄로 가능)의 그득함과 아울러, 관광지 안내, 레스토랑
가볼만한 곳들도 정보로 아울러 받게 될 수가 있다.

B&B는 여러 스타일 형태로 제공되게 되며 단순하면서도 집 같은 정경
일 수도 있고 고급스런 서비스 제공을 안내받는 곳의 형태로도 구성되게
되어 있다. 아늑한 침실 제공과 함께 욕실은 함께 사용하거나 개인 사용
으로 나뉘게 되며 아침식사는 비용에 아울러 포함되게 된다.

홈스테이: 집주인과 거실, 식당을 함께 사용하는 성격의 구성.
Bed & Breakfast: 다른 숙식객과 거실, 식당을 공용 스타일로서 구성
된다.
Farmstay: 농장일을 도와 주며 숙식을 제공하는 스타일.
Self-Contained (호별 독립식): 개인 전용의 주방, 거실, 식당 스타일.
Separate Suite (독립 스위트): 개인 전용, 주방 없음.
Guesthouse (고급 하숙집), 호텔: 레스토랑이 겸용된 대형 숙박식의
제공.
Luxury (고급): 고급 숙박식 제공 형태.

숙식 정보
집주인들로부터 직접 정보 제공의 형태로서 주, 도시 (지역)별로 알파벳
순으로 정연되어 있다.

아침식사
Continental (컨티넨탈), Light (경식): 콘 후레이크, 빵 (토스트),
과일 쥬스, 차, 커피가 제공된다.
Full (풀): 아침식사와 더불어 정식 코스를 제공한다.
스페셜: 코스로 이루어진 스페셜 형태의 아침식사.
제공: 아침식사 공급.

기타 식사 제공
B&Bs 중에서 저녁 식사를 따로 요청시 제공하는 곳도 있다 (B/A).

침대, 침실 구조
숙식인 명수, 침실 침대 갯수, 크기를 제공하는 정보가 담겨 있다.
1인 침대: 싱글 (침대 1). 트윈 (싱글 베드2). 킹 트윈 (2개의 대형 싱
글베드).
2인용 침대: 더블 (소형). 퀸 (대형). 킹 (최대형).

욕실
스위트: 개인 침실 전용.
Private (개인용): 복도 위치 전용.
Shared (공용): 기타 숙식인과 공용 형태.

로고
- 🏊 수영장
- ✿ 근사한 정경의 가든
- 🍇 와인 양조장, 와인 공정
- 🍴 레스토랑
- ☯ 생태학 관광
- 🚶 현장 활동
- ♿ 휠체어 전용
- 👫 어린이 참가 (개별 일정요)
- 🐕 애완동물 반입 가능
- 🚭 금연
- &ℬ B&B 협회
- ★★★★★ AAA Tourism (관광사업) 사정
- ✅ Tourism (관광사업) 공인

예약
호주달러 사용. 2인 (더블), 1인 (싱글)이 기본이며 아침식사가 포함
(예외의 경우 따로 안내)되는 요금율. 추가인의 경우 따로 차지가 되며
등급별, 위치별, 설치물 형태별로 요율의 형태가 달라지게 됨 – 예약시
안내 되게 되며 우편, 이메일, 전화로 예약이 가능하다.

”베드엔브랙퍼스트가 호텔과 틀린 점 하나– 떠날 때의 잊지못할 포옹담
긴 정겨운 인사.”

www.BBBook.com.au

简介
欢迎使用 Bed & Breakfast（《早餐住宿指南》）一书，这是澳大利亚最受欢迎的早餐民宿指南第一版于 1989 年出版。

Bed and Breakfasts（或 B&B）具有极为重要的价值，是感受真正的澳大利亚盛情的理想方式B&B 主人致力于确保您的入住令人愉快且值得纪念，并承诺提供最高级的殷勤招待，无论您住一晚或一周他们提供热情扬溢的欢迎、愉快的住宿和极好的早餐他们可以建议参观当地的好地方、建议最好的餐馆，甚或准备烹调的家庭美食

B&B 住宿包括各种形式，每种形式都有唯一不同的特色一些形式简单、平常，另一些形式则豪华、奢侈您的卧室通常很舒适，带有私人或套房浴室，早餐通常包含在房价内。

在当地居民家居住：和主人共用客厅或餐厅。
住宿和早餐：和其他客人共用客厅或餐厅。
农场住宿：在经营各种农场活动的农场住宿。
自主式：配备厨房、客厅和就餐区域的私人住宿
单独的套房：私人住宿无厨房。
宾馆或酒店：通常有餐馆的较大地方的住处。
华贵：较高品质的住宿。

住宿描述
所有项目均由主人自己编写按州、市或地区的字母顺序排列

早餐
欧陆式早餐或西式早餐：通常包括谷类食品、面包或烤面包片、水果或果汁、茶或咖啡。
全套早餐：西式早餐加上一道炒菜。
特别早餐：通常有几道菜的特别早餐
自助早餐：提供各种早餐供应品。

其它膳食
某些 B&B 将根据安排 (B/A) 准备夜宵

床和卧室
目录会显示床数与大小、可以入住的卧室及房客人数。
单人床数：单人房（1 张床）双人房（2 张单人床）超大双人房（2 张大单人床）。
两人床数：双人房（小床）大号房（大床）特大号房（最大床）

浴室
套房：从您的卧室专门使用。
私人：专用走廊。
共用：与其他客人共用。

标志

⊗ 游泳池
❀ 美丽的花园
🍇 葡萄酒厂或葡萄酒活动
🍴 餐馆
☯ 生态旅游
🚶 现场活动
♿ 轮椅使用者进出
👫 儿童欢迎或根据安排
🐕 宠物欢迎
🚭 禁止吸烟
B&B B&B 协会
<u>AAA Tourism</u>
★★★★★ 经过 AAA Tourism 评定
✔ 通过旅游质量认证

订房

用澳大利亚元提供的是双人（双人房）或单人（单房）房价，并包括早餐，除非另外指明对客房中的其他人额外收费房价会根据品质、位置、设施或季节有变化，应该在预订时确认通过邮件、电子邮件或电话提前预订

"酒店和 B&B 之间的差别是，您在离开时无需拥抱酒店人员。"

www.BBBook.com.au

Introducción

Bienvenido a The Bed and Breakfast Book, la Guía más popular de Alojamiento B&B en Australia. Publicado por primera vez en 1989.

Los establecimientos de 'Alojamiento y Desayuno' (en adelante B&B, del inglés Bed and Breakfast) tienen un precio muy interesante y son la manera ideal de disfrutar de la autentica hospitalidad de Australia. El compromiso de los dueños de los B&Bs es asegurar que su estancia es a la vez agradable y memorable, y le prometen una hospitalidad de primera calidad, tanto si se aloja por una noche o como una semana. Ofrecen una calurosa bienvenida, estupendo alojamiento y fantasticos desayunos. Pueden sugerir maravillosos lugares para visitar, recomendar los mejores restaurantes o incluso preparar una comida casera.

Los alojamientos de B&B incluyen una variadad de estilos, cada uno con características singulares. Algunos son sencillos y acogedores; otros son esplendidos y lujosos. La habitación será comoda, normalmente con baño privado o en suite, y el desayuno generalmente está incluido en el precio.

Alojamiento en Casa (Homestay): Los huéspedes comparten la sala de estar y el comedor con los dueños de la casa.
Alojamiento y Desayuno (Bed & Breakfast): Los huéspedes comparten la sala de estar y el comedor con otros huéspedes.
Alojamiento en Granja (Farmstay): Alojamiento generalmente en una granja en funcionamiento con actividades agropecuarias.
Alojamiento con todos los Servicios (Self-Contained): Alojamiento privado con cocina y zonas de comedor y de estar.
Habitación Independiente (Separate Suite): Alojamiento privado. Sin cocina.
Casa de Huéspedes u Hotel (Guesthouse or Hotel): Alojamiento de mayores proporciones, frequentemente con servicio de restaurante.
Lujoso (Luxury): Alojamiento de calidad superior.

Descripción del Alojamiento
Las entradas de la Guía han sido redactadas por los propios dueños del alojamiento. Están ordenadas alfabéticamente por estado y después por ciudad o región.

Desayuno
Continental o Ligero (Continental or Light): Normalmente incluye cereales, pan o tostadas, fruta o zumo de frutas, y té o café.
Completo (Full): Un desayuno ligero más un plato caliente.
Especial (Special): Un desayuno excepcional, frecuentemente con varios platos.
Provisiones (Provisions): Se suministran provisiones para el desayuno.

Comidas Extras
Algunos B&Bs preparan cenas por encargo (B/A, "by arrangement" en inglés).

Camas y Habitaciones
Las entradas muestran el número de camas y su tamaño, el número de habitaciones y los huéspedes que pueden alojarse.
Camas para 1 persona: "Single" (1 cama); "Twin" (2 camas individuales); "King twin" (2 camas individuales grandes).
Camas para 2 personas: "Double" (mediana), "Queen" (grande) o "King" (muy grande).

Cuartos de Baño

Baño en suite (Ensuite): Uso exclusivo con acceso desde dentro de la habitación.
Baño privado (Private): Uso exclusivo con acceso desde el hall.
Baño compartido (Shared bathroom): Compartido con otros huéspedes.

Logos

- Piscina
- Fantástico Jardín
- Bodega o actividades de vinos
- Restaurante
- Ecoturismo
- Actividades in situ
- Acceso para silla de ruedas
- Niños bienvenidos o con previo aviso
- Animales domésticos bienvenidos
- Prohibido fumar
- Asociación de B&B
- Evaluado por AAA Turismo (organismo nacional de los clubes de automov ilismo de Australia)
- Autorizado por Turismo

Reservas

Los precios se ofrecen en dólares australianos para 2 personas (habitación doble) o para 1 persona (habitación sencilla) e incluyen el desayuno, salvo que se indique lo contrario. Hay un cargo adicional por personas extras en la habitación. Las tarifas varían según la calidad del alojamiento, la localización, los servicios ofrecidos y la temporada, y es aconsejable confirmarlos al reservar. Haga su reserva por adelantado por correo postal, correo electrónico o teléfono.

"La diferencia entre un hotel y un B&B es que no das un abrazo al personal del hotel cuando te marchas."

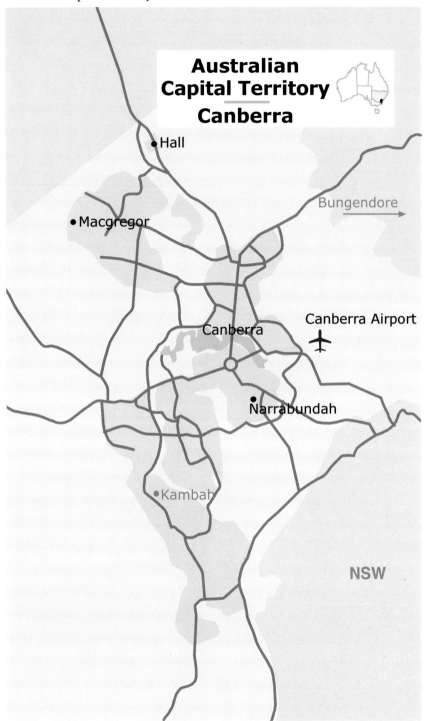

Canberra - Hall

Surveyor's Hill Winery and B&B *25 km N of Canberra*
B&B, Farmstay & Self Contained House
Leigh Hobba
215 Brooklands Road
Wallaroo (near Hall)
NSW 2618

Tel (02) 6230 2046
or 0400 564 050
survhill@westnet.com.au
www.survhill.com.au

Double $150 Single $100
Children $25 Full breakfast
Dinner $65 for 3 courses including wine
Self catering & long stay discounts
Visa MC accepted
2 Queen 1 Double (2 bdrm) plus sofa bed
Bathrooms: 1 Private

B &B and Farmstay, in 1930 farmstead, 230 acre property with vineyards & olives, overlooking Murrumbidgee River, Brindabella Ranges. Easy drive to central Canberra. Guests enjoy exclusive use of the cottage, fully private, self contained, separate from hosts' residence. Open fire in loungeroom, electric heaters in all rooms ensure cosy warmth. Gourmet meals featuring farm and local produce and premium wines provided in cottage dining room. Excellent kitchen enables self catering. Generously discounted long stay and self catering rates are negotiable. Extra B&B and self contained accommodation being added late 2008. Watch our website for details.

Canberra - Narrabundah

Narrabundah B&B *3 km SE of Parliament House*
B&B & Homestay
John & Esther Davies
5 Mosman Place
Narrabundah
ACT 2604

Tel (02) 6295 2837
or 0419 276 231
info@narbb.com
www.narbb.com

Double $120
Single $100
Continental breakfast
Dinner $40pp by arrangement
Discounts for stays of 4 days or more
Visa MC accepted
1 King (1 bdrm)
Bathrooms: 1 Ensuite

C omfortable, renovated home in quiet street. Conveniently located in relation to Canberra's main tourist attractions, such as Parliament House, National Gallery and War Memorial. Short drive to restaurants in Manuka. Close to public transport and to train station and airport. Air-conditioned (heating and cooling). Hosts are semi-retired and interests include history, genealogy, computing, music, gardening and embroidery. Miniature poodle in residence.

Canberra - MacGregor

Grevillea Lodge *11.9 km NW of Canberra GPO*
B&B & Self-contained unit
Merrill Moore
1 Florey Drive
Macgregor
ACT 2615

Tel (02) 6161 7646 or 0414 418 374
Fax (02) 6161 7646
merrill@grevillealodge.com
www.grevillealodge.com

Double $100-$130 Single $80-$100
Children 5-12 $10 pn
Full breakfast
Discounted weekly & self-catered
rates on application
Visa MC Diners Eftpos accepted
2 Queen 1 Single (2 bdrm)
Bathrooms: 2 Ensuite

Grevillea Lodge offers informal country hospitality in suburban Canberra. Comfortable & pet friendly accommodation in new energy-efficient guest wing with living room, kitchenette, private courtyard, access to large deck and native gardens, and the company of our beautiful malamute Nikki if you choose. Selection of teas, coffee, delicious treats always available. Generous breakfast includes hot dishes, fruit platter, & homemade preserves. Quality bedding, ducted heating, internet connection in rooms, BBQ. Nature reserve, walking/bike tracks 100m. Bus stop 50m. Short drive to all Canberra attractions.

Canberra
Canberra, Australia's national capital, the place to spend several days of diverse experiences for anyone interested in either Australia's important icons or natural beauties.

The Parliamentary Triangle, on the shores of Lake Burley Griffin, includes both our old and new Parliament Houses, the National Gallery & Library, the War Memorial, & the National Museum is close by.

The National Zoo & Aquarium offers fantastic wildlife experiences, national parks are nearby & cultural experiences abound. Canberra is a must to include in any visit to Australia.
Merrill Moore
Grevillea Lodge

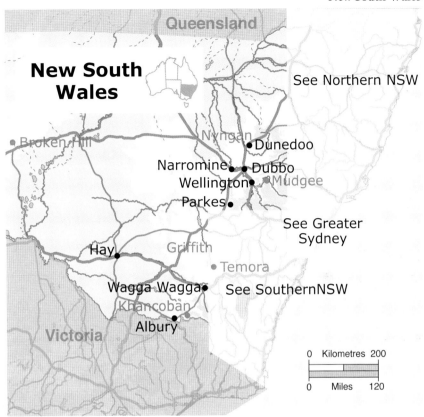

New South
Wales

Queensland

See Northern NSW

Broken Hill

Nyngan

Dunedoo

Narromine Dubbo

Wellington Mudgee

Parkes

See Greater
Sydney

Hay Griffith

Temora

Wagga Wagga See SouthernNSW

Khancoban

Albury

Victoria

0 Kilometres 200

0 Miles 120

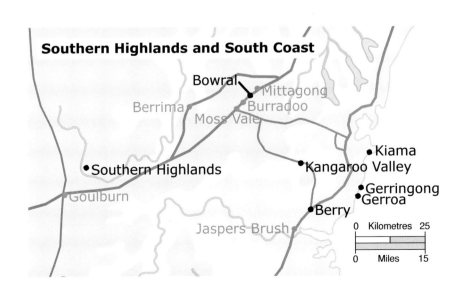

Southern Highlands and South Coast

Bowral Mittagong

Berrima Burradoo

Moss Vale

Kiama

Southern Highlands Kangaroo Valley

Goulburn

Gerringong
Gerroa

Berry

Jaspers Brush

0 Kilometres 25

0 Miles 15

Orange
Bathurst
Lithgow
See Greater Sydney
Blayney
Mandurama
Hampton
Cowra
Oberon
Jenolan Caves
Ariah Park
Crookwell
Corrimal
Wollongong
Young
Kangaroo Valley
See Southern Highlands and
South Coast
Temora
Rye Park
Kiama
Cootamundra
Yass
Gunning
Goulburn
Gerringong
Berry
Adelong
Nowra
Huskisson
Vincentia
Canberra
Jervis Bay
ACT
Milton
Braidwood
Ulladulla
Bawley Point
Adaminaby
Batemans Bay
Moruya
Cooma
Narooma
Central Tilba
Tilba Tilba
Jindabyne
Cobargo
Bermagui
Thredbo
Tanja
Snowy
Mountains
South Coast
Bega
Candelo
Merimbula
Pambula
Southern
NSW
Eden

0   Kilometres   50

0   Miles   30

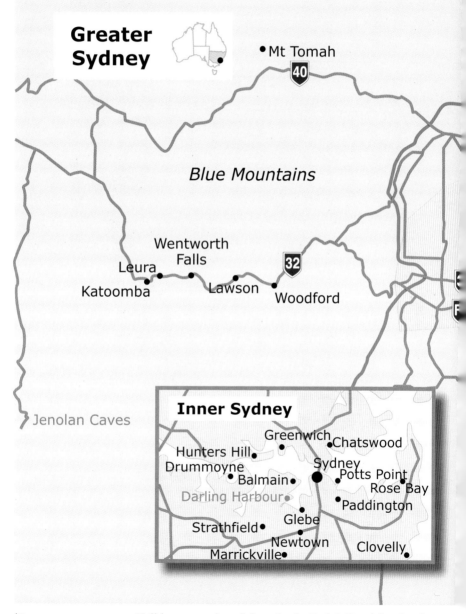

Greater Sydney

• Mt Tomah

40

Blue Mountains

Wentworth
Falls
Leura
Katoomba Lawson
Woodford

32

Jenolan Caves

Inner Sydney

Greenwich Chatswood
Hunters Hill
Drummoyne
Balmain Sydney Potts Point
Rose Bay
Darling Harbour Paddington
Strathfield Glebe
Newtown
Marrickville Clovelly

Rent a Group C (e.g Hyundai Elantra) or above for 5 days or more from the locations below and you will receive $50* off the total time and kilometre charges. Valid until 20th December 2009. Please quote coupon number **MPLA027**.

Artarmon	(02) 9439 3733	Parramatta	(02) 9630 5877
Bankstown	(02) 9792 1714	Ryde	(02) 9809 7577
Circular Quay	(02) 9241 1281	Star City	(02) 9660 7666
Croydon	(02) 9716 7052	Sydney Airport	(02) 8374 2847
Hornsby	(02) 9489 7111	Taren Point	(02) 9540 1088
Kings Cross	(02) 9357 2000	World Square	(02) 9261 0750

Travelling in an unfamiliar area?
Add Avis' portable GPS to your rental.

We try harder.

Visit www.avis.com.au or call 136 333 for bookings

*Subject to availability. $50 off is applicable to time and kilometre charges only. Cannot be used in conjunction with any other offer, coupon or promotion. Avis standard age, credit and driver requirements apply. An advance reservation is required. Non transferable and not refundable. Subject to the terms and conditions of Avis Rental Agreement at time of rental. W.T.H. Pty. Limited - ACN 000 165 855 - Avis Licensee. CT6989

... a warm welcome ... a special experience

Bed & Breakfast
and Farmstay NSW & ACT

Look for this logo as a sign for the highest quality of Bed and Breakfast and Farmstay properties in:

> **Sydney & Rural New South Wales**
> **Canberra & Australian Capital Territory**

You will find friendly hosts that are committed to ensuring your stay is an experience to remember.

Bed & Breakfast and Farmstay NSW & ACT is a non profit member association of B&B and Farmstay owners abiding by a Code of Practice with an independently assessed quality checklist.

Membership enquires: www.bedandbreakfast.org.au

To find member properties - look for the logo in this book or search for accommodation online at:

www.bedandbreakfastnsw.com

Adaminaby - Snowy Mountains

Reynella Homestead *5 km E of Adaminaby*
Farmstay & Ski Lodge, Homestead
Roslyn & John Rudd
669 Kingston Road, Reynella,
Adaminaby, NSW 2629

Tel (02) 6454 2386 or 1800 029 909
Fax (02) 64542 2530
reynella@snowy.net.au
www.reynellarides.com.au

Single $115
Children on application Full breakfast
Full 3 course dinner included (Lodge)
Horse trekks $95pp
Visa MC Diners Amex Eftpos accepted
2 King 1 Queen 4 Double 10 Twin
23 Single (19 bdrm) Lodge style
accommodation/shared bathrooms
Bathrooms: 5 Guest share

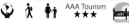
AAA Tourism
★★★

L odge accommodation on working sheep and cattle property - opportunities for some involvement. Largest horse trekking operation in Kosciuszko National Park. Operating from October to May. Stay at The Homestead $115 per night, horse riding an extra $95 per day. We require 4 people riding to take rides. Stay at the Ski Lodge in the winter only $115 per person, includes 3 course dinner. Ideal base for Skiing Accommodation. Discounts for direct bookings on ski accommodation. Superb food. BYO. Local fishing, bush walking, riding instruction. (Summer). Original operators - 37 years. Visit our website for dates and rates for trekks.

Adaminaby - Selwyn Snowfields NSW.Adaminaby
Selwyn is the perfect place to learn to ski or snowboard with it's gentle progressing terrain and caring mountain staff. Our family friendly atmosphere will make you and your family feel right at home with skiing, snow boarding, snow tubing, tobogganing, or just playing in the snow! In summer, after the snow has melted, you can go horse trekking in the Kosciuszko National Park.
Roslyn Rudd
Reynella Homestead

Albury

Elizabeth's Manor *1.5 km W of North Albury PO*

Luxury B&B & Self Contained House

Larry & Betty Kendall
531 Lyne Street
Lavington, North Albury
NSW 2641

Tel (02) 6040 4412
Fax (02) 6040 5166
bookins@elizabethsmanor.com.au
www.elizabethsmanor.com.au

Double $170-$180
Single $140-$150
Children $25
Full breakfast
Dinner $44 - $55
Visa MC Diners Amex Eftpos accepted
3 Queen 1 Double (3 bdrm)
Bathrooms: 3 Ensuite

AAA Tourism
★★★★★

Elizabeth's Manor would have to be the most luxurious and romantic adults only accommodation in Australia. On arrival guests will be presented with complimentary sparkling wine and chocolates. A gourmet breakfast can be served in your suite or the Gallery. Although we have a 'No Smoking' policy in the house, smoking is permitted anywhere outside. We also have a late check-out, twelve PM, a good excuse to try our new outside 'Therapeutic' heated spa.

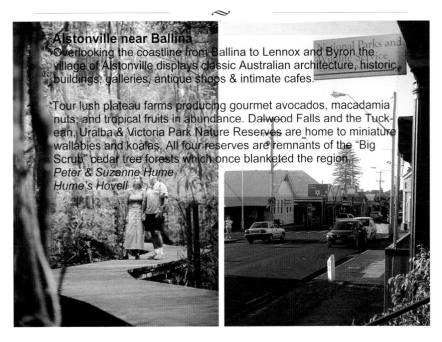

Alstonville near Ballina
Overlooking the coastline from Ballina to Lennox and Byron the village of Alstonville displays classic Australian architecture, historic buildings, galleries, antique shops & intimate cafes.

Tour lush plateau farms producing gourmet avocados, macadamia nuts, and tropical fruits in abundance. Dalwood Falls and the Tuckean, Uralba & Victoria Park Nature Reserves are home to miniature wallabies and koalas. All four reserves are remnants of the "Big Scrub" cedar tree forests which once blanketed the region.
Peter & Suzanne Hume
Hume's Hovell

Alstonville - Ballina

Hume's Hovell *8 km S of Alstonville*

Luxury B&B & Farmstay with Separate Suites
Peter & Suzanne Hume
333 Dalwood Road
Alstonville
NSW 2477

Tel (02) 6629 5371
Fax (02) 6629 5471
stay@humes-hovell.com
www.bed-and-breakfast.com.au

Double $205-$275 Single $135-$225
Children $25
Full breakfast
Dinner $35 - $45
Visa MC accepted
2 King/Twin 2 King 3 Single (4 bdrm)
Bathrooms: 3 Ensuite 1 Private

4.5 STAR RATED: AAA REVIEWED as 'ONE OF THE STATES BEST' - AN OASIS OF LUXURY - SIMPLY A GREAT PLACE TO STAY OVERNIGHT or A FANTASTIC HOLIDAY DESTINATION. Spacious Suites, Large Pool, Full Size Tennis Court, BBQ Dining Pavilion, Free Wireless Broadband, Hume's Hovell B&B: a Resort: a Retreat: - a magical experience. We're also a Macadamia Plantation in the green hills above Ballina just half an hour from Byron Bay. Explore the villages, tranquil country lanes, stroll thru nearby National Parks, see baby kangaroos, starlit night skies, enjoy fresh country air - only minutes to beaches but miles from crowds. Wake each morning to the calls of kookaburras, magpies and eastern rosellas, Full hot breakfasts & helpful friendly hosts, it's everything you dream about. Our winters are like a Tasmanian summer and summers are heaven; it's reflected by the number of guests who return again & again. Facilities include Spa Suite, King Sized Beds, TV/DVD, Free Wireless broadband, Air Conditioning, Mini-bars, Premium Tea, Local Coffee, Bathrobes, Hair-drier, Ironing boards and Complimentary Evening Drinks and Macadamias. Hume's Hovell is Non Smoking inside & casual Evening Dining is by prior arrangement.

Armidale

Poppys Cottage *6 km S of Armidale*
B&B & Farmstay & Cottage, no kitchen
Jake & Poppy Abbott
Malvern Hill
Dangarsleigh Road, Armidale
NSW 2350

Tel (02) 6775 1277 or 0412 153 819
Fax (02) 6775 1308
poppyscottage@bluepin.net.au
poppyscottage.com.au

Double $140 Single $110
Children $45 Cot available
Special breakfast
Dinner $55 (3 course candlelit
dinner+complimentary bottle wine)
2 Double 2 Single (2 bdrm)
Bathrooms: 1 Ensuite 1 Private

A rmidale Award Winning B&B - an unforgettable warm, friendly, farmstay experience awaits you in this romantic, cosy atmosphere only 6km from historic Armidale. Nestled in enchanting cottage garden with friendly company of personality farm animals, the free-standing cottage allows guests to enjoy private ensuite accommodation. Beautiful gourmet breakfasts enjoyed beneath canopy of fruit trees, are a speciality. Option of delicious and intimate candlelit dinner with complimentary bottle of wine. Relax; enjoy country hospitality at its best: "warm, friendly and generous". Magnificent waterfalls nearby.

Armidale – New England
New England is renowned worldwide for its spectacular National Parks, with pristine wilderness, rainforests and waterfalls. Geologically unique World Heritage National Parks, magnificent bushwalking & scenery.
Armidale and Uralla, at its approximate geographic centre are about 150 kms inland via the breathtaking "Waterfall Way" from Coffs Harbour.

From Sydney and Brisbane the New England Highway running north/south gives good access to the region.
Anne Thackway
Cruickshanks Farmstay and B&B

Armidale - Uralla

Cruickshanks Farmstay B&B *20 km E of Uralla*
B&B & Self-contained Cottage
Anne & Mike Thackway
(313 Mihi Road) Tourist Drive 19
Uralla, NSW 2358

Tel (02) 6778 2148
or 0427 782 148
anne@cruickshanks.com.au
www.cruickshanks.com.au

Double $120 Single $90
Children $20-$40
Complementary continental breakfast
first morning
Full breakfast extra $20pp
Dinner $25-$45 B/A
Visa MC Amex JCB accepted
2 Queen 1 Double 1 Twin 4 Single (5 bdrm)
Cottage: 3 bdrm Accomm 8;   Homestead: 2 bdrm Accomm 4
Bathrooms: 1 Ensuite 1 Guest share 1 Private
Cottage 1 Private; Homestead 1 Ensuite, 1 Private

'Try life in the slow lane, you deserve to Relax in complete comfort, enjoy good local food & premium wines, cosy log-fires for our crispy winter nights' or to participate in exciting outdoor activities. Options are 'Cottages' or 'Homestead' B&B or Self-contained. SMH journalist said 'A glimpse into a working property, fantastic for children and those seeking a break from the big smoke this New England B&B graduates with honours.'. We say 'Simply pack expectations of a great holiday and take home wonderful memories'.

Armidale – Uralla - New England
Needing a holiday to expand your horizons . . . look no further than New England "where the stars seem to touch the earth".

This area unique in Australia claims a bracing mountain altitude of about 1000 metres, provides four very distinct seasons... warm Summers, fantastically colourful Autumns, cold frosty winters, even snow, and magical springs.

Uralla steeped in history ... bushranger 'Thunderbolt' and Rocky River gold diggings.
Anne Thackway
Cruickshanks Farmstay and B&B

Ballina

Landfall *3 km NE of Ballina Township*
B&B & Homestay
Gaye & Roger Ibbotson
109 Links Avenue
East Ballina
NSW 2478

Tel (02) 6686 7555
or 0428 642 077
Fax (02) 6686 7377
landfall@tpg.com.au
www.bbbook.com.au/landfall.html

Double $100
Single $70
Full breakfast
Visa MC accepted
1 Queen 2 Single (2 bdrm)
Bathrooms: 1 Guest share

"Landfall" You're welcome in our home.

This home was the residence of Captain Tom Martin and his wife, Marjorie; he named this home "Landfall" when he retired to Ballina after many years at sea. "Landfall" is situated in East Ballina overlooking the golf course. You are invited to relax in our courtyard with its indoor solar heated pool and spa. "Landfall" is a "non smoking" home. We offer you friendly hospitality. The main part of our home is air conditioned as is the Queen Bedroom. Your hosts Gaye and Roger Ibbotson.

Ballina

The Yabsley B&B *3 km NE of Ballina*
B&B
Judee Whittaker & David Clark
5 Yabsley Street
East Ballina
NSW 2478

Tel (02) 6681 1505
or 0407 811 505
Fax (02) 6681 1505
yabsley@bigpond.com
www.yabsley.com.au

Double $135
Single $120
Full breakfast
Dinner 3 courses $40 per person
Visa MC accepted
2 Queen (2 bdrm)
Bathrooms: 2 Private

AAA Tourism
★★★★☆

The Yabsley is a two minute walk to Lighthouse Beach, Richmond River and Shaws Bay Lagoon. Also within easy walking distance to a hotel, a resort and three restaurants. The house has been refurbished and contains private guest suites, guest lounge and delightful courtyards. Watch the whales and dolphins or play tennis and golf. East Ballina gives access to day trips to Byron Bay, the Border Ranges or the Gold Coast. You can negotiate a superb meal of your choice cooked by David who specialises in seafood cuisine. Unfortunately we cannot cater for children.

Batemans Bay

Chalet Swisse Spa *10 km S of Batemans Bay*
B&B & Guest House & Self Contained
Herbert & Elizabeth Mayer
676 The Ridge Road
Surf Beach, Batemans Bay
NSW 2536

Tel (02) 4471 3671
Fax (02) 4471 1671
info@chaletswissespa.com.au
www.chaletswissespa.com.au

Double $120-$295 Single $90-$255
Children $40
Continental breakfast
S/C cabins incl. linen $120-$245
Visa MC Diners Amex Eftpos accepted
2 King 6 Queen 9 Double 2 Twin 9
Single (17 bdrm) Deluxe, 2 King, 6 Queen, Lodge
Bathrooms: 17 Ensuite

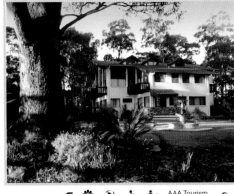

Situated on top of 'Hero's Hill' above Surf Beach our 85 ac Retreat & Health Spa offers you:- our own mineral spring water, fresh clean air, tranquillity, 120 degree ocean views from our Cafe-verandah, visits by birds and wallabies. Facilities: Indoor heated pool (28 degrees C), Spa, revitalising therapies and massages, rainforest walks, tennis, table tennis, archery. Guest lounge with large open fireplace, games corner. Friendly, widely travelled hosts. A place for you to relax, wind down and get pampered.

Bawley Point

Interludes at Bawley *26 km S of Ulladulla*
Luxury self contained cottages & B&B
Sandra Worth & Ken Purves
103 Forster Drive
Bawley Point
NSW 2539

Tel (02) 4457 1494
or 0418 665 735
interludes@bigblue.net.au
www.interludes.com.au

Double $150-$220
Full breakfast
Kitchen facilities available in B&B
Visa MC accepted
10 Queen (10 bdrm)
7 in cottages, 3 in B&B
Bathrooms: 7 Ensuite 1 Private 2 x 1 bedroom cottages have spas

Set in 26 acres of coastal bushland, Interludes boasts magnificent panoramic ocean views. Be lulled to sleep by the murmur of the sea and waken to a dazzling ocean sunrise, morning birdsong and the rustle of leaves in the trees. Enjoy the unsurpassed beauty of local beaches. Swimming, surfing, snorkelling, fishing and boating are all activities available to the energetic. Our new luxury cottages are fully self contained and self catering (breakfast not included) while a sumptuous, cooked breakfast is served in the B&B.

Bega Valley - Bemboka

Giba Gunyah Country Cottages *8 km E of Bemboka*
B&B & Farmstay & Self Contained Cottages
John and Ros Raward
224 Polacks Flat Road
Bemboka
NSW 2550

Tel (02) 6492 8404 or 0438 674 449
Fax (02) 6492 8404
ggunyah@yahoo.com.au
www.gibagunyah.com.au

Double $150-$180
Family with 3 children $170
Full breakfast provisions
2 course dinner + wine on request $40pp
Extra adult $35
1 King/Twin 1 Queen 1 Twin (2 bdrm)
2 bedrooms in each cottage
Bathrooms: 2 Private 1 cottage has disabled access

 AAA Tourism ★★★☆

Giba Gunyah cottages are perfect for that romantic weekend escape for two or for a longer, more relaxed family break. Set in more than thirty hectares of bush and rolling dairy farmland are two charming cottages furnished in country style. Cottages have 2 bedrooms, large bathroom, country kitchen, wheel-chair access, log fires, secluded fenced gardens, stunning views and prolific bird life. All linen is supplied and special little touches are provided to delight you. Your canine guests will love exploring new spaces, smells, and river.

Bellingen

Rivendell *0.1 km E of Bellingen*
B&B
Janet Hosking
10 - 12 Hyde Street
Bellingen
NSW 2454

Tel (02) 6655 0060
or 0403 238 409
rivendell@wirefree.net.au
www.rivendellguesthouse.com.au

Double $135-$150
Single $110-$150
Full breakfast
Visa MC Eftpos accepted
3 Queen 2 Twin (4 bdrm)
Bathrooms: 3 Ensuite 1 Private

 AAA Tourism ★★★★

In the heart of historic Bellingen, Rivendell is a beautifully decorated Federation home. Luxurious rooms furnished with antiques, fluffy bathrobes, open to shady verandahs and picturesque gardens. Take a refreshing dip in the freshwater pool, or in winter, relax by the log fire. After dinner enjoy complimentary port and chocolates. TV, stereo, books, games, magazines and tea/coffee making is provided in the guest lounge. "Lovely stay, fab food and cosy accommodation -we will be back! Thank you" Justin & Caroline UK.

Bellingen

Bellingen Heritage Cottages *0.25 km W of PO*
2 Luxury Self Contained Cottages
Gail & Gus Raymond
7 - 9 William Street
Bellingen
NSW 2454

Tel (02) 6655 1311
or 0428 551 311
Fax (02) 6655 1311
graymond@bigpond.net.au
www.auntylils.com.au

Double $160
Single $120
Continental provisions
Extra person $30
1 King/Twin 2 Queen (3 bdrm)
Bathrooms: 1 Private

' **A**unty Lil's' Cottage was built by the Raymond family circa 1910 and lovingly restored to the period with all comforts of home and beyond. Enjoy fascinating family memorabilia. Lots of pillows and feather doonas and warm cosy atmosphere. In heart of Bellingen in quiet street. Self contained - including lounge, dining, full kitchen, 3 bedrooms, bathroom, laundry and verandahs front and back. TV, DVD, VCR, sound system. Cottage garden/off street parking. Minutes walking distance to Heritage and craft shops, restaurants, Bellinger River, Markets, and attractions.

Berry - Kangaroo Valley

Barefoot Springs *9.5 km SE of Kangaroo Valley*
B&B & Homestay & Cottage, no kitchen
Tim & Kay
155 Carrington Road
Beaumont
NSW 2577

Tel (02) 4446 0509   Fax (02) 4446 0530
info@barefootsprings.com.au
www.barefootsprings.com.au

Double $185-$285 Single $175-$275
Full breakfast
BYO Dinner 3 courses $50, 2 courses $45
Awarded AAAT Green Star
(Environmentally Friendly)
Visa MC Eftpos accepted
1 King 3 Queen (4 bdrm)
3 in cottage & 1 in homestead
Bathrooms: 4 Ensuite Double spa in Cottages

Barefoot Springs rests high on Cambewarra Mountain; between Berry, Kangaroo Valley and the Shoalhaven. Enjoy our mountain and coastline views, while strolling through 5 acres of beautiful gardens. Many tourist destinations within a 20 minute drive. Accommodation within our homestead is a Queen bedroom with en-suite, or three separate studio cottages, each with double spa, wood fire, TV/DVD, air con. and kitchenette. Full breakfast is served overlooking panoramic views. Our 37 acre property boasts waterfalls, creeks and natural rainforest, and abundant native wildlife.

Berry - Kangaroo Valley

Wombat Hill B&B *10 km W of Berry*
Luxury B&B & Farmstay & Self
contained cottage
Trish and Ken Jessop
1010 Kangaroo Valley Road
Bellawongarah
NSW 2535

Tel (02) 4464 1924
trishandken@wombathillbandb.com
www.wombathillbandb.com

Double $205-$225
Pre school children $30 per night,
School age $45 Extra adult $70
Pets $25   Full breakfast
Extra $25 for 1 night only
Visa MC accepted
2 The Bower - QS b/r, living, bathroom, sofa bed
Wombat Cottage - QS b/r, living, kitchen, bathroom, sofa bed

E njoy luxury, perfect peace and quiet, expansive mountain views, acres of glorious gardens, friendly farm animals, great wildlife, scrumptious breakfasts. Close to Berry and Kangaroo Valley, 2 hours from Sydney, and 2.5 hours from Canberra. We can recommend local activities and venues for your enjoyment. Everyone welcome, including children and pets. Each unit has comfortable, modern amenities with Q/S bedroom, bathroom, living area with single sofa bed, A/C, fans, electric blankets, books, magazines, TV/VCR/DVD player, CD player, private deck, separate entry. (Full kitchen in cottage).

Blue Mountains - Blackheath

Amani B&B *2 km N of Blackheath*
B&B
Rosemary & Bill Chapple
31 Days Crescent
Blackheath
NSW 2785

Tel (02) 4787 8610
or 0411 111 391
Fax (02) 4787 8894
amanicottage@optusnet.com.au
www.bbbook.com.au/amanibb.html

Double $120-$140
Single $80
Children $40
Full breakfast
1 King/Twin 1 Queen (2 bdrm)
Both have wonderful views
Bathrooms: 2 Ensuite

O ur home is surrounded by lovely gardens on the edge of the National Park, overlooking the spectacular cliffs that tower above the Grose Valley. We enjoy sharing the wonderful views from our home and the many scenic bush walks that begin nearby. Our guest rooms, with private entrance, are upstairs. Two bedrooms, each with an ensuite and a guests lounge. There is central heating, TV, CD, fridge, microwave oven and tea and coffee making facilities. Blackheath is two hours by road or rail from Sydney.

Blue Mountains - Hampton - Jenolan Caves

Hampton Homestead *28 km NE of Jenolan Caves*
B&B
Deb and Richard
1991 Jenolan Caves Road
Hampton
NSW 2790

Tel (02) 6359 3337
hhomestead@ozemail.com.au
www.hamptonhomestead.com.au

Double $160-$230 **Single** $140-$210
Full breakfast
Dinner BYO from $35
Tea/coffee, TV/DVD, clock radio,
electric blankets
1 King/Twin 2 Queen (3 bdrm)
King/twin has extra bed, fridge
and external door
Bathrooms: 3 Ensuite
All 3 bathrooms with clawfoot baths

In a country setting with glorious 180 degree views and only 20mins from Jenolan Caves Mt Victoria or Oberon the centrally-heated Homestead is a great place to relax after a day exploring in the fresh air. Sit in front of the s/c fire in the guest lounge watching the sunset-lit escarpments before having a delicious candlelit dinner there in the 1920's lead-lighted B&B wing or in the 19th Century stone cottage with its open fire, and then choose from the extensive DVD library.

Blue Mountains - Hampton

Historic rural Hampton is on the ridge west of the Kanimbia Valley. The once larger community still has a small school and sandstone church (with services twice a month) and the district is home to cockatoos, eagles and a pub, with twin wind generators on the hill standing as markers. At the right time the pine forests are famous for their mushrooms, and snow falls are possible.
Deb & Richard Hunter
Hampton Homestead

Blue Mountains - Katoomba

Melba House *0.5 km E of Katoomba*
Luxury B&B
Marion Hall
98 Waratah Street
Katoomba
NSW 2780

Tel (02) 4782 4141
or 0403 021 074
stay@melbahouse.com
www.melbahouse.com

Double $195-$249
Single $185-$239
Full breakfast
Visa MC Eftpos accepted
1 King/Twin1 King 2 Queen (3 bdrm)
Bathrooms: 2 Spa Ensuite
1 Shower Ensuite

AAA Tourism
★★★★☆

I magine your own log fire and spa, central-heating, electric blankets, large comfortable suites with own sitting and dining areas, sumptuous breakfasts, that's historical 4.5* Melba House. Quiet and secluded yet close to many restaurants, galleries, antique and craft shops and walking tracks. Also, close to the best-loved attractions of Katoomba and Leura. See our website www.melbahouse.com. "Of the B&Bs around the world we have stayed, this is our best experience, it's exquisite." (W. Dallas Texas). Stay 3 consecutive nights Midweek and only pay for 2.

Blue Mountains - Leura

Broomelea *0.5 km S of Leura*
B&B
Bryan & Denise Keith
273 Leura Mall
Leura
NSW 2780

Tel (02) 4784 2940
or 0419 478 400
Fax (02) 4784 2611
info@broomelea.com.au
www.broomelea.com.au

Double $165-$215
Single $130-$190
Full breakfast
Visa MC Diners Amex
Eftpos JCB accepted
3 Queen 1 King/2 Singles (4 bdrm)
Bathrooms: 4 Ensuite

AAA Tourism
★★★★☆

A beautiful 1909 mountain home for guests who would like more than simply a bed and a breakfast. We offer spacious ensuite rooms with 4 poster beds, open fires, lounges, TV, Video, CD Players, a freshly prepared gourmet breakfast each morning and most importantly local knowledge. Broomelea is perfectly located in the Living Heritage precinct of Leura just a 10 minute stroll to famous cliff top walks with great views or our beautiful village with numerous restaurants and galleries.

Blue Mountains - Leura

Bethany Manor Bed & Breakfast *0.8 km NW of Leura*

B&B
Greg & Jill Haigh
8 East View Avenue
Leura
NSW 2780

Tel (02) 4782 9215
Fax (02) 4782 1962
bmanor@optusnet.com.au
www.bethanymanor.com.au

Double $130-$205
Single $110-$185
Full breakfast
Visa MC accepted
3 Queen (3 bdrm)
Bathrooms: 3 Ensuite

   AAA Tourism ★★★★☆

Looking for a welcoming place to call home when visiting the World Heritage Blue Mountains? Bethany Manor is a Federation style home set on over an acre of parklike grounds, with tennis court. Your ensuite bedroom incorporates a spa-bath and verandah access while the Garden View room provides the perfect setting for enjoying a sumptuous breakfast in any season. Centrally heated with a wood fire in the guest's lounge. We're an easy walk to Leura village with its speciality shops, restaurants and railway station.

Blue Mountains - Leura

The Greens of Leura *0.1 km E of Leura*

B&B
Hayley & Richard Clifton
24 - 26 Grose Street
Leura
NSW 2780

Tel (02) 4784 3241
admin@thegreensleura.com.au
www.thegreensleura.com.au

Double $125-$175
Single $105-$150
Full breakfast
Visa MC Eftpos accepted
4 Queen 1 Twin (5 bdrm)
Bathrooms: 3 Ensuite
1 Guest share 1 Private

Accommodation, Location and Value, The Greens offers the best combination in Leura and the Blue Mountains. Set in the heart of Leura just a 2 minute walk from the chic shops and restaurants, The Greens enjoys a tranquil yet convenient setting. Enjoy the full size snooker table or extensive range of books from the library before retiring to one of our comfortable rooms for a good nights sleep. Awake to our generous full cooked breakfast that will set you up for a days' exploring!

Blue Mountains - Leura

Leura's Magical Manderley *0.3 km E of Leura*
Luxury Self Contained Spa Apartments
Robyn Piddington
157 Megalong Street
Leura
NSW 2780

Tel (02) 4784 3252
or 0417 286 533
Fax (0)2 4784 1603
manderleys@bigpond.com
www.manderley.com.au

Double $170-$240
Single $150-$180
Full breakfast provisions
Stay 4 nights midweek, pay 3
Visa MC Eftpos accepted
3Queen 1 King/2 Singles (4 bdrm)
Bathrooms: 2 Private 2 double
Hydro spas and showers

Experience the Magic of Manderley - Peace, Privacy and Luxury - right in the heart of Historic Leura. Robyn Piddington proudly presents her two unique, self-contained and elegant garden apartments - Treetops and The Terrace. Guests enjoy the idyllic and secluded setting just a stroll to popular Leura Village with its' famous restaurants, galleries and tea rooms. Exquisite furnishings and decor create that special ambience. After a day exploring our beautiful Blue Mountains, pour a glass of champagne, relax and rejuvenate the body and mind, in your private, double 36 jet Hydro Spa. Tariffs include generous breakfast provisions for a self-catering, leisurely breakfast, aperitifs, champagne, chocolates, Molton Brown English toiletries and spa products. Book 4 nights mid-week - Pay for 3.
"Robyn - Another fabulous time at Magical Manderley - your superb accommodation, genuine hospitality and thoughtful touches again made us feel so pampered. Magical Manderley is the best - we will return." Dave & Jo-Ellen U.S.A

Blue Mountains - Leura

Strawberry Patch Cottage *0.5 km SW of Leura Station*
Luxury Self Contained Cottage
Lorraine Allanson
10 Wascoe Street
Leura
NSW 2780

Tel 0430 496 755
info@strawberrypatch.com.au
www.strawberrypatch.com.au

Double $200-$270
Children 10 yrs and older welcome
Accommodation only
Minimum 2 nights
Extra guests $45 per person
Visa MC Amex accepted
1 Queen 1 Double (2 bdrm)
Bathrooms: 1 Private Spa bath

Nestled within a private garden and only one and a half minutes walk to Leura village, this exquisite turn-of-the-century cottage is totally dedicated to relaxation and indulgence. Strawberry Patch is the ultimate sanctuary from everyday life. The cottage has everything from an exquisite spa, finest linen, doonas, feather and down pillows, sheepskin electric blankets, under floor heating in the bathroom, slow combustion log fire, natural gas log fire, continuous hot water, T.V., Austar, DVD Player and discs, Video, Hi Fi player, dishwasher, Washing machine, gas barbecue.

Blue Mountains - Leura

Varenna *200m from Leura centre*
Luxury Self Contained House
Lorraine Allanson
97 Railway Parade
Leura
NSW 2780

Tel 0430 496 755
bookings@varenna.net.au
www.varenna.net.au

Double $240-$280
Children 10 yrs and over welcome
Continental provisions
Minimum stay 2 nights
Additional couple $60-$100 per night
Visa MC Amex accepted
3 Queen (3 bdrm)
Bathrooms: 2 Private 1 Double Spa

AAA Tourism
★★★★

Be enchanted by the grandeur and allow the soothing ambience of Varenna create that perfect stay. Step back into a bygone era which captures the old world charm so perfectly, with the modern comforts of today and only 200m from the heart of Leura. This lavishly appointed and meticulously restored Edwardian residence is set on 1800 square metres of surrounding grounds and gardens. Varenna can assist with any occasion - be it an anniversary, honeymoon, birthday, or even a marriage proposal.

Blue Mountains - Leura

Argyll House *0.3 km S of Leura*
B&B & Guest House
Cherril & Jane Canfield
11A Craigend Street
Leura
NSW 2780

Tel (02) 4784 1555
or 0402 980 411
Fax (02) 4784 1566
stay@argyll.com.au
www.argyll.com.au

Double $135-$220
Single $110-$167
Special breakfast
Visa MC Eftpos accepted
4 Queen (4 bdrm) Spa Suite with four
poster bed, Ensuite with sun room
Bathrooms: 2 Ensuite 1 Guest share

AAA Tourism

A rgyll House is in a quiet secluded spot in the heart of the premier village on the Blue
Mountains. There are 4 accommodations including a Spa Suite with private sun room,
4 poster bed and 2 person corner spa, an Ensuite also with private sun room and 2
traditional rooms that share a bathroom, perfect for family or friends travelling together. All
rooms are spacious including a lovely sunny breakfast room and large lounge room with
wood burning fires in both public rooms in season. The house is also centrally heated and
air conditioned and we offer a comprehensive 4 course Scottish or English breakfast.

Blue Mountains - Lithgow - Hartley

Majic Views B&B *6 km E of Lithgow*
B&B & Self Contained Apartment
Allan & Jeanie Cupitt
157 McKanes Falls Road
Lithgow
NSW 2790

Tel (02) 6353 1094 or 0409 244 791
or 0421 647 898 Fax (02) 6353 1094
relax@majicviews.com.au
www.majicviews.com.au

Double $165 Single $125
Children $15-$20
Continental breakfast
Dinner $15-$25 B/A
Full breakfast B/A
Visa MC Eftpos accepted
2 King/Twin 3 Queen 3 Single (4 bdrm)
Large rooms all with views
Bathrooms: 2 Private (Ensuite b/a)

Q uiet, private rural setting on 5 acres with 'Majic Views' across the valley to the
Blue Mountains Escarpment. Contemporary styled home, with the main accom-
modation offering 1 Queen and 1 Kingtwin bedroom, living area with CD, TV,
VCR, DVD, kitchenette, luxury three way bathroom with spa and a private barbecue area.
Suitable to families with additional bedding available. Private access. Central to Jenolan
Caves, the Zig Zag Railway and Blue Mountains attractions. Discounted rate to seniors.
Private bathroom available by arrangement.

Blue Mountains - Mount Tomah - Bells Line of Road

Tomah Mountain Lodge *14 km W of Bilpin*
B&B & Homestay
Bill & Gai Johns
25 Skyline Road
Mount Tomah via Bilpin
NSW 2758

Tel (02) 4567 2111
or 0419 908 724
tomahlodge@ozemail.com.au
www.tomahmountainlodge.com.au

Double $220-$250
Single $190-$220
Full breakfast
Gourmet three course candlelit
dinners by arrangement
BYO alcohol
Visa MC Eftpos accepted
1 King/Twin 2 Queen (3 bdrm)
Bathrooms: 3 Ensuite

AAA Tourism
★★★★☆

Tomah Mountain Lodge is situated in the World Heritage Blue Mountains National Park and offers comfortable, executive style accommodation. Mount Tomah is over 1000 metres above sea level, with mountain views. This secluded setting is only two minutes drive to Mount Tomah Botanic Garden, and a short drive to the historic gardens at Mount Wilson. The lodge offers spacious & comfortable lounge rooms with log fires. Gourmet three course candlelit dinners are a speciality.

Blue Mountains – Mount Tomah
Mount Tomah Botanic Garden showcases both native and exotic plants from around the world with over 40,000 plants and set against the stunning backdrop of breathtaking views.

Discover remnant rainforest and themed plant displays that highlight biodiversity and adaptation, such as the Gondwana Walk or the Rock Garden with plantings grouped by continent of origin.
Bill & Gai Johns
Tomah Mountain Lodge

Blue Mountains - Springwood - Faulconbridge

Mountain Jewel B&B *4 km W of Springwood*
**Self Contained Suites & Self
Contained Cottage**
Betty & Warwick Reynolds
51 Summer Road
Faulconbridge
NSW 2776

Tel (02) 4751 9270 or 0418 431 341
Fax (02) 4751 1186
jewel@pnc.com.au
www.bluemts.com.au/jewel

Double $225-$450
1 small child in suites, up to 4 in cottage
Full breakfast   Dinner by arrangement
Visa MC Amex Eftpos JCB accepted
3 King 2 Queen (5 bdrm)
3 spa suites & 2 bedroom cottage
Bathrooms: 3 Ensuite

Spectacular 13 acre property adjoining the World Heritage National Park. Breathtaking views of the valley and mountains with spacious gardens and swimming pool. Many vegetables and fruit grown in our gardens. Superb gourmet breakfasts! Suites are very private with separate entrances, reverse cycle air conditioning, TV, DVD, bathrobes, hairdryers, irons and ironing boards. Some include kitchenettes, the Honeymoon Suite has a separate lounge with log fire. Complimentary flowers, chocolates, teas, coffees, fruit drinks and cheese platter on arrival. Just over one hour from Sydney. Friendly hosts who will assist you to make your stay a memorable one.

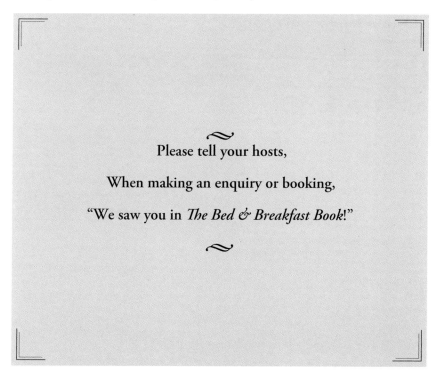

~

Please tell your hosts,

When making an enquiry or booking,

"We saw you in *The Bed & Breakfast Book*!"

~

Blue Mountains - Wentworth Falls

Blue Mountains Lakeside *1 km N of Wentworth Falls*
B&B & Self Contained Apartment
Michaela Russell
30 Bellevue Road
Wentworth Falls
NSW 2782

Tel (02) 4757 3777 or 0410 443 322
stay@lakesidebandb.com.au
www.lakesidebandb.com.au

Double $165-$240 Single $135-$190
Children 12 years plus $30
Full breakfast
Dinner by prior arrangement
Mid-week specials for longer stays
Visa MC accepted
2 Queen 1 Double 2 Single (2 bdrm)
Lake Suite B&B, Reflections S/C Spa Suite

Bathrooms: 2 Ensuite Two person Spa Bath in Reflections selfcontained suite

B lue Mountains' only Waterfront Bed & Breakfast. "At the edge of the Lake in the Heart of the Mountains." Looking for somewhere unique, secluded, plus log fire and spa? Lake Suite with delicious country cooked breakfasts home grown produce or the new self contained Reflections Spa Suite with living room, kitchenette, verandah - both with tranquil Lake views. Try a soothing in-house massage. Complimentary boats, trout fishing. Birdwatchers paradise. Minutes to Three Sisters Katoomba. "An amazing piece of paradise." Michael and Ashley (Visitors' Book).

Blue Mountains - Woodford

Braeside *19 km E of Katoomba*
B&B
Robyn Wilkinson & Rex Fardon
97 Bedford Road
Woodford
NSW 2778

Tel (02) 4758 6279
or 0414 542 860
Fax (02) 4758 8210
Braeside.BandB@bigpond.com
www.bluemts.com.au/braeside

Double $120-$140 Single $85-$100
Children from $15
Full breakfast
Dinner available $20-$35 pp
Visa MC Diners Amex accepted
1 King/Twin 1 Queen 1 Double (3 bdrm)
Bathrooms: 2 Ensuite 1 Private

AAA Tourism ★★★★

B raeside offers a quiet escape as well as being central to the attractions of the upper and lower Blue Mountains. Three bedrooms are available to suit a variety of needs including singles sharing, family groups with children and couples looking for a quiet escape. Flexible arrangements include providing an evening meal with a little notice. The guests lounge has an open log fire for cooler weather. Set in large parklike gardens Braeside offers a home away from home. No smoking inside.

Byron Bay

Victoria's Byron Bay *2 km E of Byron Bay*
Luxury Guest House
Victoria McEwen
Marine Parade & McGettigans Lane
Byron Bay
NSW 2481

Tel (02) 6684 7047
or (02) 6685 5388
Fax (02) 6684 7687
indulge@victorias.net.au
www.victorias.net.au

Double $250-$699
Full breakfast
Visa MC Diners Amex
Eftpos JCB accepted
5 King 5 Queen (10 bdrm)
Bathrooms: 10 Ensuite

    AAA Tourism ★★★★★

"Victoria's At Ewingsdale", a stately country manor, situated on 4 acres of landscaped gardens and features panoramic ocean, mountain and rural views. "Victoria's at Wategos", a stunning Tuscan style guesthouse, nestled in an exclusive ocean front valley at beautiful Wategos beach, just under the famous Cape Byron lighthouse. Both properties feature a salt-water swimming pool, open fireplaces, air-conditioning, rooms with spas and balconies. Experience personalised service in our small and exclusive boutique retreats, dedicated to providing the best in first class hospitality, quality and style.

Byron Bay and Hinterland
The sun rises first in Byron Bay and today it is still a mecca for the beach culture. But travel a few minutes west for a sub-tropical hinterland with a diverse and beautiful landscape of verdant rolling hills landscaped with macadamia plantations, friendly villages and the beautiful Nightcap National Park for romantic waterfalls.

Byron Bay Hinterland

Green Mango Hideaway *12 km W of Byron Bay*
B&B
Susie Briscoe
Lofts Road,
off Coolamon Scenic Drive
Coorabell
NSW 2479

Tel (02) 6684 7171
relax@greenmango.com.au
www.greenmango.com.au

Double $165-$250
Single $150-$220
Full breakfast
Visa MC Eftpos accepted
2 King 2 Queen (4 bdrm)
Bathrooms: 4 Ensuite

From the moment you walk down its leafy path, you'll be captivated by the tropical atmosphere of this peaceful B&B set in Byron's spectacular hinterland. With just four guestrooms, each with ensuite & verandah, you'll be escaping the crowds and yet be within 10 minutes of fabulous shops & cafes and glorious beaches. The muslin-draped beds & Oriental decor, the sparkling palm-fringed pool & lush gardens with abundant birdlife, and the wonderful breakfasts all guarantee you a relaxing and memorable stay.

Candelo - Bega Valley

Bumblebrook Farm *20 km SW of Bega*
B&B & Farmstay & Self Contained Apartment
Alan and Wendy Cross
Kemps Lane
Candelo
NSW 2550

Tel (02) 6493 2238
Fax (02) 6493 2299
stay@bumblebrook.com.au
www.bumblebrook.com.au

Double $100-$115 Single $80-$115
Children under 13 free
Full breakfast provisions
Mid week and long stay specials
Visa MC Eftpos accepted
1 King/Twin 1 King 1 Queen
2 Double 4 Single (4 bdrm)
Bathrooms: 4 Ensuite

AAA Tourism
★★★☆

A 100 acre beef property with magnificent views and lovely bush walks, fronting Tantawangalo Creek. We have four well equipped self-contained units. Breakfast is a "cook-your-own" from our fresh farm ingredients. Children are welcome and can often help feed the farm animals. BBQs are provided by the creek and in the playground near the units. Beaches and National Parks nearby. Pets welcome with prior arrangement. Relaxation massages available by your host Wendy.

Central Coast - Tuggerah

Greenacres B&B *1 km W of Tuggerah*
Separate Suite
Elizabeth & John Fairweather
8 Carpenters Lane
Mardi
NSW 2259

Tel (02) 4353 0643
or (02) 4353 0309
johnlizf@bigpond.net.au
www.greenacres-bb.com

Double $125-$160
Single $110-$145
Children over 4 years old $20 each pn
Full breakfast provisions
1 Queen 1 Double (1 bdrm)
Lounge has folding double bed
Bathrooms: 1 Ensuite

W e welcome you to Greenacres B&B, a unique tranquil/private retreat set on 3.5 evergreen acres, only minutes from Westfield Tuggerah, the railway station. Relax in your fully self contained air-con. suite with pillow top queen bed, sofa bed, TV & DVD. Games room. Home movie theatre. Free inhouse movies. For your enjoyment a 14m salt water swimming pool, Bali style gazebos, extensive landscaped gardens with ponds, fountains, waterfalls, bushwalking trails, dam. Enjoy hand feeding our Silver Perch fish. Dog/cat enclosure located next to the suite.

Central Coast
The Central Coast is a holiday playground with unique and stylish B&Bs, trendy markets, al fresco cafes, classy boutique shops. Visit the award winning National Australian Reptile Park, discover the magic of the Australian Rainforest Sanctuary, see the pelican feeding daily at The Entrance.

Visit Mt Penang Gardens, Yarramalong and Dooralong Valleys or take a scenic drive through the lush valleys and feel the natural beauty of the hinterlands.
Elizabeth & John Fairweather
Greenacres B&B

Central Coast - Terrigal

AnDaCer Boutique B&B *4 km W of Terrigal*
Luxury B&B
Gaby Schaudinn
28 Serpentine Road
Terrigal, NSW 2260

Tel (02) 4367 8368
Fax (02) 4367 8368
stay@terrigalretreat.com.au
www.terrigalretreat.com.au

Double $140-$350
Single $120-$140
Full breakfast
Book ahead for light dinner,
Seafood Platter
Romantic Weekend Accommodation
Package from $330 per night
Visa MC accepted
3 Queen (3 bdrm)
Bathrooms: 3 Ensuite

If you are looking for a romantic getaway close to Sydney, An'da'cer House Retreat provides the perfect destination with luxury boutique B&B accommodation. Stay in a secluded and relaxing resort-style atmosphere set in beautiful gardens surrounded by tranquil coastal acreages. An'Da'Cer House Retreat offers three individual luxury Suites ñ two with direct access into the garden and pool area via private gardens. The breakfast conservatory, with its casual and inviting appeal, overlooks the pool and garden and is a delightful spot to sit while indulging yourself with the fabulous breakfasts served each morning.

Central Tilba - Tilba Tilba - Narooma

The Two Story B&B *In Central Tilba*
B&B
Ken & Linda Jamieson
Bate Street
Central Tilba
NSW 2546

Tel (02) 4473 7290
or 1800 355 850
Fax (02) 4473 7992
stay@tilbatwostory.com
www.tilbatwostory.com

Double $120
Single $105
Full breakfast
Visa MC Eftpos accepted
2 Queen 1 Double 1 Single (3 bdrm)
Bathrooms: 3 Ensuite

A warm welcome awaits you at the Two Story B&B in the National Trust Village of Central Tilba. Our building is 114 years old built in 1894 and was originally the Post Office and residence, it has great character and views overlooking a superb valley of rolling hills and lush greenness. Enjoy the atmosphere, warmth in front of our log fire. Our weather is temperate and beaches are close by. We offer our guests off street parking, a choice of continental and full cooked breakfasts with tea/coffee facilities, in a totally relaxed atmosphere of pleasant old world charm.

Coffs Harbour - Woolgoolga

Solitary Islands Lodge *25 km N of Coffs Harbour*

B&B

Denise & John Hannaford
3 Arthur Street
Woolgoolga
NSW 2456

Tel (02) 6654 1335
or 0419 248 081
denise@solitaryislandslodge.com.au
www.solitaryislandslodge.com.au

Double $140-$180
Continental breakfast
Visa MC accepted
2 King/Twin (2 bdrm)
Double size room with sitting area
Bathrooms: 2 Ensuite
1 room has bath

Solitary Islands Lodge is the perfect accommodation to embrace all that the area has to offer being two minutes stroll to the beach and village. Nestled just 25km north of Coffs Harbour in the seaside village of Woolgoolga, Solitary Islands Lodge overlooks the Pacific Ocean with spectacular northerly views of the ocean, mountains and Solitary Islands Marine Park. Three unique rooms provide ample space and comfort with king beds, ensuite bathrooms, television, DVD, radio, bar fridge also tea/coffee facilities. A large deck with ocean views and barbeque is also available for guests. Airport transfers from Coffs Harbour can be arranged.

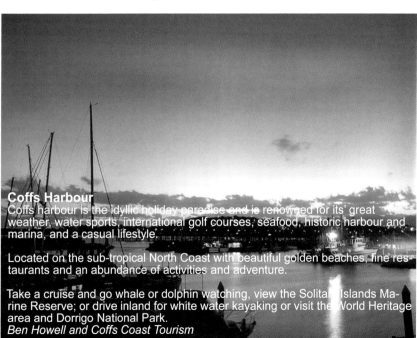

Coffs Harbour

Coffs harbour is the idyllic holiday paradise and is renowned for its' great weather, water sports, international golf courses, seafood, historic harbour and marina, and a casual lifestyle.

Located on the sub-tropical North Coast with beautiful golden beaches, fine restaurants and an abundance of activities and adventure.

Take a cruise and go whale or dolphin watching, view the Solitary Islands Marine Reserve; or drive inland for white water kayaking or visit the World Heritage area and Dorrigo National Park.
Ben Howell and Coffs Coast Tourism

fs Harbour Northern Beaches

dlands Beach Guest House *5 km N of Woolgoolga*

B&B & Guest House

Valerie & Terry Swan
17 Headland Road
Arrawarra Headland
NSW 2456

Tel (02) 6654 0364
or 0417 240 440
0417 249 500
Fax (02) 6654 0308
info@headlandsbeach.com.au
www.headlandsbeach.com.au

Double $145-$170 Single $125-$140
Full breakfast Refreshments on arrival
Visa MC accepted
3 Queen (3 bdrm)
Well appointed rooms with TV,
radio, ceiling fans, heating
Bathrooms: 3 Ensuite

 AAA Tourism ★★★★☆

Enjoy absolute beach frontage with warm hospitality at Headlands Beach Guest House located 20 mins north of Coffs Harbour on the Solitary Islands Marine National Park & 5km from Woolgoolga. A fully equipped kitchen is available for guests to use along with the BBQ poolside. Guest lounge & dining room overlook the pool, Mullawarra Beach & Arrawarra Headland. Complimentary refreshments on arrival.

Crookwell
Nestled on top of the Great Dividing Range, an hour from Canberra is the picturesque town of Crookwell - a secluded rural hideaway, protected from the harshness of modern-day intrusions.

Crookwell experiences the seasons in all their glory. Autumn is a blaze of colour - winter sees rolling hills blanketed in white powdery snow. Masses of exquisite blossoms, bulbs and flowers herald spring, and a gentle summer allows you to escape the harsh heat and humidity of coastal regions.

Great for Abercrombie and Wombeyan Caves
Mary and Geoff Ashton
Markdale Homestead

Crookwell

Markdale Homestead *40 km NW of Crookwell*
B&B & Farmstay & Self Contained House
Geoff & Mary Ashton
462 Mulgowrie Road
Binda, NSW 2583

Tel (02) 4835 3146
or (02) 8212 8599
Fax (02) 4835 3160
g_ashton@bigpond.com
www.markdale.com

Double $100-$220 Single $50-$110
Children under two no charge
Full breakfast provisions
Dinner Dinners $25 to $40
Phones and WiFi Internet
Visa MC accepted

2 Queen 3 Double 7 Twin (12 bdrm) 4 Stone House, 2 Annexe, 6 Sh Qt
Bathrooms: 1 Ensuite 4 Guest share 2 Stone House, 1 Annexe, 2 Shearers' Quarters

Food for the soul. A stunning landscape, 6000 acres, trout stocked streams, solar heated pool and all weather tennis. The Markdale Homestead and Garden combine the talents of two Australian Icons; Edna Walling, garden designer, and Professor Wilkinson, architect. Live in two adjoining, self contained, beautifully renovated, stone houses. Both have central heating, open fire, sitting room, kitchen, laundry, TV, CD Player, phone and internet access. Or stay in the comfortable Shearers' Quarters at cheaper rates.

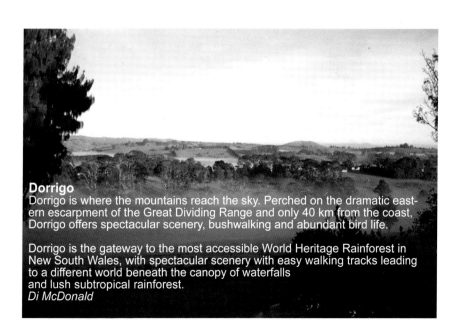

Dorrigo
Dorrigo is where the mountains reach the sky. Perched on the dramatic eastern escarpment of the Great Dividing Range and only 40 km from the coast, Dorrigo offers spectacular scenery, bushwalking and abundant bird life.

Dorrigo is the gateway to the most accessible World Heritage Rainforest in New South Wales, with spectacular scenery with easy walking tracks leading to a different world beneath the canopy of waterfalls and lush subtropical rainforest.
Di McDonald

Dorrigo

Lisnagarvey Cottage *8 km W of Dorrigo*
Luxury Self Contained Cottage
Mark & Elaine Martin
803 Whisky Creek Road
Dorrigo
NSW 2453

Tel (02) 6657 2536
or 0428 228 160
Fax (02) 6657 2053
bookings@lisnagarvey.com.au
www.lisnagarvey.com.au

Double $145-$165
Single $120-$145
Full breakfast provisions
Accommodation only rates available
1 Queen (1 bdrm)
Bathrooms: 1 Private Bath and shower

 AAA Tourism ★★★★

Nestled amidst the lush green hills of the Dorrigo Plateau and just 8 minutes to town is a beautifully renovated, luxury, one bedroom dairy bails with loads of character, charm, privacy and spectacular views over the plateau and Dorrigo township. Relax and enjoy the views from your private deck or curl up with complimentary port and chocolates in front of the wood fire. A gourmet breakfast basket can be supplied or you can choose to self cater. Fully self-contained.

Dubbo - Central West

Walls Court B&B *12 km S of Dubbo*
Farmstay & Private Cottages,
Country Hospitality
Neil & Nancy Lander
11L Belgravia Heights Road
Dubbo , NSW 2830

Tel (02) 6887 3823
or 0407 226 606
(02) 6887 3606
Fax (02) 6887 3602
nlander@bigpond.com
www.wallscourt.com.au

Double $150 Single $125
Children $30 Full breakfast
Dinner and/or picnic basket lunch b/a
Extra person $30
Visa MC Amex Eftpos accepted
1 King 1 Queen 4 Single (2 bdrm)
Bathrooms: 2 Ensuite

AAA Tourism ★★★★

Relish the tranquillity and comfort of your Walls Court suites as you laze on the veranda with a drink observing the birds in the garden. See your children's joy as they feed sheep and chooks, pat dogs and gather eggs. Gain more from your visit to the zoo; we are volunteer guides. Revel in crowd free shopping precincts or savour the tastings at nearby wineries. Explore attractions yourself or take advantage of our familiarity with the area. Your pet is welcome by arrangement. Learn a new craft - make a pair of silver earrings for a small additional cost.

Dunedoo - Central West

Redbank Gums B&B *In Dunedoo*
Self Contained Units
Sue & Lloyd Graham
41 Wargundy Street
Dunedoo
NSW 2844

Tel (02) 6375 1218
or 0428 751 218
grahamls@bigpond.com.au
www.redbankgums.com.au

Double $75-$95
Single $55
Full breakfast provisions
Dinner by arrangement
Family $110-$125
Visa MC Eftpos accepted
1 Queen 1 Double (2 bdrm)
Bathrooms: 2 Ensuite

AAA Tourism
★★★☆

W elcome to Redbank Gums B&B which is an ideal base when touring the central west. Spacious 2 bedroom unit or 2 separate units with kitchen, laundry and lounge with television and DVD. Relax in the shady garden and enjoy a barbeque. We are in a quiet area with off street parking opposite the Golf Course and are within walking distance to most amenities. Dunedoo is a friendly, hospitable town along the Golden Highway, set alongside the Talbragar River and is well known for the annual Bush Poetry Festival. Redbank Gums accepts pets by prior arrangement.

Eden
Historic Eden is the site of Australia's first mainland whaling station, established in 1828. Now it is a popular whale watching destination, with Southern Right and Humpback whales migrating between May and October. Throughout the year cruises to see Bottlenose dolphins, seals and penguins cruises are popular.

Eden is centrally located for excellent bushwalking in the National Parks such as the "Light to Light" walk along the rugged coast from Boyds Tower to Greencape Lighthouse.
Gail and David Ward
Cocora Cottage B&B

Eden

Cocora Cottage *0.2 km S of Centre of Eden*
Traditional B&B
Gail and David Ward
2 Cocora Street
Eden
NSW 2551

Tel (02) 6496 1241
or 0427 218 859
0409 961 241
info@cocoracottage.com
www.cocoracottage.com

Double $140-$160 Single $110-$120
Not suitable for children
Full breakfast
10% discount for 3 nights or longer
Visa MC accepted
2 Queen (2 bdrm)
Front room has old fireplace Back room has bay views
Bathrooms: 2 Ensuite with spas

AAA Tourism
★★★★

Heritage listed Cocora Cottage was the original Police Station in Eden. It is centrally located in a quiet area close to Eden's famous Killer Whale Museum, the Wharf and Eden's fine restaurants. Breakfast is served upstairs with spectacular views down to the Wharf and across Twofold Bay to the foothills of Mt Imlay. Both bedrooms have a Queen sized bed, an ensuite with a spa, a television and wireless internet. The front bedroom features the original open fireplace while the back bedroom offers bay views.

≈

Eden

Crown & Anchor Inn B&B *0.2 km SE of Eden Central*
B&B & Historic Inn
Lynne & Lindsay Evans
239 Imlay Street
Eden
NSW 2551

Tel (02) 6496 1017
Fax (02) 6496 3878
info@crownandanchoreden.com.au
www.crownandanchoreden.com.au

Double $180-$200
Single $160-$180
Full breakfast
Visa MC Eftpos accepted
5 Double (5 bdrm)
Period furniture, antiques and views
Bathrooms: 5 Ensuite

AAA Tourism
★★★★

Step back in time in this original 1845 inn surrounded by stunning water views. Feel at home in the delightful lounge rooms with period furniture, polished timber floors and open fires. Relax in the dining room and enjoy complementary champagne on arrival. Walk to local shops, restaurants and cafes, visit the fishermen's wharf or swim at some of the coast's finest beaches. Halfway between Sydney and Melbourne and 3 1/2 hours from Canberra, this romantic haven is a gem on the Sapphire Coast.

Gerringong - Gerroa

Tumblegum Inn *10 km S of Kiama*
B&B & Homestay
Christine & Ian Field
141C Belinda Street
Gerringong
NSW 2534

Tel (02) 4234 3555
or 0422 880 727
Fax (02) 4234 3888
tumbleguminn@hotmail.com
www.tumbleguminn.com.au

Double $120-$140
Single $90-$120
Older children welcome
Full breakfast
Visa MC Eftpos accepted
2 Queen 1 Twin (3 bdrm)
Bathrooms: 3 Ensuite

AAA Tourism
★★★★

With rolling green hills that lap to pristine beaches, Gerringong reminds visitors of Ireland. Tumblegum Inn is a newly-built Federation style home featuring antique furnishings and warm hospitality. Bedrooms contain ensuites, electric blankets, fans, clock radios and remote TV. Separate guest lounge has fridge, tea and coffee facilities, and home baked goodies. Only 1 1/2 hour south of Sydney. Local attractions include beach side golf course, saltwater pools, boutique wineries, Minnamurra Rainforest and Kiama blowhole. Winner, Illawarra Tourism Award for Accommodation.

Gerroa - Seven Mile Beach

Seven Mile Beach Bed & Breakfast *In Gerroa*
Luxury Spa Suite
Andy & Kim Reay
70 Crooked River Road
Gerroa
NSW 2534

Tel (02) 4234 2030
info@sevenmilebeachbb.com
www.sevenmilebeachbb.com

Double $250-$290
Special breakfast
Stay 3 nights receive free
lobster BBQ dinner and wine
Minimum two night stay over weekend
1 King (1 bdrm)
Designer bed linen and modern decor
Bathrooms: 1 Ensuite Spa

Seven Mile Brach Luxurious Bed & Breakfast- The name says it all, located at the top of the hill in Gerroa, offering breathtaking views of Seven Mile Beach, two hours south of Sydney. Accommodation is for couples only in your one bedroom King Spa Suite, with designer bed linen and modern decor. Enjoy wonderful views from either the indoor or outdoor spas. Facilities include: Television, DVD, music, tea and coffee, movies, board games, hair dryer, books, bicycles, golf clubs and surfboards. Enjoy a continental breakfast basket in your suite or take our full breakfast offered at the award winning Seahaven Cafe - just a two minute walk down the road.

Glen Innes

Halloran House *24 km E of Glen Innes*
Farmstay & Self Contained Cottage
Halloran Family
Gwydir Highway
Glen Innes
NSW 2370

Tel (02) 6732 3932
or 0427 323 932
www.bbbook.com.au/HalloranHouse.
html

Double $90-$100 Single $70-$75
Children free, using existing bedding
Full breakfast provisions
Dinner available by arrangement
Weekly rates available
1 Double
Bathrooms: 1 Private

Experience the warmth of New England hospitality at 'Halloran House'. Located on the Gwydir Highway in close proximity to World Heritage listed Washpool, and Gibraltar Range National Parks. A one bedroom self contained cottage, erected 2007, in a quiet garden setting. The cottage includes a double bed, ensuite bathroom with fully equipped kitchen, laundry and reverse cycle heating and air conditioning. Provisions are included for breakfast. There is a BBQ and shaded deck overlooking established gardens. Ramp access, cot and high chair available. Experience a working sheep and cattle farm, feed the chooks, ducks, calves & lambs (in season). Ideal for couples or a family retreat.

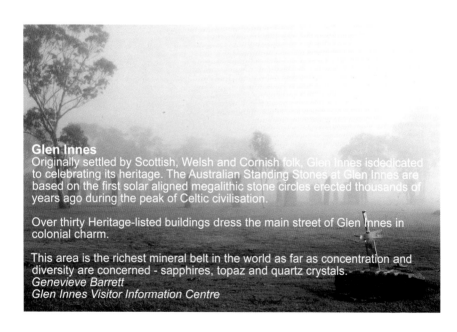

Glen Innes
Originally settled by Scottish, Welsh and Cornish folk, Glen Innes is dedicated to celebrating its heritage. The Australian Standing Stones at Glen Innes are based on the first solar aligned megalithic stone circles erected thousands of years ago during the peak of Celtic civilisation.

Over thirty Heritage-listed buildings dress the main street of Glen Innes in colonial charm.

This area is the richest mineral belt in the world as far as concentration and diversity are concerned - sapphires, topaz and quartz crystals.
Genevieve Barrett
Glen Innes Visitor Information Centre

Glen Innes - Ben Lomond

Silent Grove Farmstay B&B *32 km N of Guyra*

B&B & Homestay & Farmstay & Self Contained House
John & Dorothy Every
Silent Grove
Ben Lomond
NSW 2365

Tel (02) 6733 2117 or 0427 936 799
Fax (02) 6733 2117
silentgr@activ8.net.au
www.silentgrovefarmstay-bandb.com.au

Double $85 Single $45-$50
Children $15   Full breakfast
Dinner $18
S/C Cottage $95 per night,
2 Adults, 3 Children
Visa MC accepted
1 Queen 1 Double 2 Single (3 bdrm)
Bathrooms: 2 Guest share

AAA Tourism
★★★☆

Enjoy country hospitality in a peaceful rural setting, short detour by sealed road from the New England Highway. Working sheep and cattle property. Farm activities. 4WD tour (fee applies). Panoramic views, scenic walks, yabbying (seasonal), tennis court, fishing, occasional snow fall. Easy access to New England, Gibraltar Range, Washpool National Parks. Glen Innes Australian Stones. Smoking outdoors. Winner of 2001 Big Sky Regional Tourism Hosted Accommodation. Campervans welcome. "Lovely peaceful atmosphere, friendly hospitality couldn't be better." WC.

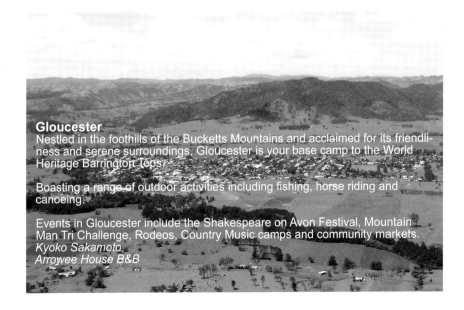

Gloucester
Nestled in the foothills of the Bucketts Mountains and acclaimed for its friendliness and serene surroundings, Gloucester is your base camp to the World Heritage Barrington Tops.

Boasting a range of outdoor activities including fishing, horse riding and canoeing.

Events in Gloucester include the Shakespeare on Avon Festival, Mountain Man Tri Challenge, Rodeos, Country Music camps and community markets.
Kyoko Sakamoto
Arrowee House B&B

Gloucester - Barrington Tops

Arrowee House B&B *1 km N of Gloucester*
B&B & Homestay & Separate Suite
Kyoko Sakamoto
152 Thunderbolts Way
Gloucester
NSW 2422

Tel (02) 6558 2050
Fax (02) 6558 2050
information@gloucester.nsw.gov.au
www.arrowee.com.au

Double $130 Single $65
Children 1-11 yrs $1 per year;
12-16 years $25 Baby cot available
Full breakfast   Dinner $35 pp
Extra adult $65 Visa MC accepted
3 Queen 6 Single (4 bdrm)
Bathrooms: 1 Ensuite 1 Guest share 3 Private

Commended Award 2005, 2006 and 2007. Established 1990. Northern gateway to World Heritage Barrington Tops. Walking distance to cafes, restaurants, shops, gallery and bushwalking on The Buckett and Mograni Mountains. Large undercover barbeque area with outdoor kitchen. Activities - bushwalking, fishing, canoeing, horse riding, scenic drives, golf, swimming, tennis. Events: Shakespeare on Avon Festival, Mountain Man Tri Challenge, rodeos, country music camps and community markets. During winter a 4 course Japanese dinner is available for only $35 per person, must pre book.

Grafton - Seelands

Seeview Farm *10 km N of Grafton*
B&B & Homestay & Farmstay
Mona Ibbott
440 Rogans Bridge Road
Seelands Grafton
NSW 2460

Tel (02) 6644 9270
or 0447 449 270
Fax (02) 6644 9270
www.bbbook.com.au/seeviewfarm.html

Double $90-$110
Single $70-$80
Children $17.50
Full breakfast
Dinner $20
1 Queen 1 Twin (2 bdrm)
Bathrooms: 1 Guest share 1 Private
Two bathrooms

AAA Tourism
★★★☆

Seeview Farm is a pretty cattle property on the banks of the Clarence River which is noted for river boat and water skiing. Grafton is famous for its Jacaranda Festival and its historical buildings. Close to beaches and mountains. Enjoy peaceful countryside - many overseas students have visited the farm, where pets are welcome. Kangaroos and bird life to watch. Good stopover from Sydney or Brisbane. Relaxing and friendly. Children are welcome. Damper and Billy Tea on the river bank can be provided.

Hay

Bank Bed & Breakfast *In Hay Central*
B&B
Sally Smith
86 Lachlan Street
Hay
NSW 2711

Tel (02) 6993 1730
or 0429 931 730
Fax (02) 6993 3440
ttsk@tpg.com.au
www1.tpg.com.au/users/ttsk

Double $120 Single $80
Full breakfast
1 King 1 Twin (2 bdrm)
2 luxurious rooms equipped
to make your stay relaxing
Bathrooms: 1 Private

This National Trust classified mansion was built in 1891 to house the London Chartered Bank, one of the historic buildings restored to its original condition in Lachlan Street. The residence consists of a large dining room complete with period furniture and decor. The cedar staircase leads to the guest suite of two bedrooms and a fully modernised bathroom (complete with spa). The guest sitting room opens onto the balcony overlooking the main street. We look forward to you experiencing the hospitality of Hay with us.

Hunter Valley - Aberdeen - Scone

Craigmhor Mountain Retreat *48 km E of Aberdeen*
Luxury B&B & Homestay & Separate Suite & Self Contained Apartment
Gay Hoskings
Upper Rouchel Road
Upper Rouchel
NSW 2336

Tel (02) 6543 6393
Fax (02) 6543 6394
bnb@craigmhor.com.au
www.craigmhor.com.au

Double $135-$165 Single $70-$85
Children $35-$45   Full breakfast
Dinner $30-$50 served
with Upper Hunter Wines
4WD tours from $100
Visa MC accepted
3 Queen 1 Twin 2 Single (4 bdrm)
Bathrooms: 2 Ensuite 1 Guest share

     AAA Tourism ★★★★

Total contrast to city living - country hospitality, seclusion, splendid views, crisp mountain air in foothills of Barrington Tops. Peace and tranquillity assured - just you, your host, 1000 ha Australian bush and all its wildlife. Homestay; B&B; Self-Catered; Mix & Match to suit. Possible activities: doing absolutely nothing, picnicking by mountain streams, bush walking (50 km of forest trails), mountain biking, fishing stocked dams, Lake Glenbawn, 4-WD touring (optional extra), exploring Upper Hunter Country - magnificent horse studs, historic towns, wineries, National Parks.

Hunter Valley - Broke

Ferguson's Hunter Valley Getaway *2 km NW of Broke*

**Luxury Self Contained Apartment &
Spacious King Suites & Spa Suites**
Susie Ferguson
130 Hill Street
Broke, NSW 2330

Tel (02) 6579 1046
Fax (02) 6579 1054
susie@huntervalleygetaway.com.au
www.huntervalleygetaway.com.au

Double $165-$270
Children welcome - no special provisions
Full breakfast provisions
We can arrange a dinner in your suite
Additional person $80
Specials and group rates available
Visa MC Diners Amex Eftpos accepted
6 King (6 bdrm) Spacious suites with sofas and views
Bathrooms: 6 Ensuite 2 spas suites and four with huge showers

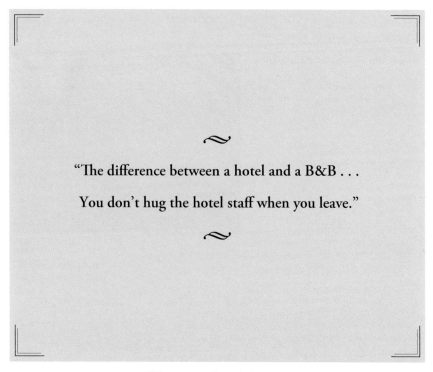

AAA Tourism
★★★★☆

Ferguson's Hunter Valley Getaway offers luxury, private suite accommodation across the Wollombi Brook from the rural village of Broke in the heart of the Hunter Valley Wine Country. Six stylish and spacious king suites with private terraces, electric BBQ and sweeping views of local vineyards and the Brokenback Range. Each suite includes a small kitchen, comfortable sofas, DVDs, reverse cycle air-conditioning and cooling ceiling fans. Gourmet breakfast hampers on weekends and generous continental breakfast midweek. Breathe fresh country air, gaze at the milky way and quite simply . . . take time out to relax.

~

"The difference between a hotel and a B&B . . .

You don't hug the hotel staff when you leave."

~

Hunter Valley - East Maitland

The Old George and Dragon Guesthouse
5 km E of Maitland

Guest House
Nicolena & Martin Hurley
50 Melbourne Street
East Maitland
NSW 2323

Tel (02) 4934 6080
or 0412 995 639
Fax (02) 4933 6076
reservations@oldgeorgedragonguesthouse.com.au
www.oldgeorgedragonguesthouse.com.au

Double $140-$240 Single $130-$190
Full breakfast
Dinner, Bed & Breakfast package
$340-$380 per couple
Visa MC Diners Amex Eftpos accepted
2 King 3 Queen (5 bdrm)
All guestrooms themed individual
Bathrooms: 5 Ensuite

Your hosts Nicolena and Martin will greet you on arrival. Our service is discreet and professional. Formerly a coach inn in the main route north from Sydney, the guesthouse has five guestrooms with ensuites, all individually decorated with high ceilings, flat LCD Television, DVD -CD Player & wireless broadband (fees apply). A spacious layout convey a comforting sense of space and privacy. The guest lounge has an open fire place for the winter months. The restaurant located next to the guesthouse features an extensive menu range with a remarkable aged wine list. The guesthouse is located close to Morpeth, famous wineries of Pokolbin , rugged glories of Barrington Tops and the sunny salty seduction of Port Stephens. The ideal place to stay for business or pleasure, special occasions, wedding night or group getaway.

Hunter Valley - Lochinvar

Lochinvar House *3 km W of Lochinvar (turn off Hwy Kaludah Ck)*

Luxury B&B & Farmstay &
Homestead (4 B/R) and Cottage (2 B/R)
Bob & Marie Cooper
Kaludah Estate,
1204 New England Highway
Lochinvar, NSW 2321

Tel (02) 4930 7873 or 0439 738 755
Fax (02) 4930 7798
lochinvarhse@yahoo.com.au
www.geocities.com/lochinvarhse

Double $121-$176 Single $99-$154
Children $66 Special breakfast
Dinner B/A
1 King/Twin 4 Queen 1 Double
(6 bdrm) plus sofabed in cottage
2 Guest share in Homestead. 1 private in Cottage

Historic Georgian-Victorian country homestead and heritage cottage circa 1841 on Kaludah Estate, an 88 acre grazing property on the Hunter River. With grand entrance and dining room, luxuriously appointed rooms featuring 13 foot ceilings and antique furnishings, Lochinvar House overlooks beautiful Loch Katrine with views over the surrounding countryside. A large swimming pool and spa with BBQ area are available. Situated 1 km north of the New England Highway, close to restaurants, Wyndham Estate, Tranquil Vale and other vineyards, equestrian centre, historic Maitland and Greta for antiques. Kennels available. Ideal for small groups and conferences.

~

Hunter Valley - Lovedale - Pokolbin

Hill Top Country Guest House *17 km N of Cessnock*

Luxury B&B & Homestay &
Farmstay & Self Contained
Apartment & Guest House
Margaret Bancroft
288 Talga Road
Rothbury
NSW 2320

Tel (02) 4930 7111 Fax (02) 4930 9048
stay@hilltopguesthouse.com.au
www.hilltopguesthouse.com.au

Double $90-$250
Full breakfast
Visa MC accepted
2 King/Twin1 King 3 Queen
4 Twin (11 bdrm)
Bathrooms: 8 Ensuite 1 Guest share
2 Private spa baths

An Australian Country Experience, staying in the colonial homestead or modern Villas. Situated on the Molly Morgan Range with spectacular views of the Hunter Valley and Wine Country. Join the 4WD Night Wildlife Safari, horse riding and encounter abundant native wildlife of kangaroos, wombats, echidnas, possums roaming in their natural environment. Winery tours leave daily. The luxury guest house offers Spa Suites, wood fires, 10' billiard table, Grand Piano, delicious meals, massages, beauty treatments, sauna, pool and air-conditioning. The guest house is ideal for couples and family and friends gatherings. The Romantic Villas are ideal for couples.

Hunter Valley - Morpeth

Bronte Guesthouse *10 km E of Maitland*
Guest House
Nicolena & Martin Hurley
147 Swan Street
Morpeth
NSW 2321

Tel (02) 4934 6080
or 0412 995 639
Fax (02) 4933 6076
reservations@bronteguesthouse.com.au
www.bronteguesthouse.com.au

AAA Tourism
★★★★

Double $120-$200
Single $110-$195
Full breakfast
Visa MC Diners Amex Eftpos accepted
4 King 3 Queen (6 bdrm)
Contemporary style accommodation
Bathrooms: 6 Ensuite
One room has a bath

Historic, charming, chic and comfortable, welcoming service with attention to detail. All rooms are themed to reflect the needs of the sophisticated traveller and offer complete luxury with ensuites, individually controlled air conditioning, LCD Flat Televisions, DVD Players, CD Players and wireless broadband (fees apply).

There are two guest lounges with open fire places for the winter months. Breakfast is served on the guesthouse's balcony overlooking the township of Morpeth and the Hunter River.

Located in the heart of Morpeth, a fascinating little village, which started life in 1821 as a river port for the Hunter River. The ideal place to stay for business or pleasure, special occasions, wedding night or group getaway.

Hunter Valley - Morpeth

Morpeth Convent Guest House *35 km NW of Newcastle*
Luxury B&B
Loris Chahl
24 James Street
Morpeth
NSW 2321

Tel (02) 4934 4176 or 1300 855 251
Fax (02) 4934 4179
info@morpethconvent.com.au
www.morpethconvent.com.au

Double $130-$165
Children only if whole house is
occupied by the party
Full breakfast   Dinner by arrangement
Special tariffs available mid-week
Visa MC Eftpos accepted
4 Queen 1 Twin (5 bdrm) polished floors, airconditioned, TV
Bathrooms: 4 Ensuite 1 Private queen rooms have ensuite, twin room private bath

Morpeth Convent Guest House is a grand two storey building once home to nuns of a teaching order, now refurbished to cater for bed-and-breakfast style accommodation with every modern comfort. The glorious house features sprawling verandas both upstairs and down, two spacious common rooms and breakfast room with bay windows. This unique accommodation experience is nestled in the heart of Morpeth NSW Australia - a town that's steeped in history and is the perfect place to get-away with family, friends or on your own.

Hunter Valley - Pokolbin

Catersfield House *23 km NW of Cessnock*
Guest House
Rosemary & Alec Cater
96 Mistletoe Lane
Pokolbin
NSW 2320

Tel (02) 4998 7220
Fax (02) 4998 7558
catersfield@catersfield.com.au
www.catersfield.com.au

Double $160-$250
Children $25 to 10 years
Extra Adult $40 Full breakfast
Dinner $55 for 3 courses (Groups)
Weekend packages from $440
Visa MC Diners Amex Eftpos accepted
5 King/Twin 3 Queen
1 Double (9 bdrm)
Bathrooms: 9 Ensuite

   AAA Tourism ★★★★

A luxury Country Resort amongst the vineyards of Pokolbin. Main House has 6 spacious guestrooms, 2 with spas and 1 with a draped 4-poster bed; the romantic Summerhouse has a glass "top-not" and a spa, and the 2-bedroom Family Suite has a log fire. Dogs up to 20 Kg are welcome. Facilities include a log fire in the Guests' lounge, a swimming pool, petanque, fishing and BBQ. A Continental breakfast is included and a hot breakfast is available. Enquire about Estate Weddings with a Reception for up to 90 guests. Mini-holiday Friday 2pm to Sunday 5pm from $500.

Hunter Valley - Pokolbin

Elfin Hill *5 km W of Cessnock*
**Farmstay & Separate Suite & Self
Contained Apartment & Guest House**
Marie & Mark Blackmore
Marrowbone Road
Pokolbin
NSW 2320

Tel (02) 4998 7543
or 0416 209 709
0406 531 709
Fax (02) 4998 7817
relax@elfinhill.com.au
www.elfinhill.com.au

Double $120-$250 Single $98-$250
Children $40 Full breakfast
Extra person $50
Visa MC Amex Eftpos accepted
7 Queen 2 Double 4 Twin 5 Single (7 bdrm)
Bathrooms: 7 Ensuite

   AAA Tourism ★★★☆

E njoy delightful country accommodation, serenely elevated with spectacular views of surrounding vineyards. Native wildlife. Rooms are comfy with everything you need to make your stay easy and enjoyable. BBQ beside the saltwater pool. Fabulous comfortable guest lounge. Easy bush walking. Close to Wine Tasting and Fantastic Cuisine, cheese, galleries etc. Excellent breakfast in your room or eat outside at one of many areas. Just completed a separate studio with mezzanine sleeping, ensuite, kitchen, amazing views, romantic and special.

Hunter Valley - Pokolbin

Holman Estate Pokolbin *120 km N of Sydney*
Self Contained House
Theo and Soula Tsironis
173 (Lot 3) Gillards Road
Pokolbin
NSW 2325

Tel 0438 683 973
Fax (02) 6842 4513
holman@mounteyre.com
www.mounteyre.com

Accommodation only
$800-$1000/night whole house
Visa MC Eftpos accepted
3 Queen 2 Single (4 bdrm)
Two double foldout futons in Games Room
Bathrooms: 1 Ensuite 2 Family share

Holman Estate is located in the heart of Pokolbin, the Hunter Valley's premier tourist location. Holman Estate offers spectacular views of the Hunter Valley, from the privacy of your own executive residence. Located on an operational vineyard, you will experience what it is like to live in a French chateau or Italian villa. The house boasts 4 generously sized bedrooms, 3 bathrooms, a billiards room and kitchen. The open-plan living and dining area features cathedral ceilings and a large open fireplace. You can simply spend a weekend drinking fine wine by the fireplace and strolling through the vineyards. Alternatively, enjoy the Hunter Valley Gardens, wine tastings, restaurants, galleries, ballooning and a myriad of other interesting pursuits. Whether you want a romantic escape, a family and friends holiday, a corporate function or even a small wedding, Holman Estate is the ideal venue. Holman Estate offers a unique opportunity to enjoy all the Hunter Valley has to offer, within easy reach of your own private residence.

Hunter Valley - Wine Country - Wollombi

Capers Guest House and Cottage *29 km SW of Cessnock*
Luxury B&B & Self Contained
House & Guest House
Jane Young
2859 Wollombi Road
Wollombi
NSW 2325

Tel (02) 4998 3211
or 0409 305 285
Fax (02) 4998 3458
stay@capers.com.au
www.capers.com.au

Double $200-$380 Single $200-$380
Full breakfast Dinner $55-$65
Cottage from $75 per person per night
Visa MC Diners Amex accepted
1 King 5 Queen 2 Double 1 Twin (9 bdrm)
Bathrooms: 8 Ensuite

  AAA Tourism ★★★★☆

Majestic Guesthouse Retreat, set in the historic village of Wollombi. Six elegantly appointed guest rooms, reverse-cycle air-conditioning and spacious guest lounge with double sided open log fire places. Includes full country breakfast, complimentary port and chocolates. Fully licensed and dinner can be arranged. Cottage: Stay two nights in luxury three bedroom cottages which accommodate up to 7 people. Open fire or A/C in the summer, large hamper breakfast, two bathrooms one with Spa bath, gourmet kitchen, sweetest garden with BBQ, TV, CD, and DVD players.

Jervis Bay - Huskisson

Dolphin Sands Jervis Bay *25 km S of Nowra*
B&B & Self Contained Cottages
Wayne and Beatrice Whitten
6 Tomerong Street
Jervis Bay, Huskisson
NSW 2540

Tel (02) 4441 5511
or 0418 476 280
Fax (02) 4441 7712
info@dolphinsands.com
www.dolphinsands.com

Double $175-$295
Children welcome in S/C Cottages
Full breakfast
Visa MC Amex Eftpos accepted
4 Queen 1 Twin (5 bdrm)
Bathrooms: 5 Ensuite
2 Queen Spa Rooms, 1 Queen with bath and shower

 AAA Tourism ★★★★☆

Dolphin Sands is what life by the ocean is all about. Dolphin Sands is a tranquil couples retreat, only minutes from the White Sands, Dolphins, and Clear Blue Waters of Jervis Bay at Huskisson. Hosts Wayne and Beatrice Whitten designed your luxury accommodations creating an intimate and relaxing atmosphere, while maintaining guest room privacy. Jervis Bay Luxury Cottage (4 bedrooms) and Dolphin Cottage (2 bedrooms) are 2 self contained cottages suitable for families, groups or a private romantic getaway.

Jervis Bay
Jervis Bay is one of nature's secrets, crystal clear waters and white sandy beaches, a place where Whales rest and Dolphins live year round. Declared a Marine Park and surrounded by national parks, the area offers a holiday experience for all ages.

Huskisson is the gateway to Jervis Bay and retains the character of a laid back coastal community offering good food, a variety of accommodation and a base to explore the generosity of nature.
Jervis Bay Tourism
www.jervisbaytourism.asn.au

Jervis Bay - Huskisson

Sandholme Guesthouse *1 km S of Huskisson on Jervis Bay*
Luxury 5 Star B&B Guesthouse
in Huskisson on Jervis Bay
Alan & Christine Burrows
2 Jervis Street
Huskisson
NSW 2540

Tel (02) 4441 8855
Fax (02) 4441 8866
guesthouse@sandholme.com.au
www.sandholme.com.au

Double $200-$310
Children under 15 not catered for
Full breakfast
Dinner by arrangement
Visa MC Eftpos accepted
5 King 2 Single (5 bdrm)
5 guestroom each 5 star
Bathrooms: 5 Ensuite 4 with Spa

 AAA Tourism ★★★★★

S andholme Guesthouse. Offering couples a romantic getaway accommodation at Huskisson on Jervis Bay, 2 hours south of Sydney. Experience the natural beauty, crystal clear waters and white sands of Jervis Bay and be pampered in a luxurious en-suite accommodation with spa. Enjoy sumptuous cooked breakfasts, relax on the verandah with a delicious espresso coffee, watch a movie in the theatre or your room. Only 200 meters from Jervis Bay, a short walk to Huskisson Village. Sandholme Guesthouse the 5 Star B&B accommodation on Jervis Bay.

Jervis Bay - Vincentia

Nelson Beach Lodge *30 km S of Nowra*
B&B
Robyn Brown
404 Elizabeth Drive
Vincentia
NSW 2540

Tel (02) 4441 6006
or 0402 263 997
Fax (02) 4441 6006
rbrown303@hotmail.com
www.nelsonbeachlodge.com.au

Double $110-$130 Single $55-$95
Children half price Special breakfast
Visa MC accepted
1 King/Twin 3 Queen 2 Twin (4 bdrm)
Beds have electric blankets
Bathrooms: 1 Ensuite 1 Family share
1 Guest share 1 Private

Just two minutes walk from white sands

Enjoy a relaxing weekend or stopover at Nelson Beach Lodge. Ideally situated 2 1/2 hours from Sydney and Canberra. A cosy comfortable home, with guest lounge and balcony overlooking Jervis Bay and secluded garden. Just two minutes walk from white sands, red cliffs and crystal clear waters of Nelson Beach. Baywatch cruises see the dolphins, seals and penguins. Also diving, fishing, swimming, sailing, golf, bike riding and bush walking tracks around the waterfront and many picnic spots in local National and Marine Park, Botanic Gardens, Winery, and historic towns nearby. Aussie Host Business.

Jindabyne - Snowy Mountains

Troldhaugen Lodge *30 km W of Berridale*
B&B & Guest House
John & Sandra Bradshaw
13 Cobbodah Street
Jindabyne
NSW 2627

Tel (02) 6456 2718
or 0409 562 718
Fax (02) 6456 2718
troldhaugen@ozemail.com.au
www.troldhaugen.com.au

Double $75-$150 Single $50-$120
Children $15- $40
Continental breakfast
cooked breakfast $7-$10
Visa MC accepted
1 Queen 8 Double 1 Single (10 bdrm)
6 dbl rooms have extra bedding for up to 5 persons
Bathrooms: 10 Ensuite

Centrally located in Jindabyne within walking distance to shops, hotels, restaurants, club and lake. Troldhaugen is situated at the end of a quiet cul-de-sac. A friendly owner/operated lodge catering for the family or couples, holiday. Facilities include guest lounge with open fireplace, TV and videos. Game room with tennis & pool tables, drying room & ski racks. All rooms are centrally heated and have own ensuites. Features include mountain and lake views.

Kiama

Bed and Views Kiama *3 km W of Kiama*
B&B
Sabine & Rudi Dux
69 Riversdale Road
Kiama
NSW 2533

Tel (02) 4232 3662
admin@bedandviewskiama.com.au
www.bedandviewskiama.com.au

Double $140-$160
Full breakfast
Lovebird Suite from $190
Visa MC accepted
1 King/Twin2 King 1 Queen (4 bdrm)
Comfortable r/c air-con. all rooms
Bathrooms: 4 Ensuite
One with spa under a glass roof

AAA Tourism
★★★★☆

Enjoy crystal clear waters at various beaches, see the world's famous Blow Hole, walk the nearby rainforest or find your favourite spot in the garden with unspoilt ocean and rural views. Only 2 minutes away from the seaside town Kiama this B&B offers modern king and queen-bed rooms, ensuites, one with spa, all air-conditioned (cool/heat). Welcoming European hospitality invites to a 'spoilt for choice' breakfast. Day-tour suggestions and booking assistance provided. "What a remarkable combination of stunning views, most comfortable bed, delicious breakfast and a warm and friendly welcome." L&D Wilson, Melbourne.

Kiama Region – Kiama Jamberoo Gerringong Gerroa and Minnamurra

Kiama, a beautiful seaside town famous for its blowholes, pristine beaches,and natural beauty of the magnificent hinterland with historic dry stone walls. The Kiama Region stretches from the Minnamurra River in the north, to the majestic Seven Mile beach in the south, bordered in the west by Jamberoo Village and the backdrop of the dramatic Illawarra Escarpment.

Visit Minnamurra Rainforest, Barren Grounds Nature Reserve and the Illawarra Fly Tree Top Walk. Try surf schools, fishing charters, dolphin and coastal cruises, Jamberoo Action Park, golf courses, vineyards and wineries.
Dianne Rendel
Seashells

Kiama

Kiama Bed & Breakfast *2.5 km W of Kiama*
Guest House & Self-catering cottage with Kitchen

AAA Tourism ★★★★☆

Tony & Marian van Zanen
15 Riversdale Road (off Jamberoo Road)
Kiama
NSW 2533

Tel (02) 4232 2844
Fax (02) 4233 1716
kiamabnb@kbb.com.au
www.kbb.com.au

Double $150-$240 Single $100-$150
Children $33
Special breakfast
Visa MC Diners Eftpos accepted
2 King 2 Queen 1 Double 4 Single (4 bdrm)
Bathrooms: 4 Ensuite

Multi Award-winning Kiama Bed & Breakfast (as seen on TVs Sydney Weekender) provides luxurious boutique-style accommodation on the outskirts of the picturesque seaside township of Kiama, overlooking the spectacular rural scenery of Jamberoo Valley and scenic rainforest escarpment. The two Guest House B&B suites, two Cottage B&B suites, or the self-catering Cottage (sleeps 8), provide the traveller with everything necessary from an overnight corporate stopover, to a romantic wedding night or extended family holiday. All rooms have ensuites, air-conditioning, TV/VCR in rooms and free movies for guest use. Guest areas include a sun-drenched dining room, comfortable lounge area with 24hr tea and coffee making, and huge furnished verandahs with spectacular views. Afternoon tea, a bottle of bubbly and a Vintage Chevrolet car ride to the Blowhole (weather permitting) can be included to enhance your experience of Kiama Bed & Breakfast (as seen on TV's Sydney Weekender). A free Jaunt is included for return guests. Meet Maysha, the playful B&B toy poodle, wander in the gardens and discover the koi pond. Treat yourself or someone you love to a little decadence. We specialize in Wedding nights, Specialty Packages and Gift Vouchers.

Kiama

Seashells Kiama *0.5 km SW of Kiama P.O.*
Luxury Self Contained House & Self Catering
Dianne Rendel
72 Bong Bong Street
Kiama
NSW 2533

Tel (02) 4232 2504 or 0414 423 225
Fax (02) 4232 3419
dianne@seashellskiama.com.au
www.seashellskiama.com.au

Double $225-$340
Children's and babies rates available
Accommodation only
2 nights min booking
Peak season wkly for whole bungalow POA
1 Queen 1 Double 2 Single (3 bdrm) + 1 porta cot
Bathrooms: 3 Private includes 1 bath & 1 separate WC

Unwind . . . Relax . . . and experience the delights of Kiama from this thoughtfully renovated 1960s bungalow. The spacious living area with sweeping town and ocean views is sunroom by day and cosy living room by night. Neat as a pin and full of light this retro-styled home has all the amenities you would expect and more . . . best of all, has personality. Whether looking for a weekend away or a longer stay Seashells Kiama is ideal for a summer holiday or winter retreat - the perfect getaway for couples, families and friends. Illawarra Tourism Award Winner.

Lismore - Clunes

PJ's *16 km N of Lismore*
B&B
Terry & Susan Hurst
152 Johnston Road
Clunes
NSW 2480

Tel (02) 6629 1788
or 0412 996 243
pjsbb@bigpond.com
www.pjsretreat.com

Double $150
Single $125
Full breakfast
Eftpos accepted
3 King (3 bdrm)
Bathrooms: 3 Ensuite

PJ's looks over some of the most beautiful countryside in NSW. All guest rooms have panoramic views that are spectacular. The stylishly purpose built B&B which features three elegant and spacious bedrooms all with the usual comforts including complimentary port, chocolates and local coffee. A personalised country breakfast is served. PJ's is the ideal spot from which to experience the many wonders of the Northern Rivers. Or just simply relax by the saltwater pool or your own private courtyard and soak up the view. Quality accommodation at an affordable price.

Merimbula

Bella Vista *In Town Centre*
B&B
Judy Hori
16 Main Street
Merimbula
NSW 2548

Tel (02) 6495 1373
Fax (02) 6495 1373
bellavistauno@bigpond.com
www.merimbulabellavista.com.au

Double $185-$225
Full breakfast
2 King/Twin (2 bdrm)
Bathrooms: 2 Ensuite

AAA Tourism
★★★★☆

B ella Vista is unique - an Award winning design and a relaxing haven. The entrance opens to a large sun drenched courtyard, private entrances to large guest room - ensuite, fridge, tea, coffee. Air conditioned, underfloor heating. Your own access to the lake and large deck where you enjoy a delicious breakfast while absorbing the spectacular views - swans, pelicans and the many birds glide by. Minutes walk to shops, restaurants & clubs. Short drive to pristine beaches, golf clubs, whale watching & fishing. We are half way between Sydney & Melbourne with daily flight taking just over an hour - 2 hours to the snow fields.

Merimbula

Robyn's Nest Guest House *2 km N of Merimbula*
Luxury B&B & Self Contained
Apartment & Self Contained Cottages
Robyn Britten
188 Merimbula Drive
Merimbula
NSW 2548

Tel (02) 6495 4956
Fax (02) 6495 2426
enquiries@robynsnest.com.au
www.robynsnest.com.au

Double $175-$250 Single $140-$215
Children $25 - $50 Full breakfast
Self Contained Villas
Visa MC Amex Eftpos accepted
5 King/Twin 10 King
11 Queen 2 Twin (28 bdrm)
Old world charm, modern comfort
Bathrooms: 28 Ensuite

   AAA Tourism ★★★★★

R obyn's Nest is a 5* multi-award winning luxury BnB set amid 100 acres of bushland with 25 acres of Absolute Lake Frontage with water views from every room. Halfway between Sydney and Melbourne on the coastal route, 2hrs from Canberra and 2hrs from the snowfields. Facilities: heated pool, spas, sauna, tennis court, jetty/boat and mooring into prime fish breeding grounds. 3mins from the town centre that has 20 restaurants, pristine beaches, whale watching, bushwalking, deep sea & rock fishing. Romantic Indulgence and adventure packages available.

New South Wales

Milton - Mollymook - Ulladulla

Meadowlake Lodge *3 km S of Milton*
Luxury B&B
Diana & Peter Falloon
318 Wilfords Lane
Milton
NSW 2538

Tel (02) 4455 7722
Fax (02) 4455 7733
enquiries@meadowlakelodge.com.au
www.meadowlakelodge.com.au

Double $200-$260 Single $170-$230
Not suitable for under 6 years old
Full breakfast
Dinner B/A Three courses $60pp BYO
Visa MC Amex accepted
1 King/Twin 2 Queen (3 bdrm)
Elegant and spacious
Bathrooms: 3 Ensuite
Separate shower and bath

In 2004, 2005, 2006 and 2007 Meadowlake won the South Coast Tourism Award in the prestigious category of Accommodation Up to Five Stars. The luxurious Five Star country house overlooks lakes and wetlands. Only 3 hours from Sydney and 2.5 from Canberra. Close to historic Milton. Near the beaches at Mollymook and bush walks in the Budawangs. Spacious and elegant rooms have en suites with baths. Dinners by arrangement. At Meadowlake Lodge luxury is a way of life. Listen to the sounds of nature.

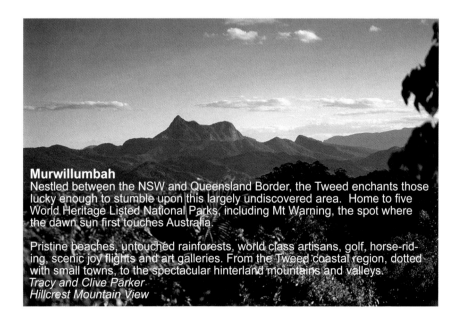

Murwillumbah
Nestled between the NSW and Queensland Border, the Tweed enchants those lucky enough to stumble upon this largely undiscovered area. Home to five World Heritage Listed National Parks, including Mt Warning, the spot where the dawn sun first touches Australia.

Pristine beaches, untouched rainforests, world class artisans, golf, horse-riding, scenic joy flights and art galleries. From the Tweed coastal region, dotted with small towns, to the spectacular hinterland mountains and valleys.
Tracy and Clive Parker
Hillcrest Mountain View

Murwillumbah - Crystal Creek

Hillcrest Mountain View Retreat *12 km NW of Murwillumbah*
Luxury B&B & Farmstay & Separate Suite & Self Contained House & Cottage full kitchen, Fully Air-conditioned
Clive & Tracy Parker
Upper Crystal Creek Road
Murwillumbah
NSW 2484

Tel (02) 6679 1023
romance@hillcrestbb.com
www.hillcrestbb.com/

Double $165-$350
Full breakfast
BBQ Packs by advance arrangement
Visa MC accepted
3 Queen (3 bdrm) in-room tv, dvd, video, a/c
Bathrooms: 3 Ensuite 2 with luxury double spa baths

AAA Tourism ★★★★☆

Multi Tourism Award winning specialists in romantic getaways offering peace, privacy, spectacular views from Mt Warning to the Springbrook rainforests, solar-heated salt-water pool, luxury double spa baths, massage, wood fire, air-conditioning & jolly good food. Choose from 2 B&B suites in the main house private guest wing or 1 fully self-contained Honeymoon Spa Cottage in its own secluded garden. Centrally located to 5 World Heritage National Parks, golf, horse-riding, galleries, markets and more. Only 35 minutes from Gold Coast airport, 75 minutes from Brisbane.

Nambucca Heads - Macksville

Jacaranda Country Lodge *3 km N of Macksville*
Luxury B&B & Guest House
Pamela and Donald Hallaran
292 Wilson Rd
Macksville
NSW 2447

Tel (02) 6568 2737
Fax (02) 6568 2769
jacaranda.lodge@hotmail.com
www.jacarandacountrylodge.com.au

Double $150-$190 Single $120-$140
Children $20 for each child
Continental breakfast
Extra Adult $25-$35
Visa MC Eftpos accepted
10 Queen 17 Single (14 bdrm)
12 in B&B, 2 in Cottage
Bathrooms: 12 Ensuite

Country club facilities with old fashioned B&B hospitality. Boutique style accommodation surrounded by beautiful gardens set amidst 230 acres of pastural landscape. Peacefully situated on the Nambucca River on the Mid North Coast of NSW. Outside facilities include tennis court, pool, sauna,walking track, golfing range and private jetty. Inside relax and enjoy our lounge area with its over-stuffed sofas, TV, billiard table and fireplace. An idyllic place for a quiet night's rest or a base for exploring the scenic delights of the Nambucca Valley.

Narooma - Tilba

Pub Hill Farm *8 km W of Narooma*
B&B & Farmstay & Self Contained cottage
Micki & Ian Thomlinson
566 Scenic Drive
Narooma
NSW 2546

Tel (02) 4476 3177
Fax (02) 4476 3177
pubhill@austarnet.com.au
www.pubhillfarm.com

Double $100-$130
Single $90-$110
Full breakfast
Karibu Cottage $160 per day
2 King/Twin 2 Queen 1 Double (5 bdrm)
Bathrooms: 5 Ensuite

Pub Hill Farm is a small farm, sitting high on a hill overlooking the beautiful Wagonga Inlet and with 2 kilometres of water frontage. The birdlife is abundant and the extreme quiet makes it an ideal place to bird watch. Small mobs of kangaroos live on the property.

All rooms have water views, private outdoor areas and private entrances, plus ensuites, microwaves, fridges, TV, and tea and coffee. We welcome guests' pets. The gardens are fully fenced for their safety. If you prefer self contained accommodation, our new Karibu Cottage is gorgeous. Just for two, with mezzanine bedroom and fabulous views over Wagonga Inlet, the Karibu sits in a secluded garden where you can enjoy water views in complete privacy. There is a cosy wood fire for winter. We have travelled extensively and lived abroad in both U K and North and East Africa and enjoy swapping travellers' tales with our guests.

"Quite the best B&B we have ever stayed at, anywhere. Superb hospitality"
J & PJ, Woodham, Surrey, England.
"Am speechless - loved every minute - your hospitality was warm and wonderful"
Mary and Bill R, Los Osos, California USA.

Narromine

Camerons Farmstay *6 km W of Narromine*
B&B & Homestay & Farmstay &
Self Contained Cottage
Ian & Kerry Cameron
Nundoone Park, 213 Ceres Road
Narromine
NSW 2821

Tel (02) 6889 2978
Fax (02) 6889 5229
www.bbbook.com.au/cameronsfarmstay.
html

Double $110-$130 Single $90
Children $40
Continental breakfast
Dinner B/A
Self Contained Cottage from $120
2 Queen 2 Double 1 Twin 4 Single (5 bdrm)
Bathrooms: 1 Ensuite 1 Guest share

    AAA Tourism ★★★☆

Our home, 30 minutes west of Dubbo. We offer 4 star S/C cottage and B&B. Our house is modern and spacious with reverse cycle air-conditioning with each bedroom having a fan/heater; guest lounge has television, video, books, tea/coffee making facilities, fridge etc. It is surrounded by large gardens, all weather tennis court, and pool. Ian and Kerry run a successful Border Leicester Sheep stud - see lambs, shearing, haymaking, cotton growing and harvesting (seasonal), tour cotton gin. Visit: Rose Nursery, Iris Farm, Aviation Museum and Gliding Centre. " Excellent, comfortable accommodation and great hospitality. So good to come back." P&G, Belgium.

Newcastle
Newcastle is thriving with its heritage as an industrial city and is a sought after weekend getaway and holiday destination.

Beautiful old buildings are a reminder of our rich architectural heritage. Beaches to die for, a vibrant harbour and great restaurants. Nature reserves like Blackbutt, the Wetlands and the Botanic Gardens are worth a visit as is the Art Gallery, the leading regional gallery in Australia.
Rosemary Bunker

Newcastle

Newcomen B&B *In Newcastle Central*
B&B & Studio SC BB
Accommodation
Rosemary Bunker
70 Newcomen Street
Newcastle
NSW 2300

Tel (02) 4929 7313
or 0412 145 104
Fax (02) 4929 7645
newcomen_bb@hotmail.com
www.newcomen-bb.com.au

Double $140-$140
Single $95-$105
Children $30
Full breakfast
Visa MC accepted
1 Queen 1 Single (1 bdrm)
Good mattress and bedding, restful decor
Bathrooms: 1 Private

B e delighted by this gem of a C19 home nestling in a vibrant garden. Explore the surrounding rich heritage area, stroll by the foreshore, enjoy the beach, savour city delights, laze by the pool, relax with every comfort, including air-conditioning, in harmonious decor featuring art works. A boutique mini holiday/work base you'll love.

Newcastle - Hamilton

Hamilton Heritage *6 km N of Newcastle*
B&B
Laraine & Colin Bunt
178 Denison Street
Hamilton, NSW 2303

Tel (02) 4961 1242   or 0414 717 688
Fax (02) 4969 4758
colaine@iprimus.com.au
www.accommodationinnewcastle.com.au

Double $120-$145 Single $90-$100
Children $10-$25 (under 3 free)
Dogs free Special breakfast
Double $80, single $60 (Shared
bathroom) Wedding night $185
Visa MC Diners accepted
2 Queen 1 Double 3 Single (3 bdrm)
All bedrooms airconditioned
Bathrooms: 3 Ensuite 1 bath, 1 spa, 3 showers

P ets Welcome. Children Welcome. Hamilton Heritage B&B, "Old World Charm", situated on Historic Cameron Hill. Close to Broadmeadow Station, Broadmeadow Race Course, Newcastle Entertainment Centre & All Major Sporting Venues. Beaumont Street the Cosmopolitan Heart of Newcastle famous for its Restaurants, Newcastle CBD, Foreshore and Beaches. Feel free to enjoy the serenity of the garden or the verandah. Breakfast of choice and time served in the Breakfast Room overlooking garden Laundry facilities available. Fax and e-mail access. We also offer a unique and memorable place to stay for newlyweds.

Newcastle - Merewether

Merewether Beach B&B *5 km S of Newcastle PO*
B&B & Self Contained Studio
Jane & Alf Scott
60 Hickson Street
Merewether
NSW 2291

Tel (02) 4963 3526 or 0407 921 670
Fax (02) 4963 7926
janescott@bigpond.com
www.bbbook.com.au/
merewetherbeachb&b.html

Double $130 Single $70-$100
Child friendly - Rates on application
Full breakfast
One family or group No stranger share
Visa MC accepted
1 Queen 1 Double 3 Single (2 bdrm)
Stunning views of city, harbour and coast from your bed
Bathrooms: 1 Ensuite 1 Guest share

Wake up to this view! Go to sleep with only the sound of waves breaking on shore. 3 minutes to beach, 5 km from CBD, 1000 km from care. Featured on "Getaway", air-conditioned, self-contained studio with kitchenette, glassed-in verandah, private entrance and garden. Children welcome. Alf's ceramics and paintings lovingly adorn the rooms. With Jane's passion for cooking, expect a breakfast extravaganza. You are our only guests. Let us spoil you! "The view is as rare as the B&B itself..." L&DF, Bowral.

Pacific Palms - Coomba

Whitby on Wallis B&B *18 km NW of Pacific Palms*
Luxury B&B & Homestay
Lew Dodds & Annabelle Lewis
1770 Coomba Road
Coomba Bay
NSW 2428

Tel (02) 6554 2448
or 0419 228 089
Fax (02) 6554 2448
info@whitbyonwallis.com.au
www.whitbyonwallis.com.au

Double $135-$160 Single $125-$135
Full breakfast
Dinner by arrangement from $35 each
Visa MC Eftpos accepted
2 King/Twin1 King (3 bdrm)
All ensuite & outdoor area
One with kitchenette & sofabed
Bathrooms: 3 Ensuite
Bath available in separate bathroom

AAA Tourism
★★★★☆

Luxurious, spacious lake-side accommodation with privacy and magnificent views. Each bedroom has its own outdoor area, TV, tea & coffee. Large guest areas - lounges, reading room, fireplaces, tea and plunger coffee makings, home-baked biscuits, fridge. Room to mix with friends or to find a quiet nook of your own. Swim in the wet-edge pool, fish from the jetty, explore the grounds, paddle on the lake or just laze the day away. Close to National Parks, recreational and tourist activities and Pacific Palms' pristine beaches.

Parkes

Kadina B&B *1.5 km E of Parkes CBD*
B&B
Helen and Malcolm Westcott
22 Mengarvie Road
Parkes
NSW 2870

Tel (02) 6862 3995
or 0412 444 452
Fax (02) 6862 6451
kadinabb@bigpond.net.au
www.kadinabnb.com

Double $130 Single $90
Children B/A
Full breakfast
Dinner B/A
Visa MC Diners accepted
2 Queen 1 Single (2 bdrm)
Deluxe King Single Trundle bed/s available
Bathrooms: 2 Ensuite

AAA Tourism
★★★★☆

Come and enjoy the tranquillity and ambience of this lovely modern spacious home. Watch TV, listen to music, play piano, read or just soak in the views. Dine in our traditionally furnished dining room, patio or secluded back garden. Mal is involved in cereal growing and merino sheep farming. Guests may visit when convenient. Come and see "The Dish". Relax in our luxurious therapeutic Hot Tub. Finalist in 2004 and 2006 Inland Tourism Awards. Regional Winners of Central West Region 2007 Local Business Awards.

Parkes
Parkes is centrally located in the Central West, easily accessible for an overnight stay. Visit our Australian icon, the world famous CSIRO Radio Telescope "The Dish". Visitors are invited to explore the world of astronomy and discover what role The Dish plays in 'listening to the stars.

Capture a picture in Trundle on New South Wales' widest main street or enjoy a weekend of fun at the Parkes Elvis Festival. Peak Hill's Open Cut Experience is now a tourist gold mine. Tyndall's Lavender farm features over 6,000 lavender plants and the Pioneer Park Antique Machinery Museum features farm equipment used in days gone by.
Helen & Mal Westcott
Kadina Bed and Breakfast

Parkes

The Old Parkes Convent *0.5 km E of Post Office*
B&B & Self Contained Apartments
Judy & Colin Wilson
33 Currajong Street
Parkes
NSW 2870

Tel (02) 6862 5385 or 0428 625 385
Fax (02) 6862 5158
parkesconvent@bigpond.com
www.parkesconvent.com.au

Double $160 Single $120
Extra Child $12 Extra Adults $20
Special breakfast Dinner B/A
1 night stay $160
Minimum of 2 nights stay $140
Visa MC Diners Amex accepted
2 Double (2 bdrm) 2 apartments
Each maximum 4, 1 double, 1 sofabed
Bathrooms: 2 Ensuite

Experience spacious living in one of our exclusive apartments. You'll enjoy your own private lounge, bathroom, kitchen, and air conditioned comfort before awaking to a full and delicious breakfast. Stay a night or a few days. Built in 1923 and set on half an acre of land in the centre of town, The Old Parkes Convent was once home to the Sisters of Mercy and girl, student boarders. The Old Parkes Convent B&B is only a short stroll to the shops, clubs, hotels, and restaurants.

Port Macquarie

Woodlands Bed & Breakfast *3 km W of town centre*
B&B & Separate Suite
Ian & Gretel McGinnigle
348 Oxley Highway
Port Macquarie
NSW 2444

Tel (02) 6581 3913
or 0412 443 277
info@woodlandsbnb.com.au
www.woodlandsbnb.com.au

Double $130-$150
Single $110-$130
Full breakfast
Visa MC accepted
1 King/Twin 4 Queen
(5 bdrm) 3 suites
Bathrooms: 1 Ensuite 2 Private

  AAA Tourism ★★★★

Luxury accommodation and hospitality in a secluded setting of gardens and trees with easy access to all local attractions. Air-conditioned accommodation options include the two bedroom Frangipani Suite which is partly self contained with lounge and equipped kitchen area, the two bedroom Magnolia Suite with its magnificently large bathroom and the Verandah Room, an ensuited queen size bedroom which opens out to the verandah and landscaped front gardens. All rooms have the full complement of expected comforts. Great dinner/accommodation package deals available.

Port Macquarie - Camden Haven

Benbellen Country Retreat
20 km S of Laurieton
Luxury B&B & Farmstay
Sherry Stumm & Peter Wildblood
Cherry Tree Lane
Hannam Vale
NSW 2443

Tel (02) 6556 7788
Fax (02) 6556 7778
info@bbfarmstay.com.au
www.bbfarmstay.com.au

Double $165-$195 Single $130-$155
Full breakfast
Dinner $40+ per person
Visa MC Diners Amex Eftpos JCB accepted
2 Queen (2 bdrm) Well appointed bedrooms are
fully ensuite with balcony
Bathrooms: 2 Ensuite

Revitalise yourself with fresh air, peace and quiet with country hospitality second to none. The large open-plan homestead, with its solar-passive design and its quietly stated elegance, is purpose built with your privacy and comfort in mind. Benbellen Country Retreat is a small working alpaca farm tucked away in a lush green hidden valley at Hannam Vale, just 40 minutes from Port Macquarie, 15 minutes from Laurieton and 30 minutes from Taree. You will fall in love with the farm itself with its magical landscape of rolling hills and lotus strewn vistas in an English-style countryside. Choose our luxury ensuite rooms and our country hospitality, not to mention locally grown produce, fresh (to die for) eggs from the farm, home-baked breads and homemade jams. Environmentally friendly. Whether on a short break escape or just "passing through", we know you will be back . . .

Port Macquarie - Camden Haven

Penlan Cottage *20 km S of Laurieton*
Luxury B&B & Farmstay & Self Contained House
Sherry Stumm & Peter Wildblood
Hannam Vale Road
Hannam Vale, NSW 2443

Tel (02) 6556 7788
Fax (02) 6556 7778
info@bbfarmstay.com.au
www.bbfarmstay.com.au

Double $155-$195 Single $155-$195
Children $10-$40
Full breakfast provisions
Dinner $40+ per person
Visa MC Diners Amex
Eftpos JCB accepted
1 Queen 1 Double 2 Single (2 bdrm)
Spacious well-designed bedrooms with quality fittings
Bathrooms: 1 Private

This charming holiday hideaway, with its uninterrupted valley views and set in its own garden of an acre and a half, is ideal for couples and families of up to six looking for a truly country experience. The main bedroom has a queen sized bed with French doors opening to the large veranda. The spacious combined living and dining area is tastefully furnished and the fully equipped kitchen/pantry has a good selection of "basic" supplies including home made jams and home baked bread. Environmentally friendly.

Port Macquarie - Camden Haven

Cherry Tree Cottage *20 km S of Laurieton*
Luxury B&B & Farmstay & Self Contained House
Sherry Stumm & Peter Wildblood
Cherry Tree Lane
Hannam Vale
NSW 2443

Tel (02) 6556 7788
Fax (02) 6556 7778
info@bbfarmstay.com.au
www.bbfarmstay.com.au

Double $155-$195 Single $155-$195
Children $10-$40
Full breakfast provisions
Dinner $40+ per person
Visa MC Diners Amex
Eftpos JCB accepted
1 Queen 3 Single (2 bdrm)
Bathrooms: 1 Private

AAA Tourism ★★★★

High overlooking the rich green paddocks and expansive dams of Benbellen Alpaca Farm, Cherry Tree Cottage is a rural hideaway ideal for couples or families of up to five. The main bedroom has a queen bed and French doors onto the expansive balcony with breathtaking views looking down Hannam Vale to South Brother Mountain. The spacious veranda provides ample room for outdoor entertaining and relaxation while soaking up the views and watching local bird life and listening to the "sounds of nature". Environmentally friendly.

Port Stephens - Shoal Bay

Shoal Bay Bed & Breakfast *3 km E of Nelson Bay*
Luxury B&B & Traditional
Philip & Christina Latham
15 Shoal Bay Avenue
Shoal Bay
NSW 2315

Tel (02) 4984 9183
or 0413 995 600
0421 880 344
rest@shoalbaybedandbreakfast.com.au
www.shoalbaybedandbreakfast.com.au

Double $135-$195 Single $105-$165
Full breakfast
2 bedroom unit, S/C self catering,
same street, from $120pn
Visa MC Amex Eftpos accepted
2 Queen (2 bdrm)
Spacious, luxurious rooms on first floor
Bathrooms: 1 Ensuite 1 Private Sunrise suite - ensuite. Sunset suite - private bathroom

Enjoy "the rest of your life", escape to Shoal Bay in our quiet, spacious and modern B&B. First floor accommodation, comfortable queen beds, ducted air, ceiling fans, televisions, DVD player in rooms. Enjoy views of Tomaree, Stephens Peak and the bay from the balcony. Guest lounge with Foxtel. A recreation room with pool table, fridge, microwave, tea and coffee making facilities. Quiet cul-de-sac, close to cafes and restaurants. 100m walk to beach. Off street parking. Share our home with us and our cat "Watson".

Port Stephens - Shoal Bay
Located on the southern headland of Port Stephens is picturesque Shoal Bay, surrounded by Tomaree National Park, ocean and harbour beaches. Experience one of the top 10 panoramic views in the world from the summit of Tomaree Head.

This coastal area is rightly known as the "Blue Water Paradise" of the North Coast of New South Wales. Go whale watching between June-October or dolphin cruising all year. Just 2½ hours drive from Sydney.
Philip & Christina Latham
Shoal Bay B&B

Scotts Head - Nambucca Valley

OceanScape Luxury Beachfront Villas *15 km SE of Macksville*
Luxury Self Contained Apartments
Jon Holcombe
2 Sea Breeze Place
Scotts Head
NSW 2447

Tel 1300 304 212
or 0416 293 256
mail@oceanscape.com.au
www.oceanscape.com.au

Villa 1 $175-$285/night (sleeps max 3)
Villa 2 $215-$425/night (sleeps max 5)
Accommodation only
Min 2 nights
Visa MC accepted
1 King (1 bdrm)
Large with WI robe & full spa bathroom ensuite
Bathrooms: 1 Ensuite large double spa, double vanity, double shower

OceanScape is small boutique development located in an idyllic secluded setting above a small beach at Scotts Head. OceanScape consists of two fully contained and extremely spacious spa villas designed to take optimum advantage of the spectacular views. Villa 1 is the upstairs single bedroom villa, with king size bed, full audio visual, ensuite bathroom with double spa. Villa 2 is the downstairs two bedroom spa villa. Each bedroom has full audio visual & large ensuite spa bathroom. Both villas have gourmet kitchens and all bedrooms have own AV, WI robe and full spa bathroom.

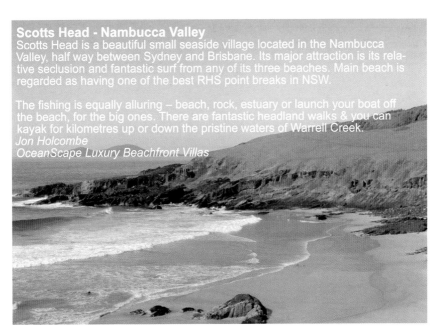

Scotts Head - Nambucca Valley
Scotts Head is a beautiful small seaside village located in the Nambucca Valley, half way between Sydney and Brisbane. Its major attraction is its relative seclusion and fantastic surf from any of its three beaches. Main beach is regarded as having one of the best RHS point breaks in NSW.

The fishing is equally alluring – beach, rock, estuary or launch your boat off the beach, for the big ones. There are fantastic headland walks & you can kayak for kilometres up or down the pristine waters of Warrell Creek.
Jon Holcombe
OceanScape Luxury Beachfront Villas

Southern Highlands - Bowral

Chorleywood B&B *2 km S of Bowral*
B&B & Self Contained Cottage
Sue Hawick
86 Burradoo Road
Burradoo
NSW 2576

Tel (02) 4861 3617
Fax (02) 4861 3617
shawick@hinet.net.au
www.highlandsnsw.com.au

Double $120 Single $75
Baby in own cot only
Full breakfast provisions
Discount for 3 nights or more
Visa MC Eftpos accepted
Cottage includes ensuite bathroom
with queen or twin beds
Bathrooms: 1 Ensuite 1 Private

Welcome to Chorleywood B&B set in an acre of private garden with a sunny terrace. Your self-contained cottage includes a double or twin-share bed, with ensuite bathroom, kitchenette, TV, radio, good heating and ingredients for a full breakfast. A second bedroom in the house with private bathroom is also available when families or friends are travelling together. The resident Cocker Spaniel is called Hamish. Local attractions include bookshops, antiques shops, Bradman Museum, wineries, restaurants and excellent walks. Canberra, Sydney and the South Coast are all less than two hours away.

~

Southern Highlands - Bowral

Chelsea Park *2.5 km S of Bowral*
B&B
Alex & Davidia Williams
589 Moss Vale Road
Burradoo, NSW 2576

Tel (02) 4861 7046
or 0414 468 860Fax (02) 4862 3597
chelsea@hinet.net.au
www.chelseapark.com

Double $150-$185 Single $150-$150
Full breakfast provisions
Candlelight supper part of weekend
package Special diet needs catered for
Visa MC accepted
1 King/Twin 2 Queen (3 bdrm)
Spacious light filled rooms
Bathrooms: 2 Private

Chelsea Park is a glamorously restored Art Deco mansion, painted in pale pink to highlight its classic Deco lines and dramatic curves. When you arrive at this Bowral gem, you soon appreciate why Chelsea Park is called the 'Hollywood Mansion in the Highlands'. Three delightfully restored and decorated rooms include: the Mayfair has award-winning 1930s furniture and balcony overlooking the woodland garden; the spacious, light-filled Chelsea with lush soft furnishings and a dramatic Hollywood-style dressing table; the Shibumi with an elegant Japanese theme. Unwind in the spa bath, sit in dappled shade in the woodland garden or enjoy a game of billiards or take drinks in the guest lounge.

Sydney

Guests, David Lucas and Pat Woodley

Bed & Breakfast Sydney Central *1 km N of Sydney Central*
Luxury Homestay
Julie Stevenson
139 Commonwealth Street
Surry Hills
NSW 2010

Tel (02) 9211 9920
or 0419 202 779
jas@bedandbreakfastsydney.com.au
www.bedandbreakfastsydney.com.au

Double $130-$160
Continental breakfast
Christmas and New Year rates apply
3 King/Twin (3 bdrm) Air-conditioned and TV
Two bedroom suite available
Bathrooms: 1 Guest share 1 Private

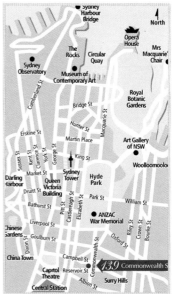

An elegant Terrace house set in the heart of the best Sydney has to offer. Relax in the tranquillity and comfort of your 'home away from home' 3 Bedrooms, two with balconies, TV, Air-Conditioned. A pretty patio garden off the breakfast room. A short walk to the The Capitol Theatre, Imax and all Theatres, Chinatown, Darling Harbour, Aquarium, Paddys and Fish Markets, Star City Casino, Chinese Garden of Friendship, Centrepoint Tower, Queen Victoria Building, Art Gallery of NSW, Museums, Law Courts, Hyde Park, Oxford Street, The Rocks, Circular Quay, the Opera House, the exciting harbour BridgeClimb. Board ferry to Manly, Zoo, Parramatta and Darling Harbour. Walk or drive to Fox Studios, the Sydney Cricket Ground, Universities, Cathedrals, Race Courses, Centennial Park, Beaches. Major attractions are Elizabeth Bay and Vaucluse House, Watsons Bay Beach 'Doyles' famous seafood restaurants. One resident cat. Not suitable for young children. KST Sydney Airporter door to door. Walk everywhere in the city from B&B.

Sydney

Manor House Boutique Hotel *1.5 km S of Central Sydney*
B&B & Boutique Hotel
Rina Park
86 Flinders Street
Darlinghurst
NSW 2010

Tel (02) 9380 6633
Fax (02) 9380 5016
info@manorhouse.com.au
www.manorhouse.com.au

Double $180-$250
Children under 8yrs old stay FREE
Continental breakfast
Visa MC Diners Amex
Eftpos JCB accepted
7 King 10 Queen 1 Twin (18 bdrm)
Individually decorated
Bathrooms: 18 Ensuite
Manor King Room with Spa Bath

Circa 1850 this grand Victorian mansion, a boutique hotel that encompasses the best of business and leisure, offers an oasis of calm elegance and sophistication for discerning travellers. The Manor House Boutique Hotel is located close to some of the city's most vibrant entertainment and restaurant precincts - Taylor Square and Oxford Street, Paddington, Darlinghurst, Woollahra, Surry Hills and East Sydney and of course Aussie Stadium, the Sydney Cricket Ground and the Entertainment Quarter (formerly Fox Studios).

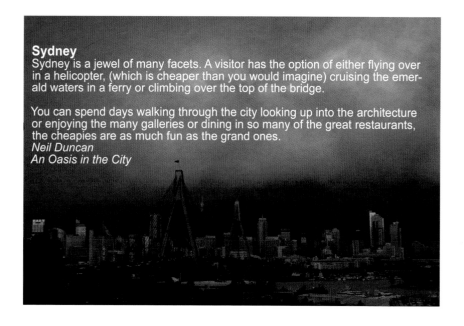

Sydney
Sydney is a jewel of many facets. A visitor has the option of either flying over in a helicopter, (which is cheaper than you would imagine) cruising the emerald waters in a ferry or climbing over the top of the bridge.

You can spend days walking through the city looking up into the architecture or enjoying the many galleries or dining in so many of the great restaurants, the cheapies are as much fun as the grand ones.
Neil Duncan
An Oasis in the City

Sydney

Y Hotel Hyde Park *1 km W of CBD*
Hotel
The Manager
5-11 Wentworth Avenue
Sydney
NSW 2000

Tel (02) 9264 2451
Fax (02) 9285 6288
res@yhotel.com.au
www.yhotel.com.au

Continental breakfast
Traditional Twin $50 per person
Studio Twin $74.50 per person
Visa MC Amex Eftpos accepted
(121 bdrm) Single, twin,
double and triple rooms
Bathrooms: 56 Ensuite

AAA Tourism

Excellent budget bed and breakfast hotel with comfy beds, warm and stylish interiors, friendly atmosphere and perfect park side location. There are backpacker, studio, deluxe and traditional rooms to choose from. City attractions are on your doorstep. Facilities include funky Cafe with internet kiosk, guest kitchen and laundry.

Sydney

Y Hotel City South *4 km S of Sydney CBD*
Hotel
The Manager
179 Cleveland Street
Chippendale
NSW 2008

Tel (02) 8303 1303
Fax (02) 8303 1300
citysouth@yhotel.com.au
www.yhotel.com.au

Continental breakfast
Double $60pp, Single $104,
Family $160 (sleep 4),
2 B/R Apt $235
Visa MC Amex Eftpos accepted
(63 bdrm) Single, double,
twin, triple and family rooms
Bathrooms: 63 Ensuite

AAA Tourism
★★★

This great value boutique bed and breakfast is surrounded by parks and the major Universities and is an ideal base to explore the inner city including Newtown, Glebe and Surry Hills. Walk to central station, Broadway and China Town. All the rooms, while compact, have been designed for comfort and feature the latest interiors. Facilities include a modern gymnasium, a roof top garden with views, cafe with outdoor terrace, secure parking, broadband in rooms, internet kiosk, guest kitchen and laundry.

Sydney - Balmain

An Oasis In The City *2 km W of Sydney*
B&B
Neil Duncan
20 Colgate Avenue
Balmain
NSW 2041

Tel (02) 9810 3487 or 0408 476 421
Fax (02) 9810 3487
anoasis@optusnet.com.au
www.bbbook.com.au/oasis.html

Double $160 Single $150
Continental breakfast
With cooked breakfast
Double $180 Single $170
2 night minimum
1 Queen (1 bdrm)
Large cathedral room with harbour view
Bathrooms: 1 Ensuite

Located in one of Sydney's most historic and charming inner suburbs, Balmain Village, An Oasis offers a very large, sun-filled room with views over Sydney Harbour. The suite is completely private, with own bathroom and entrance. We offer a substantial Continental breakfast. Included in the room are a fridge, electric kettle, toaster and hairdryer, television and DVD player and reverse cycle air-conditioner. There is a hot outdoor spa available to our guests with complimentary spa towels. An Oasis is a walk away from restaurants, cafes, pubs and bars. Public transport is also minutes away and include ferries and buses into Sydney. Dog friendly parks are also close by.

Sydney - Chatswood

The Charrington of Chatswood *10 km N of Sydney GPO*
B&B & Hotel
Robert Davies
22 Centennial Avenue
Chatswood
NSW 2067

Tel (02) 9419 8461
Fax (02) 9419 8864
charrington_hotel@hotmail.com
www.charringtonhotel.com

Double $109-$159
Single $109-$129
Children free under 12 years
Continental breakfast available at $8 pp
Visa MC Amex Eftpos JCB accepted
12 Double 4 Twin (16 bdrm)
Some rooms have an additional single bed
Bathrooms: 16 Ensuite

Recently renovated Victorian style boutique hotel with leadlight windows and tesselated tile foyer.
All rooms have a bar fridge, microwave oven, tea and coffee making facilities, IDD, ceiling fans, free wireless internet access, phone, TV, bathroom and their own balcony. There is a guest kitchen, computer room and coin operated laundry.

Sydney - Clovelly

Clovelly Bed & Breakfast *6 km SE of Sydney*
B&B & Homestay
Tony & Shirley Murray
2 Pacific Street
Clovelly
NSW 2031

Tel (02) 9665 0009
or 0419 609 276
clovellybandb@yahoo.com
www.bbbook.com.au/hosts/clovelly01.html

Double $135-$170 Single $115-$140
Full breakfast
Visa MC accepted
1 Queen 1 Double 2 Twin (2 bdrm)
Have TV/DVD, hairdryer, robes,
electric blankets, doonas
Bathrooms: 1 Ensuite 1 Private
Bathroom linen changed daily

AAA Tourism
★★★★

Clovelly, Coogee and Bronte beaches and cafes are within walking distance. Transport to Sydney's tourist attractions is nearby. Afternoon tea will be served on arrival. Tea and coffee available all day. Breakfast includes fresh fruit, juices, home made bread and a hot dish. The air conditioned bedrooms are upstairs and each has a television, DVD, hairdryer and bathrobes. Rooms are serviced daily. Guests have a separate sitting room. "Thank you for a delightful, memorable visit...so clean and personal...look forward to coming again" Robert.

Sydney - Drummoyne

Eboracum *5 km W of Sydney*
B&B & Homestay
Jeannette & Michael York
18A Drummoyne Avenue
Drummoyne
NSW 2047

Tel (02) 9181 3541
or 0414 920 975
mjyork@bigpond.com
www.bbbook.com.au/eboracum.html

Double $130
Single $100
Full breakfast
Dinner B/A
1 King/Twin 1 Double (2 bdrm)
Bathrooms: 1 Family share 1 Private

Charming water frontage home by the Parramatta River, amid beautiful trees, with glorious views. Boatshed and wharf at waters edge. Handy to transport, short stroll to the bus or Rivercat ferry wharf, off street under cover parking. Ideal central location for business or pleasure, 5km to Sydney CBD, Darling Harbour, Opera House, museums, theatres and sporting venues. Many restaurants and clubs, nearby... Enjoy the hospitality of Jeannette and Michael, with their two cats and the ambience of their comfortable home.

Sydney - Engadine

Engadine Bed & Breakfast *28 km S of Sydney*
Luxury B&B & Self Contained
Apartment
Pamela & Philip Pearse
33 Jerrara Street
Engadine
NSW 2233

Tel (02) 9520 7009 or 0412 950 606
Fax (02) 9520 7009
relax@jerrara.com.au
www.engadinebnb.com

Double $125-$175
Children by arrangement
Continental provisions
Dinner by arrangement
Weekly rates by arrangement
Visa MC Eftpos accepted
1 King 1 Queen 1 Double (3 bdrm) 1 family room
Bathrooms: 2 Ensuite 1 Private

Peaceful and quiet in leafy area close to The Royal National park, only 35 minutes from Sydney CBD and Sydney Airport. Three welcoming and spacious private en-suite apartments are ideal for business stays or a couples getaway. Each apartment is fully equipped with kitchenettes making it ideal for self catering family stays. Facilities include television, DVD, CD and barbeque. Relaxing gazebo. Tumbling waterfalls. Leafy garden courtyard with magnificent views across the valley to the city and the mountains. Guests undercover parking.

Sydney - Forestville - Manly

Jan's Forestville B&B *10 km N of Sydney CBD*
B&B & Homestay & Self Contained
Apartment
Jan Fujak
49 Keldie Street
Forestville, NSW 2087

Tel (02) 9975 6703
or 0414 351 399
Fax (02) 9975 6703
jan@accommodation-sydney.com
www.accommodation-sydney.com

Double $80 Single $60
Children negotiable
Continental provisions
Special rates are available for
long stays, families and groups
Visa MC accepted
1 Queen 2 Twin (3 bdrm) Fold up beds available
Bathrooms: 1 Guest share includes a bath and shower

Jan's B&B provides travellers with fantastic Sydney accommodation at a budget price. Self contained three bedroom accommodation with fully equipped kitchen, bathroom and lounge/dining room Separate entrance, off-street parking and pool. Relax in the comfort and privacy of our forest getaway. There are no carpets and the furnishing is child friendly. The deck overlooks the national park and the tropical pool, which guests are welcome to use. We are just a twenty minute drive from Sydney CBD, a fifteen minute drive to the beach and a ten minute drive to Chatswood Shopping Centre.

Sydney - Glebe

Bellevue Terrace *2.3 km W of Sydney Central*
Homestay
Vikki Butler
19 Bellevue Street
Glebe
NSW 2037

Tel (02) 9660 6096
Fax (02) 9660 6096
bellevuebnb@pocketmail.com.au
www.babs.com.au/bellevue

Double from $110
Single from $80
Continental provisions
1 Queen 1 Double 2 Single (3 bdrm)
Bathrooms: 2 Guest share

M y spacious, elegant townhouse is situated on a quiet residential street in the inner city suburb of Glebe, where you will find a great variety of restaurants, boutiques, galleries, pubs, and the Sydney University campus. Walk to Darling Harbour, Chinatown, Paddy's Market and the Powerhouse Museum, or take a bus to the City centre (just 2.3 kms away) or Coogee Beach. We are happy to supply maps, brochures and ideas for things to see and do in Sydney.

~

Sydney - Glebe

Cathie Lesslie Bed & Breakfast *3 km SW of Sydney*
Homestay
Cathie Lesslie
18 Boyce Street
Glebe
NSW 2037

Tel (02) 9692 0548
cathielesslie@gmail.com
cathielesslie.net

Double $110-$120
Single $80
Children $15
Full breakfast
Visa MC accepted
3 Double 2 Single (3 bdrm)
Bathrooms: 2 Guest share

Q uiet leafy inner city, close to transport, cafes, cinemas, universities and Darling Harbour. Large comfortable room with cable TV, fridge and tea and coffee facilities. Hot "bacon and eggs" breakfast, your choice including fruit, juiced oranges and freshly baked croissants. We want you to feel welcome and at ease. Please phone first for bookings.

Sydney - Glebe

Tricketts *2.5 km W of Sydney Central*
B&B & Guest House
Elizabeth Trickett
270 Glebe Point Road
Glebe
NSW 2037

Tel (02) 9552 1141
Fax (02) 9692 9462
trickettsbandb@hotmail.com
www.tricketts.com.au

✿ AAA Tourism
★★★★☆

Double $198-$225
Single $176-$198
Special breakfast
Visa MC Diners Amex Eftpos accepted
1 King 6 Queen 1 Twin (7 bdrm)
Bathrooms: 7 Ensuite

Tricketts is a lovely Victorian mansion whose magnificent ballroom was once used as the Children's Court. Today this historic building has been fully restored to its original splendour. Large bedrooms with high ceilings, all beautifully decorated, all with ensuite, have top range Sealy beds.
Breakfast is served in the conservatory and in summer out on the secluded deck overlooking the garden with bottle brush trees providing a wonderful splash of colour.The tranquillity makes one forget the city is a short 431 bus ride away and Darling Harbour, Fish Markets, Power House Museum, the Chinese Temple and Sydney University are close by.Glebe is an historic suburb full of interesting old homes that have been lovingly restored; and old fashioned gardens giving strong overtones of a bygone era.We are at the quieter "waterend" of Glebe Point Road, and a little further up lies the restaurant heart of Glebe, well known all over Sydney.
Off street parking is available. We enjoy providing a luxury homestay for travellers and business people. Also at Tricketts, the resident cats Bandit and his two friends ignore us. Children over 12 in B&B. Tricketts is fully centrally heated and air-conditioned. We ask guests to smoke outside on verandahs.

Sydney - Glebe

Pompei Bed and Breakfast *3 km W of Sydney*
Luxury B&B
Penelope Chapple & Paull Mayne
1 Forest Street
Glebe, NSW 2037

Tel (02) 9660 0969 or 0416 266 179
email@pompeibedandbreakfast.com.au
www.pompeibedandbreakfast.com.au

Double $185-$200 Single $165
Full breakfast
Visa MC Eftpos accepted
2 Queen (2 bdrm)
Individually styled guest rooms with queen size beds
Bathrooms: 1 Ensuite 1 Private

Pompei Bed and Breakfast offers luxury accommodation in Sydney for tourist and corporate business travellers alike. It offers an elegant, peaceful retreat and warm hospitality. Individually styled guest rooms possess period features and contemporary amenities. Luxurious touches include fine linen, antiques and original art works. Ideally located in the vibrant inner city suburb of Glebe, it is close to restaurants, cafes and shops. Most importantly it is located only minutes from the centre of Sydney. Close by are Darling Harbour, Sydney Convention and Exhibition Centre, Chinatown, Star City Casino and Sydney Fish Markets. Easily accessible are the Sydney Opera House, Harbour Bridge, QVB (Queen Victoria Building), historic Rocks district and Circular Quay. Pompei Bed and Breakfast is within easy walking distance of Sydney University, University of Technology and Royal Prince Alfred Hospital. Features include spacious air-conditioned double bedrooms with ensuite or private bathrooms, comfortable queen size beds, tea and coffee making facilities, LCD televisions, CD/DVD players, gourmet cooked breakfasts and a private Japanese courtyard. Your hosts Penelope and Paull offer guests an appropriate balance of high quality service, comfort and privacy as well as informative advice tailored to individual needs and interests.

Sydney - Greenwich

Greenwich B&B *5 km N of Sydney*
B&B & Homestay & Self Contained
Apartment
Jeanette & David Lloyd
15 Hinkler Street
Greenwich
NSW 2065

Tel (02) 9438 1204
or 0411 409 716
Fax (02) 9438 1484
info@greenwichbandb.com.au
www.greenwichbandb.com.au

Double $111-$165
Single $90-$140
Continental provisions
Visa MC Amex accepted
1 King/Twin 1 Queen (2 bdrm)
Bathrooms: 1 Ensuite 2 Private

Relaxed and friendly hosted accommodation in leafy Greenwich just 5km from the Sydney CBD. Enjoy spacious and private guests air-conditioned lounge/dining areas in a classic Australian Federation home. Kitchenette & laundry facility is available. Two resident dogs offer a friendly welcome. Internet and E-mail access is available. Ample off street parking. Greenwich B&B is ideal for business or leisure stays and is conveniently located to public transport (Bus, Train, Ferry) shopping, entertainment and restaurants. Transport to St Leonard's station can be arranged. Airport shuttle is available.

~

Sydney - Hawkesbury - Colo

Ossian Hall *26 km NE of Windsor*
Romantic Self Contained Cottages
Diane & Jim Swaisland
1928 Putty Road
Colo, NSW 2756

Tel (02) 4575 5250 or 0428 640 435
Fax (02) 4575 5169
info@ossianhall.com.au
www.ossianhall.com.au

Full breakfast provisions
Dinner by arrangement
Cottages from $215 per night
Packages available
Visa MC Amex accepted
4 Queen (4 bdrm)
4 Self Contained Cottages for Couples
Bathrooms: 4 Ensuite

AAA Tourism
★★★★☆

Awarded best unique accommodation in NSW State for 2007 by NSW Tourism. Ossian Hall, your romantic retreat located in a secluded valley fronting the beautiful Colo River surrounded by natural bush with abundant bird life. Cottages are self contained designed for romance with 2 person spa, logfire, air conditioned, TV, DVD, video, CD stereo. 4 person hot tub spa, sauna, solar heated pool, games room, bikes and kayaks or dinghy to explore the pristine river - available to all guests. Complete privacy with beautiful outlook. Breakfast basket supplied. Picnic/BBQ, evening meals and massages are available on request. Ask about our Romantic Horse & Carriage packages.

Sydney - Hunters Hill

Magnolia House Bed & Breakfast
7 km NW of Sydney
B&B & Homestay
Fofie Lau
20 John Street
Hunters Hill
NSW 2110

Tel (02) 9879 7078
or 0418 999 553
Fax (02) 9817 3705
fofie@magnoliahouse.com.au
www.magnoliahouse.com.au

Double $150-$220
Full breakfast
Dinner B/A
Visa MC Diners accepted
1 King/Twin 1 Queen (2 bdrm)
Bathrooms: 2 Ensuite

Magnolia House is conveniently located only 7 km from the heart of Sydney and is placed within easy reach of transport that takes you directly to the city centre. Bus or ferry transport is close by.

Sydney Airport, The Sydney Opera House, Sydney Harbour and The Harbour Bridge, the CBD, galleries, museums, are all within easy reach.

Taking the ferry to Sydney Harbour and The Opera House is a memorable trip. Hunters Hill is one of Australia's oldest residential areas. Located on a peninsula between the Lane Cove and Parramatta Rivers, much of the suburb enjoys spectacular views over Sydney Harbour. Transfers from the airport can be easily arranged.

Sydney - Manly - North Balgowlah

Pepper Tree B&B *14 km NE of Sydney*
Self Contained Apartment
Conal & Louise Gain
9 Worrobil Street
North Balgowlah
NSW 2093

Tel (02) 9400 3900
or 0403 138 903
Fax (02) 9400 3900
lougain@optusnet.com.au
www.peppertreebb.com.au

Double $130-$150
Breakfast provisions first night
1 King/Twin (1 bdrm)
Bathrooms: 1 Ensuite

S elf-contained separate, spacious one-bedroomed garden flat with separate dining/ kitchen/living area. French doors lead to large patio with views across leafy garden. Conveniently situated for easy access to city and beaches. Within walking distance of shops, between two golf courses and on cycle track to Manly.

Sydney - Marrickville

Michaela's Place *5 km SW of Sydney*
B&B
Michaela Simoni
1 Greenbank Street
Marrickville
NSW 2204

Tel (02) 9591 1780
or 0401 950 605
Fax (02) 9969 6219
mp.weyland@bigpond.com
www.bbbook.com.au/MichaelasPlace.html

Double $120-$130
Children $30
Continental breakfast
Child minding by arrangement
Visa MC accepted
1 Queen 1 Twin (2 bdrm)
Bathrooms: 1 Ensuite 1 Private

J ust renovated Federation charmer with original country kitchen but with mod cons. Secluded courtyard with barbecue. In quiet street 10 minutes from airport. One minute to station and city bus, delivery to airport available. Exotic ethnic eateries around the corner. Disabled access, children welcome, child minding available. Plenty of street parking.

Sydney - Newtown

Golden Grove Bed and Breakfast *2 km SW of Central Station*
Luxury B&B
Lloyd and Robyn Suttor
30 Golden Grove Street
Darlington
NSW 2008

Tel (02) 8003 5443 or 0414 328 013
Fax (02) 8569 1543
info@bedbreakfastsydney.com.au
www.bedbreakfastsydney.com.au

Double $195-$215 Single $140-$160
Children Under 10 Free
Children 10-16 +$20/head. (max. 2)
Full breakfast provisions
Woodfired Food Preparation,
combined class and meal $65/head
Visa MC Amex Eftpos accepted
1 King/Twin 1 Queen (2 bdrm)
Bathrooms: 2 Ensuite

This Boutique Art-Space BB features 2 superb units, each reflective of the surrounding cultural heartland of Newtown and Sydney University. The Gold Spa Apartment features original artworks by contemporary Australian artists. The upstairs Green Room combines rain forest cool with theatrical chic. Each unit's kitchen is fully equipped, so that guests can make the most of the full, mouth-watering breakfast provisions on offer. The fully self contained units have their own entrance. They also boast their own Tuscan courtyards graced with authentic Italian woodfired ovens

Sydney - Northern Beaches Peninsula

The Pittwater Bed & Breakfast *1 km N of Newport Beach*
B&B
Colette & James Campbell
15 Farview Road
Bilgola Plateau
NSW 2106

Tel (02) 9918 6932
or 0418 407 228
Fax (02) 9918 6485
colette@thepittwater.com.au
www.thepittwater.com.au

Double $175-$200
Single $175-$200
Special breakfast
Dinner $55 per person
Visa MC Amex JCB accepted
2 King/Twin 2 Queen (2 bdrm)
Bathrooms: 2 Ensuite

AAA Tourism
★★★★☆

Comfortable beds, ensuite bathrooms, full gourmet breakfast, peace, quiet and privacy. Close to Sydney's famous Palm Beach and great local restaurants, Colette and James would be delighted to welcome you to The Pittwater. Our family home is situated on the high plateau above Newport Beach. The guest areas have spectacular panoramic views of the ocean and coastline, including an attractive garden and large solar heated swimming pool. The Pittwater offers a range of complimentary services and may include airport pickup after a long-haul flight.

Harts *2.8 km E of Sydney Central*
Homestay
Katherine Hart
91 Stewart Street,
Nearest cross street - Gordon
Paddington 2021
NSW 2021

Tel (02) 9380 5516
paddington91@bigpond.com
www.bbbook.com.au/harts.html

Double $140-$170
Single $90-$130
Special breakfast
High season rates apply
1 Queen 1 Twin 1 Single (3 bdrm)
Bathrooms: 1 Ensuite
1 Guest share 1 Private

Conveniently located 19th Century Cottage in Sydney's Historic Paddington, courtyard garden, two minutes from Oxford Street and the bus service to the CBD, Sydney Harbour, Circular Quay, The Rocks, The Opera House, Botanical Gardens, Sydney Casino, Chinatown, and Bondi Beach. Nearby Centennial Park, Fox Studios, Aussie Stadium, Sydney Cricket Ground, Art Galleries, Antique Shops, Pubs, Restaurants, Fashion Boutiques, Cinemas, Paddington Markets.

All rooms with T.V, clock radios, electric blankets and feather quilts. Ironing facilities, varied breakfasts, fruit platters. One Abyssinian cat.

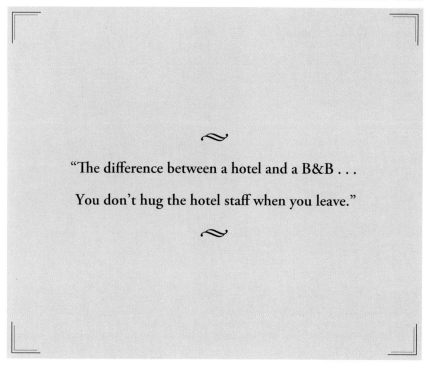

~

"The difference between a hotel and a B&B . . .

You don't hug the hotel staff when you leave."

~

Sydney - Paddington

Paddington B&B *2.8 km E of Sydney Central*
B&B & Homestay
Mary J de Merindol
7 Stewart Place
Paddington
NSW 2021

Tel (02) 9331 5777
stay@paddingtonbandb.com.au
www.paddingtonbandb.com.au

Double $95-$110
Single $60-$70
Continental breakfast
Evening meal on request
Visa MC accepted
1 Double 1 Twin 2 Single (4 bdrm)
Bathrooms: 2 Guest share

Your hosts, originally from England, have operated the B&B for 9 years since their 4 children left home. The comfortable 5 bedroom family home dating from 1880 is furnished in traditional style and located in a tranquil cul-de-sac. It is 20 minutes from the Airport, a few minutes to Football Stadium, SCG and Fox/Hordern Pavilion, and 20 minutes by frequent bus to downtown, Opera House, ferries and Bondi Beach. Paddington is a residential area of heritage architecture enlivened by many galleries, boutiques, restaurants and cafes.

Sydney - Parramatta

Harborne Bed & Breakfast *2 km S of Parramatta*
B&B
Josephine Assaf
21 Boundary Street
Parramatta
NSW 2150

Tel (02) 9687 8988
Fax (02) 9687 8998
www.bbbook.com.au/harborne.html

Double $105-$140
Single $95-$130
Continental provisions
Dinner from $20
Family suite for up to 7 adults,
$10 extra person
Visa MC Diners Amex Eftpos accepted
7 Queen 1 Single (8 bdrm)
Bathrooms: 3 Ensuite
1 Guest share 1 Private

AAA Tourism
★★★☆

Harborne is a magnificent 1858 Georgian sandstone mansion. Harborne has recently been restored as a charming 8 room B&B. The beautiful home and the lush gardens have been classified by the National Trust. A glazed breakfast atrium with Tea & Coffee facilities is available. Harborne is ideal for a relaxed stay or business or team stay. Harborne, Your Home Away From Home.

Sydney - Potts Point

Simpsons of Potts Point Boutique Hotel *2 km E of Sydney City*
B&B & Guest House
Keith Wherry
8 Challis Avenue
Potts Point Sydney
NSW 2011

Tel (02) 9356 2199 or 0408 282 802
or 0402 765 507 or 0408 292 802
Fax (02) 9356 4476
info@simpsonshotel.com
www.simpsonshotel.com

Double $235-$325 Single $215-$315
Continental breakfast
Visa MC Diners Amex accepted
5King 5 Queen 2 Family (12 bdrm)
All individually decorated with
modern convieniences
Bathrooms: 12 Ensuite 3 King-bed rooms also have bath-tub

An intimate 12-room hotel, in a restored 1892 Victorian mansion. Simpsons is located in the leafy tree-lined Potts Point, a vibrant and cosmopolitan area, with many interesting restaurants, bars, galleries and cafes nearby. Just a 20 minute stroll into the City, via the beautiful Botanic Gardens and then on to the Opera House and historic Rocks area. All rooms are decorated in traditional-style, and have private en-suite bathrooms, air-conditioning, fans, tea & coffee making facilities, direct dial phones, Wi-Fi, as well as windows that actually open.

Sydney - Potts Point

Victoria Court Sydney *1 km E of Sydney CBD*

AAA Tourism
★★★★

B&B
Manager
122 Victoria Street
Sydney, Potts Point
NSW 2011

Tel (02) 9357 3200 or 1800 63 05 05
Fax (02) 9357 7606
info@VictoriaCourt.com.au
www.VictoriaCourt.com.au

Double $99-$330 Single $88-$330
Special breakfast
Visa MC Diners Amex Eftpos accepted
22 King/Twin 3 Single (25 bdrm)
Bathrooms: 25 Ensuite

Victoria Court, whose charming terrace house dates from 1881, is centrally located on quiet, leafy Victoria Street in Sydney's elegant Potts Point; the ideal base from which to explore Sydney.

It is within minutes of the Opera House, the Central Business District and Beaches. Friendly and personalised service is offered in an informal atmosphere and amidst Victorian charm.No two rooms are alike; most have marble fireplaces, some have four-poster beds and others feature balconies with views over National Trust classified Victoria Street.

All rooms have en-suite bathrooms, hairdryers, air-conditioning, colour television, a safe, radio-clock, coffee/tea making facilities and direct dial telephones.In the immediate vicinity are some of Sydney's most renowned restaurants and countless cafés with menus priced to suit all budgets. Public transport, car rental, travel agencies and banks are nearby. An airport shuttle bus operates to and from Victoria Court and security parking is available.

Sydney - Rose Bay

AAA Tourism
★★★☆

Syl's Sydney Homestay *6 km E of Sydney*
Homestay & Self Contained Apartment
Sylvia & Paul Ure
75 Beresford Road
Rose Bay, NSW 2029

Tel (02) 9327 7079 or 0411 350 010
Fax (02) 9362 9292
homestay@infolearn.com.au
www.sylssydneyhomestay.com.au

Double $140-$160 Single $95-$110
Continental breakfast
Self Contained Apartment, Double $190
Extra person $40 Visa MC accepted
1 Queen 1 Double 4 Single (2 bdrm)
Bathrooms: 1 Guest share 1 Private

Rose Bay is one of Sydney's most beautiful harbourside suburbs and hospitality and friendliness are the essence of our modern, spacious family B&B with bush and harbour views, pet dog and that real home away from home atmosphere. We are just a short stroll from cafes, restaurants, tennis, golf, sailing and the most beautiful harbour in the world and on excellent bus and ferry routes to the City and Opera House, Bondi Beach, train stations and shopping centres. Our B&B was featured on British TV in 1991 and we

were one of Sydney's first B&Bs operating since 1980. Syl and Paul are well travelled and always ready to share their local knowledge and hospitality in a relaxed informal setting to help travellers enjoy our wonderful city. So if formality is what you seek, then Syl's is not for you! All rooms have TV and the self contained garden apartment is ideal for families. Resident gentle Pet dog. Guests are requested not to smoke inside the house.

Sydney - Scotland Island

Scotland Island Lodge *5 km N of mona vale*
B&B
Rosemary and Colin Haskell
2 Kevin Avenue
Scotland Island
NSW 2105

Tel (02) 9979 3301
Fax (02) 9979 3301
rhaskell@bigpond.net.au
scotlandislandlodge.com.au

Double $150-$190
Single $100-$120
Full breakfast
Dinner $50 per person
Visa MC accepted
1 King 2 Queen 1 Twin (3 bdrm)
Bathrooms: 2 Ensuite 1 Private

 AAA Tourism ★★★★

Unique exclusive Bed & Breakfast on beautiful Scotland Island. Ideal for couples and small groups. Kayak to Salvation Creek and experience the wonder of Pittwater. 'Too often, the breakfast part of B&B's falls by the wayside, but Rosemary is passionate about cooking and her big English breakfasts are out of this world.' 'The Beds. Perfect for a deep sleep before being woken by the birds.' Extracts from an article in the Sun Herald Travel Section by Kate Cox leading travel writer.

Sydney - Scotland Island
"The Best Kept Secret in Sydney"
From the moment you set sail for Scotland Island, you begin to experience the wonderful relaxing world of Pittwater less than an hour's drive from the city amidst the stunning natural beauty of the magnificent Ku-ring-gai National Park and stunning surf beaches on the Northern Peninsular.

A stay on Pittwater would be incomplete without experiencing the beautiful waterways on one of the regular ferries or water taxi from the wharf or take a boat or kayak and go to a secluded beach.
Rosemary and Colin Haskell
Scotland Island Lodge

Tamworth

Jacaranda Cottage Bed & Breakfast *0.4 km E of Tamworth*
Luxury B&B
Helen Hinwood
105 Carthage Street
Tamworth
NSW 2340

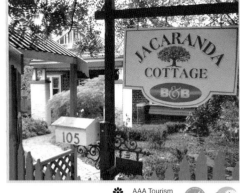

Tel (02) 6766 4281
or 0438 618 263
Fax (02) 6766 1886
rest@jacarandacottagebedandbreakfast.
com.au
www.jacarandacottagebedandbreakfast.
com.au

Double $125-$185
Full breakfast
Visa MC Amex Eftpos JCB accepted
3 Queen (3 bdrm)
Large & Comfortable
Bathrooms: 1 Ensuite 1 Guest share

 AAA Tourism ★★★★

Located in the heart of leafy East Tamworth, just a short stroll from the CBD, Jacaranda Cottage offers large comfortable bedrooms with queen-sized beds, reverse cycle air-conditioning. There is a separate guest lounge to relax in with TV, DVD, magazines, books, fridge and coffee making facilities. Delicious home-cooked breakfasts are served in the dining room or on the leafy verandah in the warmer months. At the bottom of the cottage garden is the private loft, well suited for business needs or romantic getaways.

~

Taree - Wingham

Tallowood Ridge *8 km NW of Wingham*
B&B & Farmstay & Self Contained Cabin
Shirley Smith
79 Mooral Creek Road
Cedar Party via Wingham
NSW 2429

Tel (02) 6557 0438
or 0411 035 945
Fax (02) 6557 0438
twr@ceinternet.com.au
www.bbbook.com.au/tallowoodridge.html

Double $90-$110 Single $70-$80
Children $20
Continental breakfast
2 Double 4 Single (3 bdrm)
Bathrooms: 1 Ensuite 1 Private

Come and share the country lifestyle. Enjoy the comforts of a modern air conditioned home set on 33 hectares of undulating hills, magnificent views, colourful birds, friendly cows and Jessie the dog. There is also a fully equipped air conditioned, self contained cabin accommodation up to four persons. No smoking inside please. Relax by the pool or visit the many attractions in the area, historic buildings, a museum of past history, picturesque rainforest area alongside the Manning River or visit Ellenborough Falls. Clubs, pubs and restaurants in town. "Very hospitable - scenery fantastic - so peaceful - could stay longer." M&N C, Nthn Ireland.

Taree - Wingham

The Bank Guesthouse *10 km W of Taree*
B&B & Self Contained Cottage
Bev & Rod Petterson
48 Bent Street
Wingham
NSW 2429

Tel (02) 6553 5068 or 0400 334 912
Fax (02) 6553 5863
info@thebankandtellers.com.au
www.thebankandtellers.com.au

Double $145-$165 Single $135-$155
Children 3-11 years $30 extra
Full breakfast
Dinner On request
Visa MC Amex Eftpos JCB accepted
5 Queen 1 Double 2 Single (7 bdrm)
Luxury old style Queen Rooms
Bathrooms: 6 Ensuite

The Bank Guest House & Tellers Restaurant is an oasis of stylish accommodation and dining in the beautiful Manning Valley. 5 spacious guest rooms plus a family room and Maitland Cottage (for self contained holiday accommodation). A country style breakfast is included in your tariff and is served in Tellers Restaurant. Evening meals available on request. Tellers Restaurant open for lunch from Wed to Sun & Dinner Fri & Sat. Dogs welcome by arrangement. Wheelchair accessible room available. Only 10 minutes off the Pacific Highway at Taree. 48 Bent St. Wingham. Ph: 02 6553 5068 email: info@thebankandtellers.com.au web: www.thebankandtellers.com.au.

Taree – Wingham
Wingham, first settled in 1853, is a heritage town with many National Trust listed Federation and Victorian buildings that surround the town square. A major attraction is Wingham Brush Nature Reserve, the last remaining floodplain rainforest in NSW. Giant Moreton Bay figs dominate the Brush along with one of the largest permanent maternity populations of grey headed flying foxes in NSW.
Bev & Rod Petterson
The Bank Guest House & Tellers Restaurant

The Entrance - Blue Bay

Talinga *90 km N of Sydney*
Self Contained House
Eve and Soula Tsironis
54 Werrina Parade
Blue Bay
NSW 2261

Tel (02) 4333 6333
Fax (02) 6842 4513
iannuzzi@tpg.com.au
www.bbbook.com.au/Talinga.html

Accommodation only
Seasonal: $1800-$4500/wk whole house
Visa MC Eftpos accepted
2 Queen 4 Single (4 bdrm)
Bathrooms: 2 Family share
One bathroom has a spa

Absolute beachfront with best views on the Central Coast. Blue Bay is one of the cleanest and safest beaches in NSW. Enjoy swimming, kayaking or fishing from the beach. Ideal for family escapes or even for a secluded romantic escape for a couple. Short drive to Sydney and Newcastle, meaning you can commute to work whilst the family relaxes on the beach. Terrigal, the Entrance, Erina and Tuggerah are short drives away, with all the restaurants and shopping you can hope for. This is a very popular destination, so advance bookings are essential. Guests are to provide their own linen and towels.

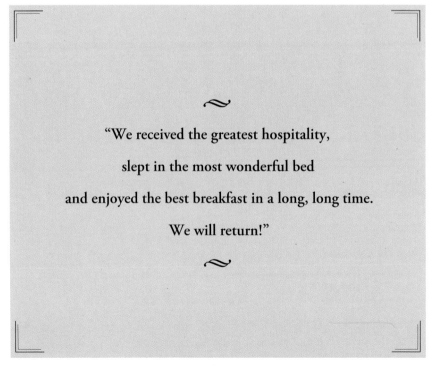

~

"We received the greatest hospitality,

slept in the most wonderful bed

and enjoyed the best breakfast in a long, long time.

We will return!"

~

Thredbo

Candlelight Lodge *33 km SW of Jindabyne*
B&B in Summer, Lodge in Winter
Jane and Mark
32 Diggings Terrace
Thredbo, NSW 2625

Tel (02) 6457 6318
or 1800 020 900
Fax (02) 6457 6049
bookings@candlelightlodge.com.au
www.candlelightlodge.com.au

Double $125 Single $90
Family $195 Seasonal rates apply in Winter
Continental breakfast in Summer, hot breakfast in Winter
Bar and restaurant open in Winter only
Visa MC Amex Eftpos accepted
4 King 2 Queen 2 Twin (14 bdrm) Plus 2 triple rooms and 6
family rooms each with 2 bedrooms - Total capacity for 44 guests
Bathrooms: 14 Ensuite

A warm and friendly European alpine atmosphere greets you on your arrival at
Candlelight Lodge. The lodge, established in 1958, is one of the original ski lodges
of Thredbo. Candlelight has comfortable, spacious rooms (ranging from single to
family) all with ensuites, small fridge, TV, telephone, DVD, wireless broadband access,
tea and coffee making facilities, superb mountain views and are serviced daily. Other
facilities include in-house masseuse, sauna, table tennis, table soccer and X-boxes for the
kids. Located in the centre of the village, Candlelight is just a short stroll to restaurants,
cafés, shops, lifts and all resort facilities. In summer, Candlelight operates as a B&B
serving continental breakfast, but in the ski season watch the snow falling on the slopes
from your breakfast table as you enjoy a full cooked breakfast daily to prepare you for a
day on Australia's longest ski runs. On a winter's night indulge in a few schnapps or local
and European beers from our licensed bar. Then choose from either our blackboard menu
or full á la carte in the restaurant which features both Australian and international cuisine
- always boasting a few Austrian and Swiss specialties. Whether you're planning a walking,
wildflower or skiing holiday, Candlelight makes your stay a truly alpine experience.

Thredbo – Snowy Mountains
Thredbo is a pretty, alpine village nestled in amongst the peaks of the 690,000 hectares that make up the beautiful Kosciuszko National Park.

In Winter Thredbo is Australia's top ski resort with the longest runs and best variety of terrain. When the snow melts Thredbo transforms with the seasons. It becomes a haven for hikers, mountain bikers and lovers of wildflowers, clean air, stunning scenery, great food and music. Kids love the summer bobsled. The chairlift gives you a great starting point for a walk to the summit of Kosciuszko. There's also tennis, golf, fishing and horse-riding.

A summer holiday in Thredbo can be pure relaxation and a chance to indulge in good food and clean air or it can be as physically challenging as you wish.
*Megan & John Leggett
Candlelight Lodge, Thredbo*

Thredbo - Jindabyne - Snowy Mountains

Bimblegumbie *9 km SW of Jindabyne*
B&B & Farmstay & Separate Suite & Self Contained House & Guest House & Self Contained Cottages
Prudence Parker
942 Alpine Way, Crackenback
Thredbo Valley
NSW 2627

Tel (02) 6456 2185 or 0412 484 966
Fax (02) 6456 2060
holiday@bimblegumbie.com.au
www.bimblegumbie.com.au

Double $152-$245 Single $80-$160
Children $5-half price depending on age
Special breakfast $18.50
Dinner $42.50 for 3-course
Visa MC Amex Eftpos accepted
2 King/Twin 2 King 6 Queen (10 bdrm)
Bathrooms: 2 Ensuite 2 Guest share 3 Private 1 has bath

AAA Tourism
★★★☆

B B, Room only & Self Contained Cottages. Pets welcome. Peaceful, private & relaxing, award winning wonderful gardens, colourful birdlife and wildlife. Delicious homemade yummy breakfasts & dinners, jams, sauces & specialities. Interesting eclectic artistic decor. A collector's delight. Resident very friendly dogs. Return guests pay 10% less. 150 acres mountain virgin bush walks, close to ski fields, horse riding, trout fishing, Lake Jindabyne. Relax, recuperate, rejuvenate, reflect, respond, remember, return.

Tilba Tilba - Narooma

Green Gables *16 km S of Narooma*
B&B
Stuart Absalom & Philip Mawer
269 Corkhill Drive
Tilba Tilba
NSW 2546

Tel (02) 4473 7435
or 0419 589 404
Fax (02) 4473 7835
relax@greengables.com.au
www.greengables.com.au

Double $150-$170
Single $90-$110
Children $20-$40
Full breakfast
Dinner $30-$40 B/A
Visa MC Diners Amex accepted
3 Queen 1 Twin (3 bdrm)
Bathrooms: 2 Ensuite 1 Private

AAA Tourism
★★★★

Mesmerising views, stylish accommodation, generous hospitality, fine food, endless relaxation at any time of the year, close to all the Tilba area has to offer. Set in lush gardens there are three large bedrooms with ensuite/private bathrooms and an inviting guest sitting room. Dinner is available by arrangement either served on the verandah or in the private dining room. What better way to experience the natural beauty of the unique Tilba area with its irresistible combination of mountains and unspoilt ocean beaches.

Tilba
Tolkienesque rocky outcrops among rolling green hills entice visitors to the National Trust villages of Central Tilba and Tilba Tilba. Set in the Tilba Valley with the majesty of Gulaga (Mt Dromedary) as a backdrop, the area is well known for its cheese, gold mining past, gardens and more recently art, craft, heritage and indigenous culture.

Within easy driving distance from Narooma and Bermagui the area has access to a pristine coastline with many secluded beaches. The temperate climate – the area's best kept secret – means that visitors can discover, explore and enjoy what's on offer all year round.
Stuart Absalom
Green Gables

Ulladulla Guest House

0.1 km S of Ulladulla

B&B & Self Contained Apartment & Guest House

39 Burrill Street
Ulladulla
NSW 2539

Tel (02) 4455 1796 or 1800 700 905
Fax (02) 4454 4660
ugh@guesthouse.com.au
www.guesthouse.com.au

Double $158-$318 Single $100-$248
Children $50
Full breakfast
Dinner $40-$90
Visa MC Diners Amex Eftpos accepted
 1 King/Twin2 King 6 Queen 1 Double 3 Single (10 bdrm)
Bathrooms: 10 Ensuite

Located only 100 metres south of the picturesque harbour on the beautiful South Coast.

Accommodation: All rooms with ensuites, queen bed, custom-designed furniture and original artwork. Executive suites have marble bathroom with private spa and king size bed. Two self-contained units have private entrances and cooking facilities

Restaurant: Elizans French Restaurant is 2007 Winner Best Restaurant South Coast. Our executive chef applies French cooking techniques to fresh local produce, Elizans is fully licensed with an award winning wine list.

Art Gallery: With permanent exhibiting Artists David Benson, Dianne Gee, Tracey Creighton and Judy Trick.

Features: Excellent recreational facilities include heated salt-water pool, internal and external spas, sauna, in-room massage and gym. Ulladulla Guest House is recommended by number of reputable guides Frommers (US), Rough (UK), Time-Out (London), Johansens.

Urunga

Aquarelle Bed & Breakfast *6.5 km S of Urunga*
Luxury B&B
Helen & John
152 Osprey Drive
Urunga
NSW 2455

Tel (02) 6655 3174
or 0427 553 174
info@aquarelle.com.au
www.aquarelle.net.au

Double $145-$175 Single $120-$145
Full breakfast
Dinner in winter months
by prior arrangement only
Visa MC Eftpos accepted
1 King suite 1 Queen suite (2 bdrm)
King bed can be configured as twin beds
Bathrooms: 2 Ensuite

AAA Tourism
★★★★☆

Aquarelle's two peaceful, elegant A/C suites suit the discerning traveller. Tall forests and a waterlily-covered lake surround the contemporary property, ensuring total privacy. Folding glass doors let you bring the outdoors into your private sitting room - gourmet breakfast accompanied by the call of the whip bird is an inspirational way to start your day. Fresh seasonal produce features on your daily breakfast menu, and we cater for special dietary requirements. "A wonderful break in this gorgeous part of the world" David & Gill UK

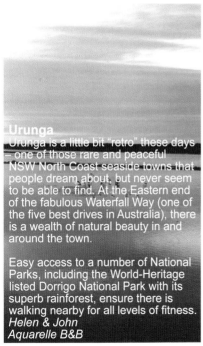

Urunga
Urunga is a little bit "retro" these days - one of those rare and peaceful NSW North Coast seaside towns that people dream about, but never seem to be able to find. At the Eastern end of the fabulous Waterfall Way (one of the five best drives in Australia), there is a wealth of natural beauty in and around the town.

Easy access to a number of National Parks, including the World-Heritage listed Dorrigo National Park with its superb rainforest, ensure there is walking nearby for all levels of fitness.
Helen & John
Aquarelle B&B

Wagga Wagga

Dunn's B&B *2 km S of Wagga Wagga PO*
B&B
Les and Kate Dunn
63 Mitchelmore Street
Wagga Wagga
NSW 2650

Tel (02) 6925 7771
or 0435 043 079
choc1001@gmail.com
www.dunnsbedandbreakfast.com.au

Double $120
Full breakfast
Visa MC Eftpos accepted
3 Double (3 bdrm)
Bathrooms: 3 Ensuite

D unn's B&B is a magnificent spacious Federation home with old world charm. There are three generous bedrooms furnished for comfort with elegant appointments. Featuring brass beds, mahogany tables and country hospitality, modern ensuites, television, tea and coffee making facilities and refrigerator. Guests have the use of their own sitting room and balcony upstairs or they are welcome to join our family downstairs. There are facilities for wireless internet, undercover parking and a private entrance. We also provide homemade afternoon tea, maps, complimentary vintage car ride and friendly service. Complimentary pick up from airport or train station in Vintage Buick.

Wellington

Carinya B&B *0.5 km S of Wellington*
B&B
Miceal & Helen O'Brien
111 Arthur Street (Mitchell Highway)
Wellington, NSW 2820

Tel (02) 6845 4320
or 0427 459 794
Fax (02) 6845 3089
carinya@well-com.net.au
www.bbbook.com.au/carinyabb.html

Double $95-$105
Single $85-$91
Children $12-$15
Full breakfast
Visa MC accepted
1 King/Twin 2 Queen 2 Single
(3 bdrm) 1 Family Room,
1 Queen Room & 1 King room
Bathrooms: 2 Guest share

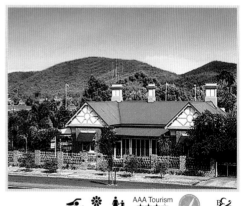

AAA Tourism ★★★☆

C arinya is an old homestead in a lovely garden setting. Pool and tennis court available. Off street parking a plus. Situated Sydney side of Wellington, on the Mitchell Highway. Family friendly. Billiard table is always popular. Close to everything, especially Wellington Caves and Japanese Garden. Walk Mt Arthur or inspect significant historic buildings and acclaimed Cameron Park. Drives to Burrendong Botanic Garden & Arboretum and Burrendong Dam make Wellington a pleasant stopover. Other attractions; Dubbo Zoo, Mudgee and Parkes are ideal for short excursions.

Wollongong - Corrimal

Corrimal Beach Bed & Breakfast *10 km N of Wollongong*
B&B & Homestay
Sue & Daryl Thomson
56 Dobbie Avenue
East Corrimal
NSW 2518

Tel (02) 4283 2899
Fax (02) 4283 2899
inquiries@corrimalbeach.com
www.corrimalbeach.com

Double $250-$390 Single $220-$360
Full breakfast
2 or 3 course dinner on request
Alfresco dining if requested
Visa MC accepted
3 Queen (3 bdrm)
All have ensuites & private courtyards
Bathrooms: 3 Ensuite

Enjoy a quiet weekend escape in a modern architecturally designed home, 45 minutes south from Sydney airport, 2 hours from Canberra, and minutes from central Wollongong. A short walk to the Illawarra cycleway or Corrimal beach, where you can stroll along the beach, surf, fish or just sunbake. 10 eighteen-hole golf courses and 10 bowling clubs within 30 minutes drive. Close to many fine restaurants, renowned gardens and picturesque beaches. Board a train to exciting Sydney or visit the Southern Highlands. All rooms have TV, Ensuite and courtyard.

Please tell your host,

"I found you in *The Bed & Breakfast Book*."

Wollongong - Mount Pleasant - South Coast

Above Wollongong at Pleasant Heights B&B *5 km NW of Wollongong*
Luxury B&B & spa suites with kitchenette
John & Tracey Groeneveld
77 New Mt Pleasant Road
Wollongong, NSW 2519

Tel (02) 4283 3355 or 0415 428 950
Fax (02) 4283 1655
info@pleasantheights.com.au
www.pleasantheights.com.au

Double $185-$450
Children by arrangement
Full breakfast provisions
Dinner by arrangement
Midweek specials available
Visa MC Diners Amex accepted
1 King/Twin 2 Queen (3 bdrm)
Bathrooms: 1 Ensuite 2 spa suites

Award winning boutique B&B, 'Above Wollongong at Pleasant Heights' provides exquisite accommodation which opens into a lush, tropical garden setting, complete with sweeping coastal views.Guests choose between an eclectic trio of suites: two stylish spa suites in exotic, modern themes, and our chic, adorable studio with The View . . . serenity - harmony - solitude.This is high quality accommodation offering privacy and relaxation . . . each suite has its own entrance with a courtyard, terrace or balcony and also offers a range of indulgences, including aromatherapy massage. And of course, a lavish breakfast hamper is provided for each stay.Above Wollongong is a popular wedding destination and also great for pampering weekends. We are within minutes of local restaurants, beaches , 5 kilometres from the Wollongong CBD, University and The Nan Tien Temple.Within one hour of Sydney and the International Airport, Southern Highlands, Jervis Bay, Kangaroo Valley and The Blue Mountains - all this makes Pleasant Heights the perfect base for day tripping! Above Wollongong at Pleasant Heights is popular for that special occasion, anniversary or weekend getaway.

Yass

Kerrowgair *1.5 km N of Yass*
B&B
Judy & John Heggart
24 Grampian Street
Yass
NSW 2582

Tel (02) 6226 4932
or 0417 259 982
info@kerrowgair.com.au
www.kerrowgair.com.au

Full breakfast
$130-$150
Visa MC Diners Eftpos accepted
3 Queen 1 Twin (4 bdrm)
Bathrooms: 4 Ensuite

  AAA Tourism ★★★★☆

Kerrowgair - A beautifully restored Georgian house (C.1853), in historic Yass, one hour from the Nation's capital. This outstanding heritage house has large bedrooms, all with ensuites, and gracious sitting and dining rooms, with open fires, for the use of guests. It is complimented by the shady verandahs and covered terrace. Set in over an acre of beautiful gardens, guests can enjoy the peace and tranquillity of the ancient trees, rose gardens and pond. Kerrowgair has become renowned for it's warm hospitality and superb breakfasts.

Yass - Rye Park

The Old School *20 km SE of Boorowa, 40 km N of Yass*
B&B & Self Contained House &
Country House (self-contained)
Margaret Emery
76 Yass Street
Rye Park
NSW 2586

Tel (02) 4845 1230 or 0418 483 613
(02) 6227 2243
Fax (02) 4845 1260
theoldschool@bigpond.com
www.theoldschool.com.au

Double $140-$160 Single $110-$130
Children $25 Special breakfast
Dinner $65
Country House $1500 per week
Visa MC Amex accepted
1 King 2 Queen 1 Double 1 Twin 2 Single (5 bdrm) 2 suites, 3 rooms
each, ensuite
Bathrooms: 2 Ensuite 1 Family share 1 Private Orchard Wing suite has a bath

Fine food, warm fires, good books and a piano make this retreat a return to life's simple pleasures. Set on four acres amidst trees, roses, gardens and ponds an atmosphere is created that encourages relaxation. Margaret has built a reputation for her food and offers a seasonal menu, with influences from Belgium, the Mediterranean and Asia. The Old School won an Award of Distinction in the 2000 Capital Country Awards for Excellence in Tourism. Rye Park is half an hour north of Yass.

Young - Cootamundra

Old Nubba Schoolhouse *3 km N of Wallendbeen*
Self Contained House & Self-
Contained Farm Cottages
Fred & Genine Clark
Old Nubba
Wallendbeen
NSW 2588

Tel (02) 6943 2513
or 0438 432 513
Fax (02) 6943 2590
oldnubba@bigpond.com
www.bbbook.com.au/
oldnubbaschoolhouse.html

Double $100-$120 Single $75-$95
Children $10-$20
Full breakfast provisions
2 Queen 2 Double 8 Single (7 bdrm)
Bathrooms: 3 Private

Old Nubba is a sheep/grain farm between Cootamumdra and Young, 3 ¹/₂ hours Sydney, 1 ¹/₂ hours Canberra. The Schoolhouse, Killarney Cottage and Peppertree Cottage are all fully self-contained and have slow-combustion heating, reverse cycle air-conditioning, electric blankets and linen/towels provided. They sleep 4-8 and are set in their own gardens thru the trees from the homestead. Farm attractions include peace and quiet, bush walks, birdlife, bike riding, fishing and olive picking. Well behaved doggies and cats welcome. Many local tourist attractions nearby.

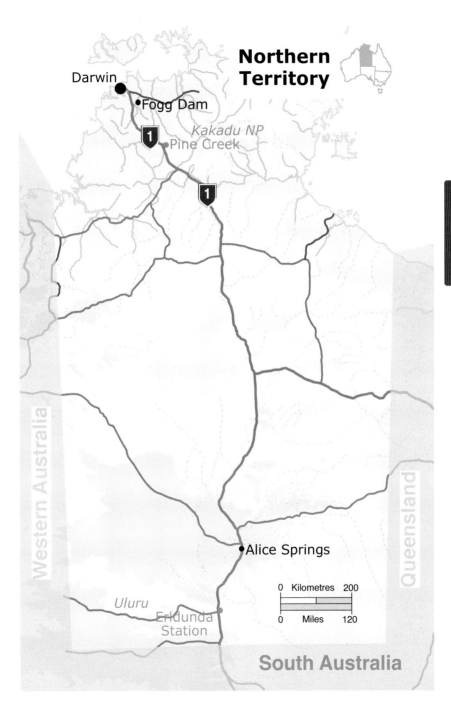

Alice Springs

Nthaba Cottage B&B *2.5 km N of Town Centre*
B&B Cottage
Anne & Will Cormack & Pets
83 Cromwell Drive
Alice Springs
NT 0870

Tel (08) 8952 9003
or 0407 721 048
Fax (08) 8953 3295
nthaba@nthabacottage.com.au
www.nthabacottage.com.au

Double $185-$200
Single $145
Full breakfast
Visa MC accepted
1 King/Twin (1 bdrm)
Bathrooms: 1 Ensuite

 AAA Tourism ★★★★

S urrounded by the spectacular MacDonnell Ranges, Nthaba features a quality cottage separate from the main house. The cottage has one kingsize or two single beds and the cosy sitting-room with television has Edwardian chairs and other favourite pieces. The cottage opens onto a lovely garden with many visiting birds. Close to convention centre and many great walks. Your host, Will, is keen to share his local bird knowledge with you. Two resident friendly dogs.

Alice Springs

The Hideaway *500 km NE of Ayers Rock*
B&B & Self Contained Apartment
John & Pauline Haden
18 Lewis Street
Alice Springs
NT 0871

Tel (08) 8953 1204
or 0428 531 204
Fax (08) 8953 1204
info@hideawayinalice.com
www.hideawayinalice.com

Double $120
Full breakfast provisions
Family $180
1 Queen 2 Single (2 bdrm)
Bathrooms: 1 Private

B assa and Cocoa the resident cats will be there to add to the welcome. All rooms have fans, electric blankets and the apartment has ducted air-conditioning, a gas heater is available in winter in the separate lounge/dining area. Your hosts John and Pauline have a combined 80 years of personal local experience, we look forward to sharing this knowledge with you. We are within 5 minutes walk from the famous Cultural Precinct and a 5 minute drive from the World acclaimed Desert Park.

Alice Springs

Kathy's Place Bed & Breakfast *3 km E of Alice Springs*

B&B & Homestay & Friendly & personalised
Kathy & Karl Fritz
4 Cassia Court
Alice Springs
NT 0870

Tel (08) 8952 9791
or 0407 529 791
Fax (08) 8952 0052
kathy@kathysplace.com.au
www.kathysplace.com.au

Double $140 Single $80
Children $10 per child
Full breakfast
Additional person in same room $30
Visa MC Eftpos accepted
2 Queen 1 Single (2 bdrm) 3 in B&B
Bathrooms: 1 Family share 1 Guest share Separate toilet

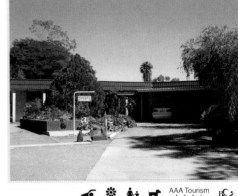

 AAA Tourism ★★★☆

Friendly Australian home, courtesy arrival transfers, tours arranged and help provided so you can enjoy the treasures the "Alice" has to offer, taking at least two days to enjoy. Air conditioning, swimming pool and garden outdoor area with native birds that come in. Combustion heating in the cooler months providing a cosy atmosphere to chat, read, watch T.V.

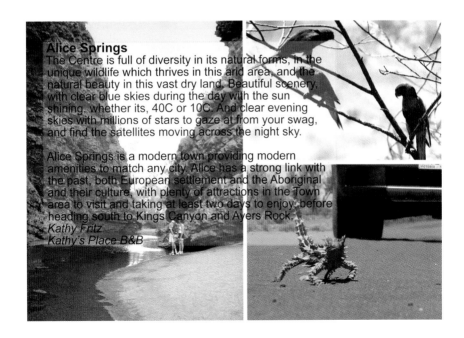

Alice Springs
The Centre is full of diversity in its natural forms, in the unique wildlife which thrives in this arid area, and the natural beauty in this vast dry land. Beautiful scenery, with clear blue skies during the day with the sun shining, whether its, 40C or 10C. And clear evening skies with millions of stars to gaze at from your swag, and find the satellites moving across the night sky.

Alice Springs is a modern town providing modern amenities to match any city. Alice has a strong link with the past, both European settlement and the Aboriginal and their culture, with plenty of attractions in the Town area to visit and taking at least two days to enjoy, before heading south to Kings Canyon and Ayers Rock.
Kathy Fritz
Kathy's Place B&B

Darwin - Fogg Dam - Humpty Doo

Eden at Fogg Dam *25 km E of Humpty Doo*
B&B & Self Contained Apartment
Heather Boulden & Jeremy Hemphill
530 Anzac Parade
Middle Point
NT 0836

Tel (08) 8988 5599
Fax (08) 8988 5582
eden@foggdam.com.au
www.foggdam.com.au

Double $130-$185
Single $110-$165
Full breakfast
Dinner Bookings required $35 pp
Special diets accommodated
Visa MC accepted
2 Queen 1 Double 2 Single (3 bdrm)
Cross breeze, overhead fans, a/c
Bathrooms: 2 Private
Upstairs, spa bath with shower

Enjoy the bush and stay in comfort on an organic tropical fruit farm registered with Land for Wildlife, on the doorstep of internationally renowned Fogg Dam: a wildlife sanctuary reputed as paradise for birdwatchers, photographers and biologists. It's also known for spectacular sunrises and sunsets. Sunrise has the added magic of a dawn chorus of birds. Why not take a picnic breakfast! We're close to other tourist attractions and en route to Kakadu National Park. A unique location just 65km (40 miles) from Darwin.

Fogg Dam
Worth visiting on the way to Kakadu is Fogg Dam Conservation Reserve, created in 1956 as part of the failed Humpty Doo Rice Project which planned to grow and export rice to Asia. Fogg Dam is a habitat for numerous animals, Australian and migratory birds.

The reserve is in the Adelaide River wetlands and known internationally to biologists, birdwatchers and photographers for its rich biodiversity. It's the only Top End wetland accessible throughout the year.
Heather Boulden & Jeremy Hemphill
Eden at Fogg Dam, B&B and Certified Organic Tropical Fruit Farm

Darwin - Malak

Beale's Bedfish & Breakfast *5 km N of Airport*
B&B & Lodge

Heather & Allan Beale
2 Todd Crescent
Malak, Darwin
NT 0812

Tel (08) 8945 0376
Fax (08) 8945 0379
bealesbedfish@aapt.net.au
www.bealesbedfish.com.au

01/11-28/03 $80-$120 per room
01/03-31/10 $150-$200 per room
Continental breakfast
Visa MC accepted
3 Queen 8 Single (3 bdrm)
Bathrooms: 3 Ensuite

Beale's Bedfish & Breakfast is a dual purpose built establishment. Designed to cater for the B&B traveler and also to the Individuals, Families and Groups that also wish to partake in the adrenalin packed adventure of Barra or Bluewater Fishing in the Northern Territory.

It is the home of Darwin's Barra Base Fishing Safaris, which can cater for all types of fishing, from Barramundi & Bluewater fishing in coastal reefs, rivers and sheltered waters to being able to fish 10 nautical miles to sea to complete adrenalin packed pelagic and deep sea fishing.

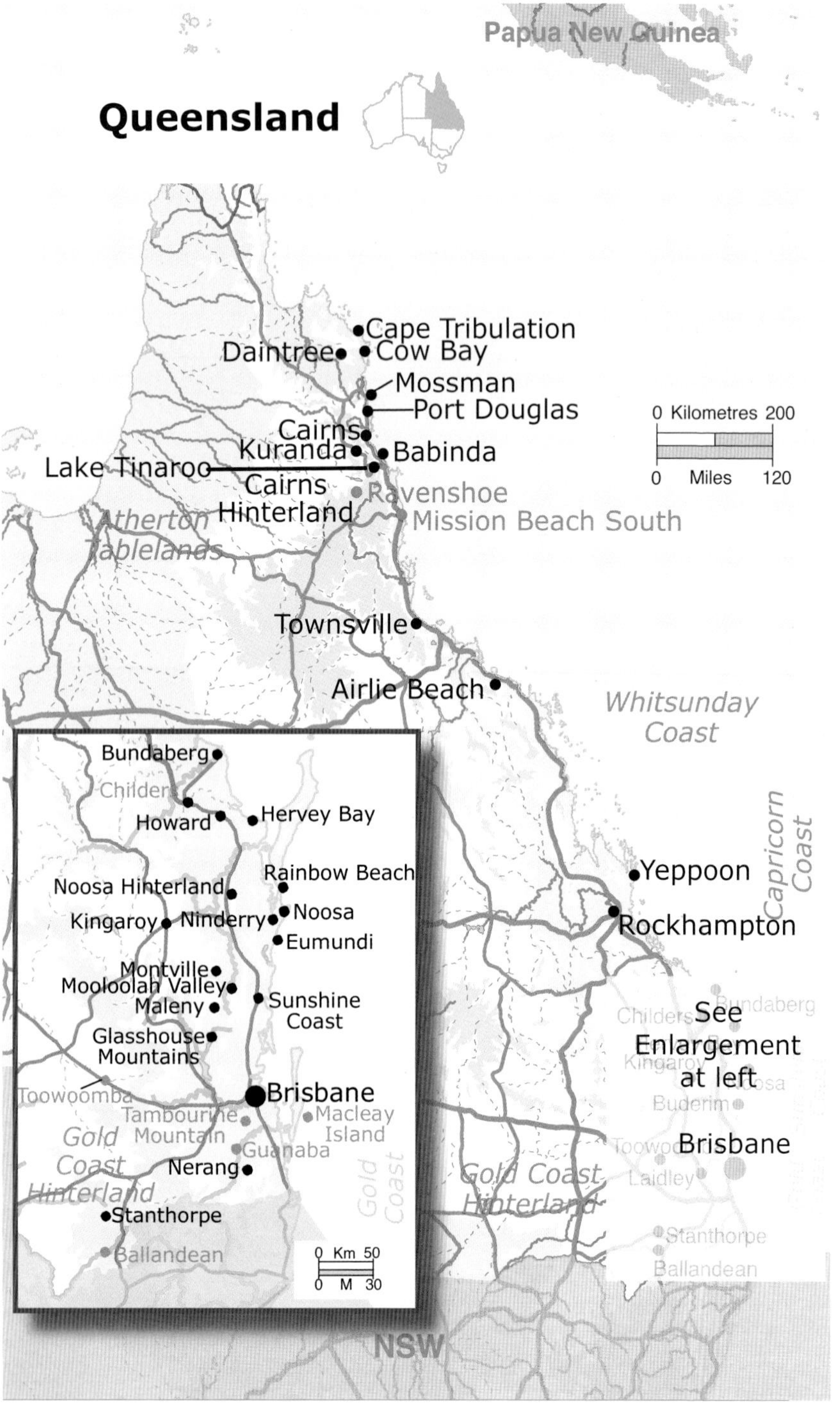

Queensland

Papua New Guinea

Cape Tribulation
Daintree • • Cow Bay
Mossman
Port Douglas
Cairns
Kuranda • • Babinda
Lake Tinaroo
Cairns Ravenshoe
Hinterland Mission Beach South
Atherton
Tablelands

0 Kilometres 200

0 Miles 120

Townsville

Airlie Beach

Whitsunday
Coast

Bundaberg
Childers
Howard
Hervey Bay

Rainbow Beach
Noosa Hinterland
Kingaroy • Ninderry • Noosa
Eumundi

Montville
Mooloolah Valley
Maleny • Sunshine
Coast
Glasshouse
Mountains

Toowoomba
Brisbane
Tambourine
Gold Mountain Macleay
Coast Guanaba Island
Hinterland Nerang

Stanthorpe

Ballandean

0 Km 50

0 M 30

Capricorn Coast

Yeppoon

Rockhampton

Childers Bundaberg
Kingaroy
Buderim

See
Enlargement
at left

Toowoomba Brisbane

Laidley

Gold Coast
Hinterland

Stanthorpe

Ballandean

NSW

Far North Queensland

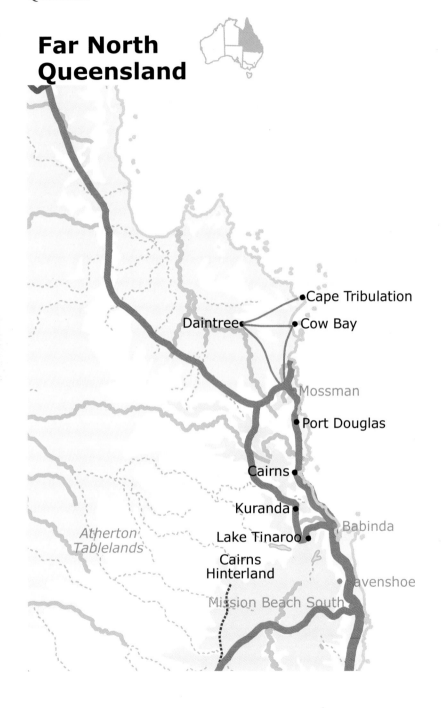

Cape Tribulation

Daintree

Cow Bay

Mossman

Port Douglas

Cairns

Kuranda

Babinda

Lake Tinaroo

Atherton Tablelands

Cairns Hinterland

avenshoe

Mission Beach South

Airlie Beach - Whitsunday

Whitsunday Moorings B&B *0.3 km SW of Airlie Beach*
B&B
Peter Brooks
37 Airlie Crescent
Airlie Beach
Qld 4802

Tel (07) 4946 4692
Fax (07) 4946 4692
info@whitsundaymooringsbb.com.au
www.whitsundaymooringsbb.com.au

Double $185 Single $165
Children $35
Full breakfast
$35 extra person above two
Visa MC Diners Amex Eftpos accepted
2 Queen (2 bdrm)
Bathrooms: 2 Ensuite

Studio apartments, private terrace, swimming pool, overhanging Abel Point Marina and Coral Sea. Spectacular views. Traditional English breakfast, includes, squeezed juice, tropical fruit, cereals, choice cooked mains, homemade jams, teas, coffee. Apartments feature crisp starched linen, daily servicing, air-conditioning, ceiling fans, satellite TV, ensuite with shower, hairdryer, 'Gilchrist & Soames' toiletries, kitchen, refrigerator, microwave, equipped light meals, clock radio, laundry, computer and wireless facility for laptops. Relax in the pool, a cool drink, watching the sun setting on boats returning to Abel Marina below.

~

Airlie Beach - Whitsunday

Whitsunday Heritage Cane Cutters Cottage *7 km SW of Airlie Beach*
Self Contained House
Suzette & Adrian Pelt
PO Box 59
Airlie Beach
Qld 4802

Tel (07) 4946 7400
or 0419 768 195
Fax (07) 4946 1373
cottage@whitsunday.net.au
www.whitsundaycottage.com

Double $150-$190
Rollaway or sofabed available for children
Breakfast basket $35 by arrangement
2 people option
Air conditioned, secluded
Visa MC accepted
1 Double (1 bdrm) Main bedroom in cottage
Bathrooms: 1 Ensuite

This Award Winning 100 year old beautifully restored Cane Cutters Cottage is a special and unique place to stay during your visit to the Great Barrier Reef and Whitsunday Islands. During the restoration, many of the original building materials were recycled into a modern kitchen and bathroom whilst still retaining all the charm and interest of the past. Located closed to Airlie Beach it is the perfect location from which to relax and enjoy the best of the Whitsundays.

Brisbane - Birkdale

Birkdale Bed & Breakfast *17 km E of Brisbane CBD*
B&B & Traditional and private
Geoff & Margaret Finegan
3 Whitehall Avenue
Birkdale, Brisbane
Qld 4159

Tel (07) 3207 4442
glentrace@bigpond.com
www.bbbook.com.au/birkdalebb.html

Double $100-$110 Single $70-$80
Children $20
Full breakfast
Visa MC Diners Amex accepted
2 Queen 1 Double 2 Single (3 bdrm)
Spacious and private
with separate guest entrance
Bathrooms: 2 Ensuite 1 Private

Only 20 minutes from Brisbane CBD and airport, but with a lovely country atmosphere. Set in half an acre of beautifully landscaped gardens, Birkdale B&B is a modern English style country home, with a new luxurious guest wing with separate entrance. All bedrooms have private facilities and reverse cycle air conditioning for your comfort. Off street parking. Enjoy feeding the birds, go whale watching in nearby Moreton Bay or meet the local koalas. Qualified Aussie Hosts. Dual Tourism Award Winner. Corporate and weekly rates.

Brisbane - Paddington - Rosalie

Fern Cottage B&B *2.5 km W of Brisbane*
B&B
Mary & Geoff
89 Fernberg Road
Paddington - Rosalie
Qld 4064

Tel (07) 3511 6685
or 0423 096 254
Fax (07) 3511 6685
info@ferncottage.net
www.ferncottage.net

Double $145-$155 Single $115-$125
Children under ten $15
Continental breakfast
Extra person $35
Visa MC Eftpos accepted
3 Queen 1 Single (3 bdrm)
Bathrooms: 3 Ensuite

AAA Tourism
★★★★

Fern Cottage is a charmingly refurbished 1930s 'Queenslander' located in trendy Paddington/Rosalie . . . a village, only 2.5km west of Brisbane City Centre . . . Enjoy modern conveniences and comforts of home in our 3 fabulously decorated, air conditioned ensuited bedrooms. Kitchenette, lounge room and individual patios assures your privacy. Sidewalk cafes, fine restaurants, boutiques, antique shops and galleries are within walking distance. A fresh tropical breakfast starts your day . . . in the leafy green garden courtyard with gazebo. One resident pet.

Brisbane - Shorncliffe

Naracoopa Bed & Breakfast *21 km NE of Brisbane*
B&B & Self Contained Pavilion
Grace & David Cross
99 Yundah Street
Shorncliffe
Qld 4017

Tel (07) 3269 2334
or 0412 147 456
narabnb@bigpond.net.au
www.naracoopabnb.com.au

Double $155-$185 Single $135-$155
Children $45 Extra person $45
Special breakfast
S/C $165 double, 4 night minimum.
Weekly double from $780
Visa MC Eftpos accepted
3 Queen 1 Double (3 bdrm)
Bathrooms: 3 Ensuite

 AAA Tourism
★★★★

The perfect getaway: 4 star Naracoopa offers luxury, privacy; your seaside destination on Moreton Bay; close to water, cliffs, cafes, train, pier. Two designer decorated B&B rooms, with private ensuites, verandahs, refrigerator, tea & coffee facilities, air conditioning, outdoor hot spa. The Self-contained Pavilion provides more space and comfort for extended stay. It includes all the above guest amenities and a fully equipped stainless steel kitchenette, superbly appointed lounge and bedroom, wireless broadband, Foxtel digital, DVD/CD. Breakfast not included. Handy to airport, coasts, city, waterfront.

Brisbane - West End

Eskdale Bed & Breakfast *2 km SW of Brisbane*
B&B & Homestay
Paul Kennedy
141 Vulture Street
West End
Qld 4101

Tel (07) 3255 2519
eskdale_brisbane@yahoo.com.au
eskdale.homestead.com

Double $120 Single $70
Children ¹/₂ price
Continental breakfast
Every 5th night free;
see web site for special offers
Visa MC accepted
1 King 1 Queen 1 Double
1 Twin (4 bdrm)
Bathrooms: 1 Family share 1 Guest share

Eskdale Bed & Breakfast is a typical turn-of-the century Queensland house close to the restaurant district of West End. It's 2 km to the city centre across the Victoria Bridge, and just 1 km from the Southbank Parklands and the Brisbane Convention and Exhibition Centre, the Queensland Performing Arts Centre, Museum and Art Gallery. You'll be close to all the action and still be able to relax on the back deck and watch the birds feeding on the Australian native plants in the garden.

Queensland

Bundaberg

Inglebrae *1 km W of Bundaberg*
Luxury B&B
Christina & John McDonald
17 Branyan Street
Bundaberg
Qld 4670

Tel (07) 4154 4003
or 0418 889 971
Fax (07) 4154 2503
inglebrae@people.net.au
www.inglebrae.com

Double $130-$150
Single $110-$120
Full breakfast
Visa MC Eftpos accepted
2 Queen 2 Single (3 bdrm)
Beautifully furnished bedrooms with many extras
Bathrooms: 2 Ensuite 1 Private
Ensuites in keeping with old word charm

Inglebrae is a restored Queenslander circa 1910 with beautifully appointed air-conditioned rooms and ensuites. Take a leisurely stroll to the city centre where you will find great shopping and many fine restaurants in which to dine. Bundaberg is situated at the Southern tip of the Great Barrier Reef and is the departure point for Lady Elliott Island. Enjoy a sumptuously cooked breakfast on the verandah overlooking beautiful gardens.

~

Cairns – Brinsmead

Jenny's Homestay *10 km W of Cairns*
B&B & Homestay
& Self-Contained Flat
Jenny & Lex Macfarlane
12 Leon Close,
Brinsmead, Qld 4870

Tel (07) 4055 1639
or 0428 551 639
jennysbb@jennysbandb.com
www.jennysbandb.com

Double $80-$100
Single $65-$85
1 Self contained Flat $90-$120
Breakfast: Special
1 King 1 Twin (3 bdrm)
Total capacity for 6 guests
Bathrooms: 2 Ensuite 1 Private

AAA Tourism
★★★★

Jenny and Lex invite you to our home in Cairns. Wake to the sound of birds and our beautiful rainforest garden. A continental breakfast is served in the sunroom or around the pool. My husband and I are Photographers and enjoy outdoor activities. Only a short distance to tropical beaches, great restaurants, golf courses and the famous Kuranda Train and Skyrail. We are booking agents for all tours and rental cars. A complimentary pick up on arrival. "This was our 4th stay and we enjoy it more each stay" Gary & Helen Young, Seattle Washington, USA."

Cairns - Edge Hill

Galvin's Edge Hill Bed and Breakfast *0.2 km N of Edge Hill Post Office*

Luxury B&B & Self Contained Apartment
Julie and Jesse Low
61 Walsh Street
Cairns
Qld 4870

Tel (07) 4032 1308
or 0409 345 726
Fax (07) 4032 5968
info@galvinsonedge.com.au
www.galvinsonedge.com.au

Double $125-$140
Single $95
Family rates available
Special breakfast
1 Queen 2 Single (2 bdrm)
1 with Queen and 1 with 2 single
Bathrooms: 1 Family share

   AAA Tourism ★★★★

One of Cairns' oldest & finest Queenslanders, located in quiet, leafy Edge Hill, we are one of the most conveniently located B&Bs in Cairns - five minutes drive from downtown and 5 minutes from the airport. Relax in your own private two-bedroom apartment (we only take one booking at a time so there's no need to share). Enjoy our magnificent swimming pool and gardens. Three minutes walk and you're in the village of Edge Hill with restaurants, shops, the Cairns Botanic Gardens walks, and more.

Cairns - Holloways Beach

Billabong B&B *10 km N of downtown Cairns*

B&B
Vicky & Ted Riddle
30 Caribbean Street
Holloways Beach,
Cairns
Qld 4878

Tel (07) 4037 0162
or 0427 370 044
Fax (07) 4037 0162
info@cairnsbb.com
www.cairnsbb.com

Double $155-$165
Single $120-$125
Full breakfast
Visa MC accepted
2 Queen 1 Single (2 bdrm)
Bathrooms: 2 Ensuite

Billabong is your perfect accommodation in Cairns located on an island in the heart of a large lily-covered Billabong, close to downtown Cairns and the airport. Two queen guest suites with contemporary décor include ensuite bathrooms, air conditioning and ceiling fans. Your facilities include television, CD, wireless internet, fridge, tea/coffee making, BBQ and separate entrance. Large French doors open onto a private deck overlooking the Billabong featuring spectacular bird life. A short walk to the beach and restaurants. The delicious gourmet breakfast is Billabongs specialty.

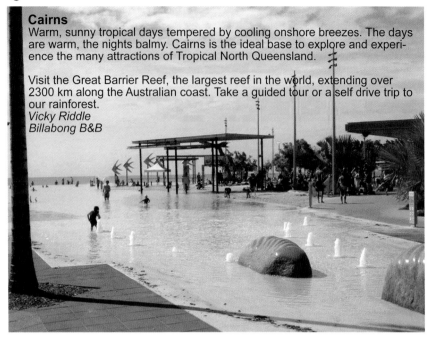

Cairns
Warm, sunny tropical days tempered by cooling onshore breezes. The days are warm, the nights balmy. Cairns is the ideal base to explore and experience the many attractions of Tropical North Queensland.

Visit the Great Barrier Reef, the largest reef in the world, extending over 2300 km along the Australian coast. Take a guided tour or a self drive trip to our rainforest.
Vicky Riddle
Billabong B&B

Cairns - Lake Tinaroo

Tinaroo Haven Holiday Lodge *5 km S of Kairi*
Luxury Self Contained Pole House and Cottage
Michael and Tania Taylor
Lot 42 Wavel Drive
Tinaroo Waters (via Kairi)
Qld 4872

Tel (07) 4095 8686
or 0437 344 973
Fax (07) 3319 7232
tinlodge@fire-break.com
www.fire-break.com

Double $90-$185
Children $16 per child
Continental provisions
No charge for children under 2
2 Queen 1 Double 3 Single (4 bdrm)
2 bedrooms in Pole home 2 bedrooms in cottage
Bathrooms: 3 Private
2 bathrooms in Polehome 1 in cottage

   AAA Tourism
★★★★

The property consists of a pole house and a cottage both hidden in the tree tops on 2.5 acres of bushland. They are both fully self-contained with all amenities, which includes Austar with National Geographic, Discovery, News, Sports, Movies, Cartoon Network, DVD Player, large selection of DVDs, a selection of games. There is also a laundry. Both units have dining areas and log fireplaces. The balconies area equipped with a BBQ.

Cairns - Stratford

Lilybank *8 km N of Cairns*
B&B
Mike & Pat Woolford
75 Kamerunga Road
Stratford Cairns
Qld 4870

Tel (07) 4055 1123
Fax (07) 4058 1990
lilybank@bigpond.net.au
www.lilybank.com.au

Double $110-$132
Single $94.60
Special breakfast
Extra person in room $33
Visa MC Amex Eftpos JCB accepted
2 King/Twin1 King 3 Queen
4 Twin 5 Single (5 bdrm)
Bathrooms: 5 Ensuite

'**L**ilybank' - a fine example of traditional 'Queenslander' architecture. 'Lilybank' owes its success to the happy blend of hospitality and privacy offered to our guests. Bedrooms are air-conditioned, there's a guests' lounge with TV, video, salt-water pool, laundry, BBQ and off-street parking. We'll serve a wonderful breakfast and help you choose and book tours which are right for you. Our excellent local restaurants are within walking distance. Two spoodles and a galah live in our part of house. There's a beautiful tropical garden and guests are welcome to pick their own fruit in season.

Cairns - Yorkeys Knob

A Villa Gail *17 km N of Cairns*
B&B & Self Contained Apartment
Gail Simpson
36 Janett Street
Yorkeys Knob Cairns
Qld 4878

Tel (07) 4055 8178
or 0417 079 575
Fax (07) 4055 8178
gail@avillagail.com
www.avillagail.com

Double $110-$180 Single $75-$120
Special breakfast
Self Contained Apartment $180-$200
1 King 1 Queen 1 Double
1 Twin (3 bdrm)
Bathrooms: 2 Ensuite

"**V**illa Gail" on Millionaires Row was designed to make the most of our unique elevated location at Yorkey's Knob. Our cool Mediterranean-style house is set within lush tropical gardens overlooking the beach with breathtaking views across the Coral Sea. From the delightful in-ground swimming pool spacious guest's verandah or your own large room, you can relax and enjoy our tropical lifestyle. Villa Gail is only 15 minutes from Cairns, near to the Skyrail, golf course, tours to the World Heritage Wet Tropics Rainforest, the Outback and the Great Barrier Reef. All pick ups from our door.

Cairns Hinterland - Kuranda

Koah Bed & Breakfast *40 km W of Cairns*
B&B & Homestay & Farmstay & Self Contained Chalets
Greg Taylor
Lot 4 Koah Road
MSI 1039 Kuranda
Qld 4881

Tel (07) 4093 7074
Fax (07) 4093 7074
koah@internode.on.net
www.kurandahomestay.com

Double $77 Single $55
Children 50% (under 15)
Continental breakfast
Cabin $110-$135
Visa MC accepted
2 Queen 2 Double 4 Twin 2 Single
(6 bdrm) 2 cabins sleep 4 each,
2 dbl in homestead
Bathrooms: 1 Ensuite 1 Private

Comfortable country home on 10 acres 10 mins from Kuranda the township in the Rainforest Kuranda and 30 mins from Cairns and Great Barrier Reef. Offering fully self contained cabins for families with balconies overlooking native bushland and large dam. Also homestead accommodation of 2 double bedrooms with double opening doors onto verandah 1 guest bathroom (ensuite) fully insulated and screened with ceiling fans. Each bedroom can be fitted with single folding bed for children, pets also welcomed.

~
Travelling to New Zealand?

Use *The New Zealand Bed & Breakfast Book*!

www.bnb.co.nz
~

Daintree - Cape Tribulation

Cape Trib Exotic Fruit Farm *80 km N of Mossman*
B&B & Cottage, no kitchen
Digby and Alison Gotts
Lot 5 Nicole Drive
Cape Tribulation
Qld 4873

Tel (07) 4098 0057
digby@capetrib.com.au
www.capetrib.com.au

Double $140-$160
Children age 6 and over welcome
Full breakfast
Four cafes in walking distance
2 nights minimum
Extra person $30
Visa MC Eftpos accepted
2 Queen 2 Double (2 bdrm)
1 Queen + 1 Double folding divan per open-plan cottage
Bathrooms: 2 Ensuite

Two private, high set timber pole-framed cottages on the edge of our privately owned World Heritage Rainforest. Breakfast is a sumptuous repast, based around farm produce. The property is in a remote wilderness area and runs on solar power. We offer an ECO Certified Ecotourism experience. Located one kilometre from the beach, and the Great Barrier Reef is 45 minutes offshore.

Daintree
The Daintree Coast combines breathtaking beauty with exceptional biodiversity and offers a unique holiday destination. Visitors have long been attracted by the World Heritage Listed Wet Tropics Rainforest and The Great Barrier Reef which meet spectacularly along the Daintree Coast and offer an unparalleled richness of rare and primitive flora and fauna.
Alison Gotts
Cape Tribulation Exotic Fruit Farm

Daintree - Cow Bay

Cow Bay Homestay *58 km N of Mossman*
B&B & Homestay
Marion Esser
160 Wattle Close
Cow Bay
Qld 4873

Tel (07) 4098 9151
marion@cowbayhomestay.com
www.cowbayhomestay.com

Double $140
Single $140
Children over 6 years
Full breakfast
Dinner please advise
Visa MC accepted
1 Queen 2 Double 1 Twin (2 bdrm)
Bathrooms: 2 Ensuite

Cow Bay Homestay is adjacent to two World Heritage Wilderness areas the Daintree Rainforest and the Great Barrier Reef. Wake up to nature: views into vast tropical gardens and rainforest, swim in our fresh water creek, sit under trees or on the deck spotting birds, stars, butterflies or the goanna. Get active with walks to stunning Cow Bay Beach and big range of guided tours. Great breakfast. Marion can arrange all your tour bookings. Action Packed Relaxation.

Daintree
Holidaying on the Daintree Coast, experiencing the stunning beauty of the Daintree Rainforest and the Great Barrier Reef, relaxing in comfortable accommodation with local hosts, is forever to be remembered. Numerous activities to participate as well as the total bliss effect of just nature's noises.
Marion Esser
Cow Bay Homestay

Eumundi

Eumundi Rise B&B *0.2 km W of Eumundi*
B&B
Faye Kenney
37-39 Crescent Road
Eumundi
Qld 4562

Tel (07) 5442 8855
or 0419 042 810
Fax (07) 5442 8859
fayekenn@bigpond.com
www.eumundirisebandb.com.au

Double $165-$185
Children over 5 welcome $40
Full breakfast   Dinner B/A
Extra person $40
Visa MC Eftpos accepted
2 King/Twin 2 Queen (4 bdrm)
Bathrooms: 4 Ensuite

High overlooking the Valley & Ranges you'll find this Relaxing Scenic Gem. Great hospitality, fully cooked breakfast, own en suite and under cover parking. Enjoy sipping a glass of your favourite wine or have a cuppa with home made cookies in peace and tranquillity on the veranda. Eumundi Rise is within walking distance to our Famous Eumundi Markets, restaurants, hotels, cafés, art galleries and shops, plus our newly opened public swimming pool. Conveniently situated 15 minutes to Noosa, 10 minutes to Buderim Ginger Factory or 45 minutes to the hinterland.

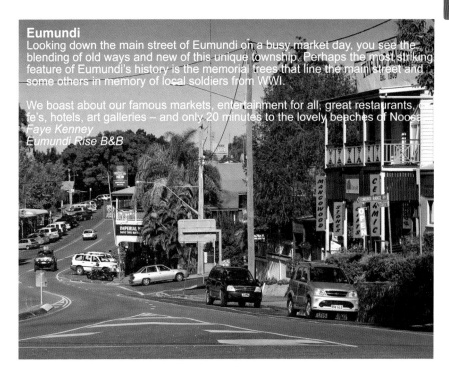

Eumundi
Looking down the main street of Eumundi on a busy market day, you see the blending of old ways and new of this unique township. Perhaps the most striking feature of Eumundi's history is the memorial trees that line the main street and some others in memory of local soldiers from WWI.

We boast about our famous markets, entertainment for all; great restaurants, cafe's, hotels, art galleries – and only 20 minutes to the lovely beaches of Noosa.
Faye Kenney
Eumundi Rise B&B

Gold Coast Hinterland - Nerang

Riviera Bed & Breakfast *6 km S of Nerang*
B&B & Retreat
Robert & Caroline Marchesi
53 Evanita Drive
Gilston/Nerang, Qld 4211

Tel (07) 5533 2499 or 0421 853 189
Fax (07) 5533 2500
rivbandb@bigpond.net.au
www.rivierabandb.com.au

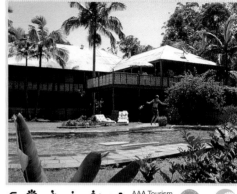

Double $115-$140 Single $95-$115
Children $15-$30 Extra adult $45
Continental breakfast
Dinner B/A: $25-$45
Children's meals $10-$35
High Season tariff 20th Dec-3rd Jan
Visa MC Eftpos accepted
4 Queen 3 Single (4 bdrm)

AAA Tourism
★★★☆

Bathrooms: 1 Ensuite 1 Guest share 1 Private Ensuite has bath & shower

Unique French Experience in Exquisite 100 year old Queenslander in Gold Coast Hinterland. Close proximity to all Theme Parks and National/Wildlife Parks. Peaceful, secluded in an exotic location on 7 acres of sub-tropical bushland. Franco-Australian hosts offer French Speciality Breakfasts on weekends and wholesome breakfasts of homemade/homegrown produce on weekdays. Exotic native birds to handfeed from deck while kangaroos graze nearby. Authentic French Gourmet meals by arrangement. Aussie host offers Therapeutic Massage. Pet friendly.

Hervey Bay

The Chamomile Bed & Breakfast *0.5 km NW of Hervey Bay Marina*
B&B
Diane & Brian Scruton
65A Miller Street
Hervey Bay
Qld 4655

Tel (07) 4125 1602
or 0408 781 886
Fax (07) 4125 6975
info@chamomile.com.au
www.chamomile.com.au

Double $125-$150
Single $105-$125
Full breakfast
Visa MC accepted
2 Queen 1 Twin (3 bdrm)
Bathrooms: 1 Ensuite 1 Guest share

Relax on the verandah as you sip a cappuccino, listen to the calming sound of water spilling over the waterfall and enjoy the peaceful sounds of the birdcalls. Stroll down to the Hervey Bay Marina and enjoy the sights and colours of the boats and people. Recharge in the garden spa. Relish the delicious breakfast and afternoon tea. A free booking service for Fraser Island, Lady Elliot Island and Whale Watch tours. A very warm welcome awaits you.

Hervey Bay

Alexander Lakeside B&B *1 km N of Hervey Bay*
B&B & Separate Suite
Sharon & John Lagan
29 Lido Parade
Hervey Bay
Qld 4655

Tel (07) 4128 9448
Fax (07) 4125 5060
alexbnb@bigpond.net.au
www.herveybaybedandbreakfast.com

Double $130-$140
Full breakfast
Self Contained Suites $150
Visa MC Eftpos accepted
3 Queen (3 bdrm)
2 Queen Rooms & 1 S/C Suite
Bathrooms: 3 Ensuite

AAA Tourism
★★★★☆

Luxury accommodation located beside a peaceful wildlife lake. Wake up and enjoy a full tropical breakfast while watching our wildlife. Guests can participate in turtle feeding. Indulge yourself in our heated Lakeside Spa. Fully equipped kitchen and laundry. BBQ facilities. We can organise your tours to view the majestic Humpback Whales Aug, Sept, Oct. World Heritage listed Fraser Island the largest sand Island in the world and Lady Elliott Island beginning of the Great Barrier Reef. A warm welcome awaits you. Your Home Style Resort.

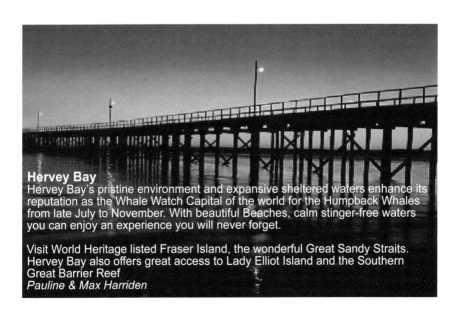

Hervey Bay
Hervey Bay's pristine environment and expansive sheltered waters enhance its reputation as the Whale Watch Capital of the world for the Humpback Whales from late July to November. With beautiful Beaches, calm stinger-free waters you can enjoy an experience you will never forget.

Visit World Heritage listed Fraser Island, the wonderful Great Sandy Straits. Hervey Bay also offers great access to Lady Elliot Island and the Southern Great Barrier Reef
Pauline & Max Harriden

Hervey Bay - Howard

Montrave House B&B Home & Pet Stay *30 km N of Maryborough*
B&B
Jackie & George Adams
20 Pacific Haven Drive
Howard
Qld 4659

Tel (07) 4129 0183
or 0407 930 106
montrave@bigpond.com
www.bbbook.com.au/MontraveHouse.html

Double $95-$105
Full traditional Aussie or Scottish
breakfast included
Refreshments on arrival included,
tea/coffee & evening port
2 Queen 1 Double 2 Twin (4 bdrm)
Bathrooms: 2 Guest share Spa bath

E njoy the elegance of a bygone era, traditional Scottish hospitality in the ambiance of a high set historic Queenslander in a tranquil atmosphere on rural acreage. Modern comforts, spa bath, wide verandahs and comfortable air conditioned tastefully decorated federation rooms. Close to the golf course boat ramps for two saltwater rivers and within walking distance of Howard CBD. Bookings available for all tours of Fraser Island also Lady Elliot Island and whale watching trips as well as vehicle and boat hire. Central for Hervey Bay and the historic towns of Maryborough and Childers.

Kingaroy

Rock-Al-Roy B&B *5 km S of Kingaroy*
B&B
Max & Lyn Lehmann
15 Kearney Street
Kingaroy
Qld 4610

Tel (07) 4162 3061
rockalroybb@burnett.net.au
www.rockalroy.southburnett.com.au

Double $100-$130
Single $80-$100
Children $20
Special breakfast
Dinner available
Visa MC accepted
1 Queen 1 Double 2 Single (3 bdrm)
Bathrooms: 2 Guest share

 AAA Tourism
★★★☆

J ust five minutes from Kingaroy, this warm modern Queenslander style house set on 7600 m2 with extensive shrub, gardens and pot plants offers quiet, peaceful surroundings with panoramic views overlooking Kingaroy. "Very welcoming and friendly, even the pets welcomed us." "Great meals. Thank you for making us feel so welcome in your beautiful home." Hosts Lyn & Max Lehmann.

Noosa - Lake Weyba

Eumarella Shores Lake Retreat *7 km SW of Noosa*
**B&B & Self Contained House & Self
Contained Cottages and Pavlions**
Bill & Christine Tainsh
251 Eumarella Road
Lake Weyba, Qld 4562

Tel (07) 5449 1738 Fax 07 5449 1738
stay@eumarellashores.com.au
www.eumarellashores.com.au

Double $136-$295
Children $25 per night
Full breakfast provisions
BBQ Hampers available
Extra guests $25-$40 pn
Complimentary use of canoe
Visa MC Eftpos accepted
5 King/Twin 5 King 7 Queen 8 Double
1 Single (14 bdrm) 7 queen & 7 king twin or king
Bathrooms: 7 Private 3 x pavilions with king single spa

AAA Tourism
★★★★

Aunique lake front retreat, nestled in temperate rainforest on the shores of pristine Lake Weyba. Only minutes from cosmopolitan Noosa: world class beaches, national parks, restaurants and boutiques. Enchanting traditional cottages and contemporary pavilions on the lake's edge; self contained to preserve your privacy with individual lake access and beach area. Explore the creeks and lake in a canoe; go bushwalking; bird & wildlife watching; fish virtually from your doorstep; or simply relax on your verandah, listening to the gently lapping lake. Sheer bliss!

Noosa and the Noosa Hinterland
Noosa - "gem" of the Sunshine Coast is renowned for its squeaky clean white sandy beaches, azure seas, the secluded beach coves of the Headland Section of the Noosa National Park, and as a mecca for serious foodies with a mouth watering selection of outstanding restaurants.

Snuggled behind the bustling coastal strip is the Noosa Hinterland; a patchwork of tranquil lakes and rivers, lush forests and pastures, quaint, historic villages guarded by striking volcanic formations, shrouded in Aboriginal legends.
Christine
Eumarella Shores and Tourism Noosa

Noosa - Noosa Valley

Noosa Valley Manor Luxury B&B *6 km SW of Noosa*
Luxury B&B
Kathleen & Murray Maxwell
115 Wust Road
Doonan, Noosa Valley
Qld 4562

Tel (07) 5471 0088
or 0400 280 215
Fax (07) 5471 0066
noosavalleymanor@bigpond.com
www.noosavalleymanor.com.au

Double $220-$260
Full breakfast
Candlelight dinners by arrangement
Visa MC Eftpos accepted
1 King/Twin 3 Queen (4 bdrm)
All with air conditioning
Bathrooms: 4 Ensuite

Noosa Valley Manor is a custom built Bed & Breakfast that truly reflects its 4.5 star AAA rating. Set in 1.5 acres of award winning tropical gardens yet you are only 10 minutes pleasant drive to the heart of Noosa. All bedrooms are air conditioned with ensuites. Gourmet fresh food is a feature of your stay with us. Here is what some guests have said: "Divine food, beautiful house, perfect hosts." "So lovely to be spoilt by wonderful people in a beautiful setting."

Noosa - Peregian

Lake Weyba Cottages *14 km S of Noosa*
B&B & Self Contained Cottages
Philip & Samantha Bown
79 Clarendon Road
Peregian Beach
Qld 4573

Tel (07) 5448 2285
or 0404 863 504
Fax (07) 5448 1714
info@lakeweybacottages.com
www.lakeweybacottages.com

Double $280-$415
Not suitable for children under 14 years
Full breakfast provisions
3 course dinner $185 per couple
Extra person $90 per night
Visa MC Amex Eftpos accepted
4 King/Twin 5 Queen 2 Single (10 bdrm)
Bathrooms: 8 Ensuite 1 Guest share Double spa in each cottage

Luxury cottages for couples with double spas, wood fires, air-conditioning and fabulous views. Peace and privacy assured. Enjoy breakfast on your private verandah, perfect for relaxing and watching passing kangaroos and the abundant bird life. LCD televisions with home theatre systems and digital reception in all cottages. Only 5 minutes to Peregian Beach and 15 minutes south of Noosa. Complimentary facilities include canoeing, cycling, fishing and a DVD library. Additional services include in-house dinners, massage treatments and eco tours. Perfect for weddings and conferences.

Noosa Hinterland - Cooroy

Cudgerie Homestead B&B *7 km NW of Cooroy*
B&B
Veronica & Steve Hall
42 Cudgerie Drive
Cooroy
Qld 4563

Tel (07) 5442 6681
or 0408 982 461
Fax (07) 5442 6681
cudgerie@hotmail.com
www.cudgerie-noosa.com

Double $155-$167 Single $90-$95
Infants free with cot in parent bedroom
Full breakfast
Delicious evening meals available b/a
Massage therapy available b/a
Visa MC accepted
3 Queen 1 Double 2 Twin (5 bdrm)
Bathrooms: 4 Ensuite 1 Private

Multi-award winning Cudgerie Homestead is one of the Sunshine Coast's most popular bed and breakfasts, offering you a unique blend of hospitality and cuisine. Unwind by the sensational swimming pool in summer or around the pot belly in winter. A quiet and secluded location with fantastic views across the Noosa Hinterland. Guest Comments: "A place to indulge, superb breakfasts on the veranda. Charming hosts with helpful touring advice." "It doesn't get any better than this, splendid location, warm and friendly hosts and top notch food."

~

Rainbow Beach

Rainbow Ocean Palms *75 km E of Gympie*
Luxury Self Contained Apartments
Mark & Tanya Beech
103 Cooloola Drive
Rainbow Beach
Qld 4581

Tel (07) 5486 3211
Fax (07) 5486 9797
oceanpalms@westnet.com.au
www.rainbowoceanpalms.com

Double $200-$350
Breakfast by arrangement
10 one-three bedroom apartments
Visa MC Amex Eftpos accepted
1 King 1 Queen 2 Single (3 bdrm)
Ocean views
Bathrooms: 1 Ensuite 1 Private

Rainbow Ocean Palms Resort is a small boutique resort positioned on the highest point in Rainbow Beach, offering panoramic ocean views to World Heritage listed Fraser Island. Nestled against Great Sandy National Park, walking trails and wildlife viewing opportunities are on your doorstep. The spacious luxury apartments open out to sweeping views of the bushland and seascape beyond the infinity style heated pool. All apartments have spa baths and quality guest toiletries. Escape to a world of natural charm and enjoy Mark and Tanya's hospitality.

Rockhampton - Capricorn Coast

Brae Bothy B&B *20 km NE of Rockhampton*
B&B
Judy & Keith Brandt
1184 Yeppoon Road
Iron Pot, Rockhampton
Qld 4701

Tel (07) 4936 4026
or 0427 364 026
Fax (07) 4936 4038
stay@braebothy.com.au
www.braebothy.com.au

Double $120-$150 Single $105-$115
Children 12 and under $15
Full breakfast
Dinner $25 B/A
Extra adult $30
Visa MC accepted
1 King/Twin1 King 2 Queen (3 bdrm)
Bathrooms: 2 Ensuite 1 Private

   AAA Tourism
★★★★☆

An award winning B&B located on 4.2 hectares of Bush. Relax in a tranquil setting with abundant bird life. Bedrooms tastefully furnished, air-conditioned, Queen size beds, ensuite and private outdoor garden. Each room has a television set. The King room has an external spa. Guest BBQ facility and swimming pool. Fifteen minutes to Yeppoon's beautiful beaches and ten minutes to Rockhampton shopping centres. Brae Bothy has the very friendly Kelpie dog called Molly and a ginger cat called Rusty.

Stanthorpe

Jireh *7 km S of Stanthorpe*
B&B & Homestay
Margaret Taylor
89 Donges Road
Severnlea
Qld 4380

Tel (07) 4683 5298
ktaylor3@vtown.com.au
www.bbbook.com.au/jireh.html

Double $100-$120
Single $70-$80
Children $40
Full breakfast
Dinner $30
Extra adult $50
3 Double 1 Single (3 bdrm)
Feather doonas, electric blankets
Bathrooms: 1 Ensuite 1 Guest share

Old-fashioned country hospitality in a quiet rural setting, close to the wineries and national parks of the Granite Belt. Antiques and country decor reflect family history and include many examples of Margaret's embroidery, patchwork, dolls and bears. Hearty country breakfasts are served and dinner (Traditional or Indian) is by arrangement. The combination of country home, personal attention, household pets, farm animals, and country rambles offers both a unique experience and value for money. "Wonderful friendly atmosphere and simply great food." B&B Book Commended, 2004, 2005.

Stanthorpe

The Granite Belt, so called because of its spectacular granite outcrops, is situated just north of the New South Wales border, around the small town of Stanthorpe.

Because of its altitude, the area has become well-known as the coldest place in Queensland, when locally produced red wines, 'Christmas in July' dinners and cosy log fires attract large numbers of tourists to the area.
Margaret Taylor
Jireh B&B

Sunshine Coast - Ninderry - Yandina - Coolum

Ninderry House *5 km E of Yandina*
B&B
Mary Lambart
8 Karnu Drive
Ninderry
Qld 4561

Tel (07) 5446 8556
Fax (07) 5446 8556
enquiries@ninderryhouse.com.au
www.ninderryhouse.com.au

Double $150 Single $95
Full breakfast
Dinner $25-$35, provided if requested
on booking
Visa MC accepted
2 King/Twin 1 Queen (3 bdrm)
Beautiful outlook to mountains, valley and ocean
Bathrooms: 3 Ensuite

Central Sunshine Coast location, views overlooking Mt Ninderry and Maroochy Valley to the Ocean. Close to beaches, native plant nurseries, ginger factory, art galleries, craft and produce markets of Eumundi and Yandina. First class restaurants nearby. Three ensuite guestrooms, comfortable sitting room with fire, deck for summer breezes or winter sun. Imaginative meals using fresh local produce. Special diets catered for. Dinner available if requested on booking. Full breakfast included in tariff. Ph/Fax: 07 5446 8556. Email: enquiries@ninderryhouse.com.au.

Sunshine Coast Hinterland - Glasshouse Mountains

Glass on Glasshouse *60 km N of Brisbane*
B&B Luxury Cottages with kitchenettes
Bill & Misao Rogers
182 Glasshouse-Woodford Road
Glasshouse Mountains, Qld 4518

Tel (07) 5496 9608
or (07) 5496 9603
or 0431 101208
info@glassonglasshouse.com.au
www.glassonglasshouse.com.au

Double $265-$440 Single $250-$425
Full breakfast
Nearest restaurants are 6 km away
Extra person $70/night
Max 3 people/cottage (3rd on sofabed)
Visa MC Eftpos accepted
3 King (3 bdrm) King or Twin beds
Bathrooms: 3 Ensuite Freestanding spa

Experience the mystical beauty of the Glasshouse Mountains. We offer three architect-designed cottages, featuring two walls of floor-to-ceiling glass with wonderful Mountain views. Sit on the deck and watch the kangaroos, or listen to the sounds of the Kookaburras and Black Cockatoos. Ideal for those who just want to relax. King-size bed, freestanding spa, open fire, Blu-Ray DVD, flat-screen TV, kitchenette, and a BBQ. Breakfast in our cafe or in your cottage. Australia Zoo is close. Nearby are: beaches, Woodford, Maleny, Eumundi markets and Noosa.

Sunshine Coast Hinterland - The Glasshouse Mountains

The Glasshouse Mountains are ancient volcanic plugs about 25-27 million years old and form the backdrop to the beautiful hinterland region forty minutes North of Brisbane. The area is popular with bushwalkers, climbers, cyclists, bird-watchers, artists and photographers.

It's a great base to explore the other attractions of the Sunshine Coast: Australia Zoo, the hinterland towns of Maleny and Montville, the beaches of Caloundra and Mooloolaba, the Big Pineapple, Eumundi markets and Noosa.
Bill Rogers
Glass on Glasshouse

Sunshine Coast Hinterland - Maleny

Maleny Country Cottages *8 km W of Maleny*
Self Contained House
Claude & Teresa Goudsouzian
347 Corks Pocket Road
Reesville Via Maleny
Qld 4552

Tel (07) 5494 2744
Fax (07) 5494 2744
reception@malenycottages.com.au
www.malenycottages.com.au

Double $225-$245
Children $20-$50
Breakfast hampers by arrangement
$35 per couple per morning
Two nights from $360-$395
Extra adult $30-$50
Visa MC Diners Amex Eftpos JCB accepted
1 Queen 1 Twin (2 bdrm) All linen included
Bathrooms: 1 Ensuite 2 Guest share

AAA Tourism
★★★★

M ountain hideaway on 60acres of forested property. Fully self-contained air conditioned cottages with all linen, spa, fireplace and verandah BBQ. Abundant wildlife, alpacas and bush walking tracks.

Sunshine Coast Hinterland - Maleny - Montville

Lillypilly's Country Cottages *6 km S of Town*
5 B&B Cottages with kitchenettes
Josef & Adele Gruber
584 Maleny-Montville Road
Maleny
Qld 4552

Tel (07) 5494 3002
or 0408 943 002
Fax (07) 5494 3499
adele@lillypillys.com.au
www.lillypillys.com.au

Double $198-$308
Single $187-$297
Full breakfast
Dinner $28.60-$33.00 (Main Course)
$^1/_2$ to 1 hour massage $49.50-$88
Visa MC Diners Amex Eftpos accepted
5 Queen (5 bdrm)
Bathrooms: 5 Ensuite 5 Private

AAA Tourism
★★★★☆

L illypilly's Cottages for couples overlook picturesque Lake Baroon or are situated in a rainforest garden setting. All cottages are air conditioned and feature log fires, dual-system double spas, separate ensuite, lounge area with television, video, DVD and CD player, kitchenettes, and private verandahs with double hammocks. Gourmet Breakfasts are included in the rate and Candlelit Dinners are available Tues-Sat and served to your individual cottage. An on-site masseuse and saltwater pool are also features of Lillypilly's.

Sunshine Coast Hinterland - Montville

Secrets on the Lake *5 km SW of Montville*
Luxury B&B & Luxury Treehouse Cabins
George and Aldy Johnston
208 Narrows Road
Montville
Qld 4560

Tel (07) 5478 5888
Fax (07) 5478 5166
aldy@secretsonthelake.com.au
www.secretsonthelake.com.au

Double $320-$390
Continental provisions
Visa MC Amex Eftpos accepted
1 King/Twin 13 Queen
2 Single (14 bdrm)
Bathrooms: 1 Ensuite 11 Private

Secrets on the Lake offers the perfect opportunity for romance, relaxation and intimate accommodation. Elevated wooden walkways lead you through the rainforest to 10 individually themed treehouses offering total privacy, superb attention to detail and a completely unique world-class experience. Each retreat features carved cedar furniture, double shower, kitchen facilities, special home baked treats, toasty log fire, AC, TV, CD/DVD, sunken double spa and your own balcony with BBQ. What a way to indulge... we provide a stunning view, chocolates, roses & champagne. All you need to bring is that special someone to share it with.

Sunshine Coast Hinterland - Mooloolah Valley

Mooloolah Valley Holidays *1 km SW of Mooloolah*
Self Contained Holiday Houses
Atalanta Moreau
93 King Road
Mooloolah Valley
Qld 4553

Tel (07) 5494 7109
or 0408 224 668
info@mooloolahvalley.com
www.mooloolahvalley.com

Double $175-$250
Breakfast by arrangement
Ask about our wonderful parties,
weddings and celebrations
Visa MC accepted
4 Double 4 Single (4 bdrm)
One 2 bedroom house, two 1 bedroom houses
Bathrooms: 4 Private

Discover the glorious pleasures of a country horse riding holiday at Mooloolah Valley. For romantic couples, Jacaranda Cottage is charming and full of olde-world splendour. Funky Piccaninny Cottage featuring the rainbow serpent sleeps four. For families and celebrations, Frangipani House is dazzling! Guests are treated to a fun-filled holiday. Try the tropical Hot-tub Jacuzzi spa, fabulous heated swimming pool and wood-fire pizza oven . . . Great for parties! There are fun games like giant chess set, bikes to explore picturesque Mooloolah Valley, safe Horses and cute Ponies to trek into Rainforest and Mountain-tops. Come and enjoy!

Yeppoon - Capricorn Coast

While Away B&B *2.4 km N of Yeppoon*
Luxury B&B
Sharyn McClelland
44 Todd Avenue
Yeppoon
Qld 4703

Tel (07) 4939 5719
Fax (07) 4939 5577
whileaway@bigpond.com
www.whileawaybandb.com.au

Double $120-$140
Single $100
Special breakfast
Visa MC Eftpos accepted
1 King 3 Queen 1 Twin (4 bdrm)
Bathrooms: 4 Ensuite

 AAA Tourism ★★★★☆

W hile Away B&B is a purpose built B&B. We offer style, comfort and privacy in a modern home less than 100 m to beach. This property is ideal for couples but unsuitable for children under 10. All rooms have ensuites, television plus air-conditioning. We offer a generous tropical/cooked breakfast - tea/coffee-making facilities with cake/biscuits are available at all times. Dining room facilities available for use of guests. We will do our best to ensure you enjoy your stay in this area.

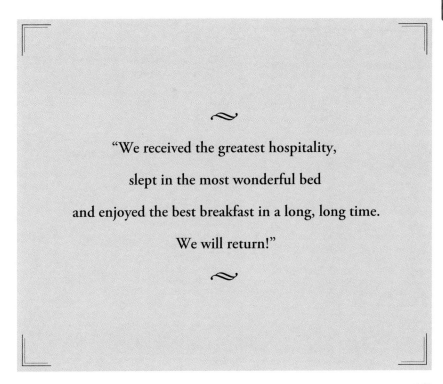

"We received the greatest hospitality,

slept in the most wonderful bed

and enjoyed the best breakfast in a long, long time.

We will return!"

South Australia

Barossa Valley

Tanunda

Mt Pleasant

Port Lincoln

Mannum

Adelaide

McLaren Vale

Strathalbyn

Fleurieu Peninsula

Port Elliot

Victor Harbor

Goolwa

Kangaroo Island

Middleton

Meningie

Port Augusta

Naracoorte

Limestone Coast

Beachport

Mount Gambier

0 Kilometres 100

0 Miles 60

Adelaide

Largs Bay

Basket Range

College Park

North Adelaide

Rostrevor

Adelaide

Norwood

Burnside

Adelaide Airport

Goodwood

Glenunga

Glenelg

Hawthorndene

Somerton Park

Stirling

Adelaide Hills

0 Kilometres 5

0 Miles 3

Seacliff Park

South Australia

lide - Burnside - St Georges

ndale 5 km SE of Adelaide
> & Self Contained Apartment
Jenny & Steve Studer
16 Inverness Avenue
St. Georges
SA 5064

Tel 0413 414 140
or (08) 8338 2768
kirkendale@ozemail.com.au
www.kirkendale.com.au

Double $135-$155
Single $125-$135
Children $30 - $40
Continental provisions
Not suitable for children under 10 years
Visa MC accepted
1 Queen 2 Twin (2 bdrm)
Bathrooms: 1 Private

I dyllic "Country-style" 3 room apartment, nestled in peaceful, leafy garden, sun-dappled patio, French doors, terracotta floors, rose garden. Hint of the Provence. Fresh flowers, fruit basket, generous breakfast provisions, books, tourist information. Separate entrance, private bathroom, living room, kitchenette, sole occupancy. Quiet location. 5km city, near restaurants, wineries, wildlife parks. Jenny and Steve are extremely well travelled, this is reflected by their gracious but unobtrusive hosting. Smoking outdoors. "We loved our accommodation - our best yet in 6 weeks of travel," SS & DC, USA.

Adelaide - College Park

Possums Rest Bed & Breakfast _2 km NE of Adelaide CBD_
Separate Suite
Sue & Phil Ogden
8 Catherine Street
College Park
SA 5069

Tel (08) 8362 5356
or 0412 092 881
Fax (08) 8362 5356
possumsrest@gmail.com
www.possumsrestbedandbreakfast.com.au

Double $135
Single $125
Special breakfast
2 night minimum stay
1 Queen (1 bdrm)
Bathrooms: 1 Ensuite

P ossums Rest Bed & Breakfast is ideally located in the leafy heritage area of Adelaide. Accommodation is quiet and luxurious, yet only 2 km from the CBD - within walking distance of Adelaide events such as WOMAD, Clipsal 500, Fringe Festival and Festival of Arts. Walk to the Adelaide Zoo, Museum, Art Galleries and numerous shopping and restaurant precincts. Guests are welcome to enjoy the pleasant garden and inground swimming pool in summer. Home cooked breakfasts cater for special dietary requirements. Comfortable accommodation, has wireless internet connection, television, DVD and cooking facilities. Laundry facilities are available.

Adelaide - Glenelg

Water Bay Villa Bed & Breakfast *11 km SW of Adelaide*
Luxury B&B - Self Contained Suite
Kathy & Roger Kuchel
28 Broadway
Glenelg South
SA 5045

Tel 0412 221 724
glenelg@waterbayvilla-bnb.com.au
www.waterbayvilla-bnb.com.au

Double $240-$275
Single $200
Children $20-$45
Full breakfast provisions
Visa MC Diners Amex accepted
2 Queen 2 Single (2 bdrm)
Bathrooms: 1 Ensuite

Indulge! Experience the luxury of this 1910 Queen Anne Villa in seaside Glenelg. 'The Attic' - your upstairs 4 room suite with private entry and off street parking. Welcoming bottle of wine, fresh flowers, fruit and chocolates. Antiques, open fire, claw foot bath and laundry. Kitchenette with cooking facilities. Living area with tourist info, TV, DVD player, CD/Radio. A few minutes stroll via the award winning garden to the nearby beach, Jetty Road, trams, restaurants, cinema, 7-day shopping, summer markets, The Beachouse, fun park and marina. Close to airport and public transport. Come and enjoy! "A little piece of heaven." HF, Canada.

Adelaide - Goodwood

Rose Villa *2 km S of Adelaide*
B&B & Homestay
Doreen Petherick
29 Albert Street
Goodwood
SA 5034

Tel (08) 8271 2947
Fax (08) 8271 2947
doreen@rosevilla.com.au
www.rosevilla.com.au

Double $125-$145
Single $100-$120
Children $10
Continental breakfast, cooked breakfast available for extra $10 per person
1 King 1 Queen (2 bdrm)
Bathrooms: 1 Ensuite 1 Guest share

Treat yourself to a romantic candle lit breakfast in my newly decorated Tea Rose salon. Rose Villa offers an elegant private suite (own entrance) overlooking the garden. Inside is an additional guest room with the use of the exquisite Blue-White-Russian Tea Cup bathroom. Stroll to trendy Hyde Park Road with its delightful cafes and coffee shops, boutiques and flower shops. Close by are buses and trams (to the Bay) and city and The Ghan Terminal. "Rose Villa" is roses, romance and caring hospitality. You are most welcome. "A romantic and warm place to be. Great hospitality." Erwin Zwijnenburg, The Hague, Holland.

Adelaide - Largs Bay

Seapod B&B *18 km NW of Adelaide*
B&B & Separate Suite
Bernadette McDonnell
146 Esplanade
Largs Bay
SA 5016

Tel (08) 8449 4213
or 0418 851 680
info@seapod.com.au
www.seapod.com.au

Double $180-$195
Single $150-$160
Children $50
Full breakfast
Visa MC Diners Amex
Eftpos JCB accepted
1 Queen (1 bdrm)
Bathrooms: 1 Private

S eapod is wonderful hosted bed & breakfast accommodation right on the beachfront with great views and within walking distance of shops, restaurants, cafes, and public transport. Delicious breakfasts served daily in your own suite overlooking the sea. Natural, free range and organic produce with unlimited freshly brewed coffee and tea are standard. See dolphins and magnificent sunsets from your table, go for a run on the track across the road, walk along the jetties, swim with the dolphins, or stroll along the beach for miles.

Adelaide - North Adelaide

Cornwall Park Heritage Accommodation *1 km N of Adelaide city centre*
B&B & Self Contained Apartment
Judy Fitzhardinge
84 Mills Terrace
North Adelaide
SA 5006

Tel (08) 8239 0155
or 0411 171 807
judy@seekshare.com.au
www.seekshare.com.au

Double $135-$250
Single $120-$165
Children B/A
Special breakfast
Visa MC Diners Amex Eftpos accepted
(3 bdrm)
Including spa suites

C ornwall Park is an 1873 state heritage listed property, situated around north Adelaide golf course and parklands. Only 1 kilometre from Adelaide city and 500m from some of the best restaurants and cafes in Adelaide. The bluestone residence was sympathetically renovated in 2002-3 to include lovely spacious bedrooms, including large spa and bedrooms with ensuites in the heritage side. Open fireplaces and reverse-cycle air-conditioning throughout. A romantic place suitable for people on holiday, weddings as well as the business person. Internet is available for guests. Secure off street parking.

Adelaide - Seacliff Park - Brighton

Homestay Brighton *2 km S of Brighton*
B&B & Homestay
Ruth & Tim
PO Box 319
Brighton
SA 5048

Tel (08) 8298 6671
or 0417 800 755
Fax (08) 8298 6671
rimbb@hotmail.com
www.bbbook.com.au/brighton.html

Double $65-$75
Single $45-$55
Full breakfast
1 Double 2 Single (2 bdrm)
Bathrooms: 1 Guest share 1 Private

Spacious home and grounds in quiet suburb close to Brighton/Seacliff beach. Public transport to the city and nearby large Westfield Shopping Centre. Ideal for day trips to the Fleurieu Peninsula with its picturesque wine areas and southern vales and coast. Guest rooms are upstairs including a television lounge with heating and cooling. Laundry and off-street parking are available. Sascha, our friendly Border Collie dog, stays outside the house "Great value in a relaxing suburb of Adelaide. Outstanding host, helpful, supportive and friendly." J&GB, UK. "Home from Home." LJ, UK.

Adelaide - Somerton Park

Forstens Bed & Breakfast *2.5 km S of Glenelg*
B&B & Homestay
John & Marilyn Forsten
19 King George Avenue
Somerton Park
SA 5044

Tel (08) 8298 3393
forstens_bandb@hotmail.com
www.bbbook.com.au/forstensbb.html

Double $77
Single $60
Full breakfast
1 King 2 Single (2 bdrm)
Bathrooms: 1 Ensuite 1 Guest share

AAA Tourism
★★★☆

Located in a residential area 600 metres from beautiful Somerton Beach, 2.5km south of the bustling seaside resort of Glenelg with its 'mile' of shopping and dining along Jetty Road. A city bus passes the house en route to Glenelg and Adelaide. Guests are accommodated in a lovely bedroom with a rear garden view, ensuite bath, TV, private entrance, reverse cycle air conditioning, and off-street parking. Warm fresh bread is included in the cooked breakfast. Laundry facilities available.

Adelaide Hills - Basket Range

Bishops Adelaide Hills *20 km E of Adelaide*
Self Contained Cottages
Douglas Bishop
Lobethal Road, Basket Range, SA 5138

Tel (08) 8390 3469 **Fax** (08) 8390 0450
enquiries@bishopsadelaidehills.com.au
www.bishopsadelaidehills.com

Cottage $240 per night
Min 2 night booking w/ends & public hols
Portacot and high chair available
Breakfast provisions first night
Visa MC accepted
Henry's 1 Queen. The Waterfalls 1 Queen.
Willow Cottage 1 Queen, 4 Single
Henry's double shower & double spa
The Waterfalls shower & double spa
Willow Cottage bath/shower

Enjoy the freedom, beauty and tranquillity of the Bishop family's 300 acre historic property - with easy access to restaurants, pubs and vineyards. Three self-contained cottages at Basket Range, just 30 minutes from Adelaide - perfect for both weekend getaways and extended breaks. Henry's is a fully restored Federation cottage, The Waterfalls was rebuilt from the ruins of a pioneer cottage. Both are suitable for couples and include open log fireplace, luxurious bathroom with spa bath, queen sized bed, digital television and DVD. Willow Cottage can accommodate up to 6 and also offers ducted reverse cycle air conditioning and a barbeque. Bishops Adelaide Hills - minutes from everywhere, hours from anywhere.

Adelaide Hills - Mt Pleasant

Saunders Gorge Sanctuary *18 km E of Mt Pleasant*
Family cottage & 5 Self contained buildings for couples
Brenton & Nadene Newman
18km east of Mt Pleasant
Mt Pleasant, SA 5237

Tel (08) 8569 3032
nature@saundersgorge.com.au
www.saundersgorge.com.au

Double $120-$160 Single $90-$130
Children $10 per night
Continental provisions
Restaurant availabile on the property
Family Cottage $20 per additional adult
per night (sleeps 6) Visa MC accepted
4 King 3 Queen 2 Single (7 bdrm)
Bathrooms: 5 Ensuite
1 Guest share in family cottage

  AAA Tourism ★★★☆

ECO Tourism accredited Saunders Gorge Sanctuary is a private property of 1364 ha on the rugged Eastern slopes of the Mt Lofty Ranges (Adelaide Hills). Offering visitors the opportunity to experience the rugged Australian landscape, learn about and enjoy the natural environment. The property is a combination of conservation and sheep grazing. Relax in self contained accommodation. Experience the tranquility & beauty of the property. Explore the many scenic walks or drive the 4WD trail. Enjoy an evening meal in the licensed restaurant.

Adelaide Hills - Stirling

The Retreat at Stirling *4 km E of Stirling*
French Provincial Style Villa
Helen & Brian Rohan
9 Hoylake Avenue
Stirling
SA 5152

Tel (08) 8339 4702
or 0412 127 045
info@the-retreat.com.au
www.the-retreat.com.au

Double $260
Full breakfast provisions
Extra person $60/night
Visa MC Amex accepted
1 King 1 Queen (2 bdrm)
Bathrooms: 1 Private Double spa bath

Designed with elegance and indulgence in mind, The Retreat is a fully self contained, two bedroom Bed & Breakfast elegantly furnished and finished in French Provincial style, with wide-open spaces and breathtaking views of the Adelaide Hills. Tastefully appointed and decorated in all rooms, the Retreat features a beautifully appointed kitchen plus a roomy lounge with open look fire place, formal dining area and an outside courtyard ideal for barbeques.The two large bedrooms - one king and one queen size - both reflect French elegance, and The Retreat's 12.5 metre indoor heated pool and double spa bath are wonderful extravagances.

Barossa Valley - Lyndoch - Tanunda - Angaston

Bellescapes *1 km N of Barossa Valley*
Self Contained B&B Cottages
Mandy & Mark Creed
PO Box 481
Lyndoch
SA 5351

Tel (08) 8524 4825
or 0412 220 553
Fax (08) 8524 4046
escape@bellescapes.com
www.bellescapes.com

Double $150-$250 Single $140-$250
Children welcome in properties
with more than one bedroom
Full breakfast provisions
Dinner platters and BBQ packs b/a
Tours b/a Visa MC accepted
13 properties, ranging from 1 bedroom to 3 bedrooms
Each property has its own bathroom facilities some with spas

Bellescapes properties are exclusively yours, private & self contained, properties can accommodate between 2-12 guests. Indulge in one of our stunning B&B's designed to spoil, all located within the beautiful Barossa Valley. Choose from either heritage or contemporary properties, 9 with spa and 9 with cosy log fires. Your choice between vineyard views, the townships of Angaston, Lyndoch, Tanunda or getaway from it all in the Barossa foothills of Eden Valley. We pride ourselves on providing quality service and accommodation with a very personalised touch.

Barossa Valley - Tanunda

Goat Square Cottages *75 km N of Adelaide*
B&B & Self Contained Apartment
Ngaire Ingham
33 John Street
Tanunda
SA 5352

Tel 1800 227 677
or (08) 8524 5353
info@goatsquarecottages.com.au
goatsquarecottages.com.au

Double $190 Extra couple $120
We can provide a baby's cot at no extra cost
Full breakfast provisions
Close to the 1918 Restaurant
Visa MC accepted
3 cottages (one 2 bedroom)
3 King 1 Queen
Bathrooms: 3 Private Fully heated, with
modern double spa and shower.

AAA Tourism
★★★☆

These 3 adjoining cottages date from 1847, incorporating original features from the 1840s, including the old baker's oven. Recent renovations include a modern spa baths, under-floor heating and a superbly appointed kitchen. You are welcomed with warm country hospitality and a selection of local products for your breakfast. Very close to some of SA's most famous wineries - a great chance to visit this historic area and then relax sitting in the flowery garden, where you can pick your own fruit in season.

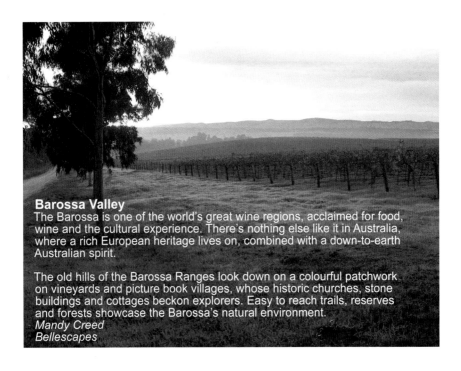

Barossa Valley
The Barossa is one of the world's great wine regions, acclaimed for food, wine and the cultural experience. There's nothing else like it in Australia, where a rich European heritage lives on, combined with a down-to-earth Australian spirit.

The old hills of the Barossa Ranges look down on a colourful patchwork on vineyards and picture book villages, whose historic churches, stone buildings and cottages beckon explorers. Easy to reach trails, reserves and forests showcase the Barossa's natural environment.
Mandy Creed
Bellescapes

Goolwa

Vue de M B&B *0.1 km S of Goolwa*
B&B
Pam & Bob Ballard
11 Admiral Terrace
Goolwa
SA 5214

Tel (08) 8555 1487
or 0414 760 232
admin@vuedemerde.com.au
www.vuedemerde.com.au

Double $180
Single $170
Full breakfast
Visa MC accepted
2 Queen (2 bdrm)
Bathrooms: 2 Ensuite

 AAA Tourism ★★★☆

M?? Mysterious, Mighty, Murray, Mouth, Muesli, Milo, Milk or Munchies?? Ask us about the real name of our 1850's Riverside Cottage. Relax and enjoy the superb river view from the balcony adjoining your room. Two Queen-sized bedrooms, each with Ensuite. Breakfast is served in the Sun Room with magnificent views from the Hindmarsh Island Bridge to the Goolwa Barrage.

Travelling to New Zealand?

Use *The New Zealand Bed & Breakfast Book*!

www.bnb.co.nz

Kangaroo Island - Emu Bay

Seascape on Emu Bay *1 km N of Emu Bay*
Luxury B&B & Small Luxury Lodge
Mandy and Paul Brown
Bates Road, Emu Bay
Kangaroo Island
SA 5223

Tel (08) 8553 5033
Fax 08 8559 5088
info@seascapelodge.com.au
www.seascapelodge.com.au

Double $552 Single $379
Children under 12 by prior arrangement
Full breakfast
Dinner 3 course set menu + wine etc.
included in tariff
Luxury 4WD island tours available
Visa MC Eftpos accepted
2 King/Twin3 King (3 bdrm)
Bathrooms: 3 Private Private bathroom in each suite

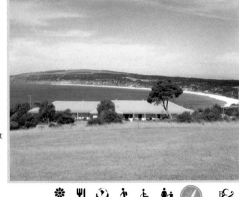

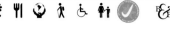

Explore Australia's premier wildlife destination on one of our exclusive 4WD tours. Our hosted dinner, bed and breakfast property provides an intimate, homely experience whilst Enjoying stunning beach, sea and rural views from every room in the house. Sit back on the open deck in summer, nestle up against the wood fire in winter or simply relax with a wine in the privacy of your room and soak up the quiet tranquillity. This together with Mandy's elegant home-style cooking will make for a memorable experience.

Kangaroo Island

Kangaroo Island is renowned for its spectacular scenery and abundant and diverse variety of wildlife and flora. The spectacular South Coast is buffeted by winds from the Southern Ocean that have produced incredible rock formations, whilst the calmer north coast has rolling hills, secluded bays and beautiful beaches.

Blessed with a temperate 'Mediterranean' climate not unlike the French Riviera, the warm dry summers and cool mild winters make it a year-round destination.
Jenny Bloemendal

Limestone Coast - Beachport

Bompas of Beachport *In Beachport*
B&B & Boutique Hotel
Corinne & Steven Spadotto
3 Railway Terrace
Beachport
SA 5280

Tel (08) 8735 8333
Fax (08) 8735 8101
bompas@bigpond.com
www.bompas.com.au

Double $80-$145
Single $60-$130
Children free if using existing bedding
Special breakfast
Cafe breakfast, lunch & dinner
Visa MC Eftpos accepted
2 King 3 Queen 1 Double
2 Twin (8 bdrm)
Bathrooms: 5 Ensuite 2 Guest share

Historic, family run boutique hotel in stunning seaside town. Several rooms have balcony with uninterrupted sea views. Relax and unwind as you watch the fishing boast return to the jetty. Licensed café/restaurant downstairs, open breakfast, lunch and dinner 7 days serving great food with a wide range of local wines. Cooked or continental breakfast available, please enquire in included in tariff. Most rooms upstairs. Beachport is central to all attractions of the Limestone Coast region.

~

McLaren Vale

Willunga House *44 km S of Adelaide*
B&B
Valerie Bainbridge and Nick Scarvelis
1 St Peter's Terrace
Willunga
SA 5172

Tel (08) 8556 2467
Fax (08) 8556 2465
willungahouse@internode.on.net
www.willungahouse.com.au

Double $220-$250
Single $150-$220
Special breakfast
Tariffs for stays of 2 or more nights
$180 - $220
Visa MC accepted
5 Queen (5 bdrm)
Bathrooms: 3 Ensuite 2 Private

Willunga House is situated in a prime location in one of South Australia's most picturesque historic townships 12 kilometres from the beach and minutes from vineyards, a golf course, restaurants, shops, markets and galleries. Willunga House is a State Heritage listed Georgian stone residence built in 1850. Its guest wing offers 5 bedrooms beautifully appointed with antique furnishings and modern digital TVs. A sitting room opens onto a large balcony where guests can relax and enjoy the tranquility of the house and its surrounds. Breakfast is served in dining facilities downstairs.

Naracoorte

Willowbrook Cottages B&B's *1 km E of Post Office*
2 Self Contained B&B Cottages
Lynette & John Lauterbach
3 & 3A Jenkins Terrace
Naracoorte
SA 5271

Tel (08) 8762 0259
or 0419 802 728
stay@willowbrookcottages.com.au
www.willowbrookcottages.com.au

Double $120-$140
Single $90-$100
Children $15 per child
Full breakfast provisions
Visa MC Amex accepted
2 Queen 1 Twin (3 bdrm) per cottage
Bathrooms: 1 Private per cottage

  AAA Tourism ★★★★

The allure and charm of bygone years combined with all the modern conveniences expected by today's traveller - that's the brilliant blend of Willowbrook Cottages B&Bs. Centrally located in Naracoorte, within walking distance to shops and eateries, Willowbrook Cottages are the ideal base for exploring the Limestone Coast including World Heritage Fossil site, Coonawarra & Padthaway wine regions.

Naracoorte
Halfway between Adelaide and Melbourne is the picturesque pastoral township of Naracoorte. Naracoorte Caves National Park is South Australia's only World Heritage Site and a premier visitor attraction. The park is the only site on Earth that preserves a continuous fossil record of the past 500,000 years.

Bool Lagoon is a seasonal wetland of international importance inhabited by up to 155 different species of birds.

Naracoorte is central to four renowned wine-growing regions – Coonawarra, Wrattonbully, Padthaway and Mt. Benson. With cellar door outlets in all areas, it is truly a wine lover's paradise.
Lynette & John Lauterbach
Willowbrook Cottages B&Bs

Strathalbyn - Fleurieu Peninsula

Watervilla House *55 km S of Adelaide*
B&B & Cottage, no kitchen
Jane Littlejohns
2 Mill Street
Strathalbyn
SA 5255

Tel (08) 8536 4099
jane@watervillahouse.com
www.watervillahouse.com

Double $160
Single $140
Full breakfast
3 Queen (3 bdrm)
Bathrooms: 1 Ensuite
1 Family share 1 Private

Watervilla House Bed & Breakfast - This charming 1840's homestead invites you to enjoy a unique and friendly experience, surrounded by 1½ acres of tranquil gardens. The three bedrooms, guest lounge and dining room feature comfortable, elegant antique decor. Situated in the heart of historic Strathalbyn, centrally located within the Fleurieu Peninsula and close to The Southern Vales and Langhorne Creek wine Regions. Watervilla House has been featured on The Great Outdoors and Discovery.

Victor Harbor

Encounter Hideaway Cottages *4 km S of Victor Harbor*
B&B & 2 Self Contained Cottages
Jill Fairchild
26 Giles Street
Encounter Bay
SA 5211

Tel (08) 8552 7270
or 0409 527 270
Fax (08) 8552 8386
jill@encounterhideaway.com
www.encounterhideaway.com

Double $160
Single $100
Full breakfast provisions
$50 per extra person per night
Visa MC accepted
1 Queen 2 Single (2 bdrm)
Bathrooms: 1 Private, includes spa

Encounter Hideaway has two self-contained cottages. Ruby and Bud Cottages are situated just one street back from the sea in the historic part of Encounter Bay, only five minutes drive from the centre of Victor Harbor. Set in a charming garden, each cottage has a queen-size bed in the main bedroom, plus twin beds (Ruby) or double bed (Bud) in the second bedroom, a sparkling bathroom with a large spa, a well equipped kitchen with generous provisions for a cooked breakfast, a comfortable living room with A/C, TV, VCR, CD player, flowers, port and fresh fruit.

Beauty Point

Pomona Spa Cottages *40 km NW of Launceston*
Luxury B&B & Self Contained Cottages
Paula & Bruce Irvin
77 Flinders Street
Beauty Point
Tas 7270

Tel (03) 6383 4073
relax@pomonaspacottages.com.au
www.pomonaspacottages.com.au

Double $180-$250
Single $180-$240
Full breakfast provisions
Visa MC Eftpos accepted
4 King/Twin 2 Single (4 bdrm)
Spacious bedrooms with river views
Bathrooms: 4 Ensuite
Spa and seperate shower

AAA Tourism
★★★★☆

R elax and enjoy a wine or a delicious breakfast in your private Rotunda, overlooking beautiful views of the Tamar River/valley. Spoil yourself in the new luxurious, spacious, sunny S/C Spa Cottages. Water views from your king bed or in front of your cosy wood fire. Stroll in the rambling gardens, orchard, vines and along river to Restaurants, Seahorses, Platypus House. Explore the Tamar Valley Scenic Wine Route, National Parks, Penguins. Ferry & Airport - within 1 hour. Ideally located between Freycinet and Strahan. B.B.Qs.

Deloraine

Bowerbank Mill B&B *52 km W of Launceston*
Heritage B&B, Self Contained Cottages and Separate Suites
Anne and JD
4455 Meander Valley Road
Deloraine, Tas 7304

Tel (03) 6362 2628
info@bowerbankmill.com.au
www.bowerbankmill.com.au

Double $139-$229 Single $129-$209
Children $29-$59 depending on age
Special breakfast Extra adult $49-$59
Visa MC accepted
7 Queen 1 Double 5 Single (11 bdrm)
Bathrooms: 3 Ensuite 3 Guest share

The 1853 Colonial icon on Deloraine's outskirts is where magnificent mountains and wilderness meets picturesque farmland. Here at Bowerbank Mill B&B and Art Gallery you have the best of both worlds- the great outdoors meets the great indoors. To call this Heritage Mill a B&B is to undermine its uniqueness as guests explain: 'a wonderful experience in old world charm and ambience. The Mill is a maze of character' and 'Superb restoration of a true Tasmanian gem'.

The Mill's uniqueness is in the poetic blend of its original features - huge pit-sawn beams, stone walls, the six storey chimney etc. - antiques, curios, plus warm hospitality and pampering. Your gourmet breakfast, port/cheese and afternoon tea are brought to your Cottage, Suite or room.
NEW ON OFFER: Deloraine Hill Retreat - Spacious and modern with 180 degree views over pretty Deloraine and the spectacular Great Western Tiers Mountains.
Both conveniently located (Central North) near pristine lakes, wilderness, Cradle Mountain, wineries and galleries. 30 minutes to Launceston and Devonport (Airports and Ferry).

Derwent Bridge

Derwent Bridge Chalets & Studios *0.5 km E of Lake St Clair Turnoff*
Self Contained Chalets & Studios
John & Louise
15478 Lyell Highway
Derwent Bridge
Tas 7140

Tel (03) 6289 1000
or (03) 6289 3210
Fax (03) 6289 1230
info@derwent-bridge.com
www.derwent-bridge.com

Double $155-$385
Single $155-$385
Children 11 years and younger $25
Over 12 years $35
Continental breakfast
Visa MC Diners Amex Eftpos accepted
2 King/Twin 2 King 10 Queen 4 Single
(14 bdrm) 10 in Chalets, 4 in studios
Bathrooms: 10 Ensuite

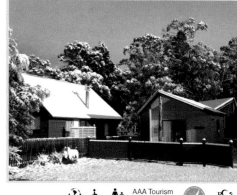

AAA Tourism
★★★☆

Edged by a snow gum forest and the Derwent River, 5km from the World Heritage listed Cradle Mountain Lake St Clair National Park - half way between Hobart and Strahan this quality 3½ star property is "simply magic" in summer or winter. Featuring 6x Chalets (2x spa bath) and 4x Studios, with complimentary port wine, chocolate mints, ground coffee and a morning newspaper. All with TV, DVD, microwave etc. Check-in from 3pm.

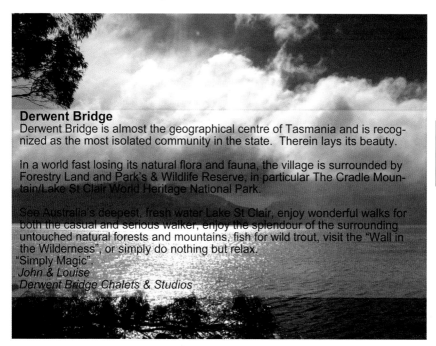

Derwent Bridge

Derwent Bridge is almost the geographical centre of Tasmania and is recognized as the most isolated community in the state. Therein lays its beauty.

In a world fast losing its natural flora and fauna, the village is surrounded by Forestry Land and Park's & Wildlife Reserve, in particular The Cradle Mountain/Lake St Clair World Heritage National Park.

See Australia's deepest, fresh water Lake St Clair, enjoy wonderful walks for both the casual and serious walker, enjoy the splendour of the surrounding untouched natural forests and mountains, fish for wild trout, visit the "Wall in the Wilderness", or simply do nothing but relax.
"Simply Magic".
John & Louise
Derwent Bridge Chalets & Studios

Devonport - Port Sorell

Tranquilles *14 km E of Devonport*
Luxury B&B
John Kumm & Barbara Walsh-Kumm
9 Gumbowie Drive
Port Sorell
Tas 7307

Tel (03) 6428 7555
Fax (03) 6428 7775
enquiries@tranquilles.com
www.tranquilles.com

Double $120-$195
Single $110-$190
Full breakfast
3-course dinner & luncheon hampers
available by prior arrangement
Visa MC Diners Amex Eftpos accepted
1 King 2 Queen (3 bdrm)
Bathrooms: 3 Ensuite 1 shower, 2 double spas

AAA Tourism
★★★★☆

Uniquely blending elegance, relaxation, complimentary WiFi with three beautifully appointed bedrooms (two with double spas), log fire, conservatory and enclosed courtyard, set in two acres of sweeping gardens. 15 minutes from Devonport, an hour to Launceston. Port Sorell is renowned for beaches, walking tracks and the Narawntapu National Park. A perfect location to unpack once, and explore the many highlights of the region - eg Cradle Mountain, Stanley, Tamar Wine Route. Meals serving fresh Tasmanian produce available by prior arrangement - fully licensed.

Port Sorell
A sweep of golden beaches, sheltered inlets, a seaside holiday haven and magnificent outlooks - that's Port Sorell. Protected by hills and with Bass Strait to the north, the district enjoys a particularly mild climate with low rainfall and a high average of sunshine.

Port Sorell is an ideal gateway to enable you to undertake any number of day tours in the North of Tasmania, including Narawntapu National Park, Cradle Mountain, Cataract Gorge and Tamar Valley Wine Route.
John Kumm, Tranquilles

Hobart - Battery Point - Sandy Bay

Grande Vue & Star Apartments *0.8 km S of Hobart Central*
**Private Hotel, Apartments &
Townhouses**
Annette & Kate McIntosh
8 Mona Street Battery Point
22 Star St Sandy Bay , Tas 7005

Tel (03) 6223 8216 or 0419 104 417
or 0400 591 457   Fax (03) 6224 1724
jarem8@bigpond.com
www.grande-vue-hotel.com
www.starapartments.com.au

Double $165-$280 Single $125-$165
Children and Extra Guests $30
Continental provisions
Visa MC Amex Eftpos accepted
2 King/Twin 7 Queen 2 Double (7 bdrm)
Bathrooms: 7 Ensuite 5 spa suites

G rande Vue Private Hotel is located in Hobart's historic Battery Point. (8 Mona Street). This gracious Edwardian mansion c1906 has spectacular views of the Derwent River, Mount Wellington, just 5 minutes walk to the city, restaurants, Salamanca Place and Hobart's waterfront. We also offer studio, water view rooms and spa suites. Star Apartments (22 Star Street Sandy Bay) are modern contemporary design 1 and 2 bedroom stylish apartments and townhouses with kitchens, washer/dryer and central heating. Some have water views, balconies/courtyards, spas and secure undercover car parking. Walking distance to Battery Point, restaurants, Salamanca Place and the city centre.

Hobart - Lindisfarne

Orana House *6 km E of Hobart*
B&B
Maria and Tony Grincais
20 Lowelly Road
Lindisfarne
Tas 7015

Tel (03) 6243 0404
Fax (03) 6243 9017
welcome@oranahouse.com
www.oranahouse.com

Double $140-$200
Single $110-$160
Children (5 years or older only) $50
Full breakfast
Visa MC Eftpos accepted
7 Queen 3 Double 4 Single (10 bdrm)
A range of rooms to suit all tastes and budgets
Bathrooms: 10 Ensuite

A large Federation home circa 1909 offering warm hospitality. Orana House is 12 minutes from the airport and six minutes to Hobart. Situated near picturesque Lindisfarne Bay, it is a convenient base to explore southern Tasmania. Some of our many features include superb breakfasts, great views from the verandah and guest lounge, afternoon tea daily, genuine antiques and open fire. A choice of standard, deluxe or spa rooms, all with ensuites.

Hobart - Rose Bay

Roseneath Bed & Breakfast *3.5 km NE of Hobart*
B&B & Self Contained Apartment
Susan & Alain Pastre
20 Kaoota Road
Rose Bay
Tas 7015

Tel (03) 6243 6530 or 0418 121 077
Fax (03) 6243 0518
pastre@bigpond.com
www.roseneath.com

Double $115-$170
Single $100-$165
Full breakfast
Dinner $38-$50 b/a
Low season/long stay available
Visa MC Diners Amex
Eftpos JCB accepted
2 King/Twin 1 Queen 2 Double (5 bdrm)
Bathrooms: 5 Ensuite 2 rooms have baths, 1 spa, 5 showers

For true Tasmanian hospitality and warmth with a French accent. Only 5 minutes from CBD/Salamanca and 10 from airport. Spectacular views of Mt Wellington, the Tasman Bridge and Derwent River. An ideal base for exploring southern Tasmania or for business. Choose from a SC studio (kitchenette) or in-house accommodation with ensuites (1 spa). Guest lounge with log fire; conservatory; inground heated (summer) pool; spacious, secluded gardens; BBQ; off street parking. Dinner by arrangement with your French chef host. Pet on property.

~

Huon Valley

Matilda's of Ranelagh *2 km N of Huonville*
Luxury B&B
Steve and Sonia
2 Louisa Street
Ranelagh, Huon Valley
Tas 7109

Tel (03) 6264 3493
Fax (03) 6264 3492
crabapplevalley@bigpond.com
www.matildasofranelagh.com.au

Double $185-$205
Single $165-$185
Full breakfast
Visa MC Eftpos accepted
4 Queen 1 Twin (4 bdrm)
Bathrooms: 4 Ensuite

Matildas is set in parkland and gardens, bounded by Mountain River in the heart of The Huon Valley. The home is beautifully furnished with antiques while concessions to modern living include central heating, and underfloor heating in all bathrooms. The Queen took tea in what is now The Matilda Suite in 1970 during a visit to The Huon. Matildas is a warm family home as well as a luxury guest-house, and we look forward to welcoming you to share in this world of ours.

Launceston

Trevallyn House B&B *4 km N of Launceston City Centre*
Luxury B&B
Janie & Brett Reynolds
83a Riverside Drive
Launceston
Tas 7250

Tel (03) 6327 3771
Fax (03) 6327 3700
info@trevallynhouse.com.au
www.trevallynhouse.com.au

Double $140-$190
Full breakfast
Extra person $35
Visa MC Amex Eftpos accepted
2 Queen 1 Single (2 bdrm)
Bathrooms: 2 Ensuite

AAA Tourism
★★★★☆

With 7 hectares of gardens and bushland and sweeping views of the Tamar River this secluded and peaceful new luxury accommodation is only five minutes from Launceston's City Centre. Located on the Tamar Valley Wine Route Trevallyn House offers comfort and convenience. You are assured of a special experience with two beautifully appointed guest rooms. The Guest Lounge with open fire is a perfect place to experience the changing seasons of the Tamar Valley and your gourmet cooked breakfast served in the Dining Room.

Launceston

Alice's Cottages and Spa Hideaways *0.5 km W of Launceston*
Cottages and Spa Hideaways
Rob and Louise Widdowson
129 Balfour Street
Launceston, Tas 7250

Tel (03) 6334 2231 Fax (03) 6334 2696
alicescottages@bigpond.com
http://alicescottages.com.au

Double $170-$206 Single $130-$170
Children can be accommodated in fold
out beds All cottages have their own
cooking facilities Hearty continental
breakfast provisions are provided
Visa MC Diners Amex Eftpos accepted
6 Queen (6 bdrm)
6 cottages each with a queen bed
3 with spas baths and 3 with showers and baths

AAA Tourism
★★★★

A wickedly wonderful romantic retreat awaits for lovers in one of Alice's Spa Hideaways tucked away in the historic heart of Launceston. The accommodation, which welcomes pets and children by arrangement, is fully self-contained for your privacy. Roaring log fires and bubbling spas warm the bodies and stir the passion whilst being cocooned in a different world with all the modern comforts. Launceston's finest restaurants and fabulous Cataract Gorge are a pleasant stroll away, or you may decide to prepare and enjoy dinner in the intimacy of your own fireside. Saviour the complimentary bedtime port, chocolate truffles, brewed coffee and sweet treats which all just tops a tremendous experience.

Launceston

Edenholme Grange *1.5 km SW of Post Office*
Luxury B&B & Self contained
apartments & 2 bed cottage
Paul & Rosemary Harding
14 St Andrews Street
Launceston
Tas 7250

Tel (03) 6334 6666 or 0419 894 269
Fax: (03) 6334 3106
sales@edenholme.com
www.edenholme.com

Double $150-$240 Single $130-$220
Children: $25 up to age 13
Full breakfast
Visa MC Diners Amex Eftpos JCB accepted
2 King/Twin 2 King 4 Queen
3 Double 2 Twin (10 Bedrooms)
Themed Heritage Rooms   Total capacity for 28 guests
Bathrooms: 10 Ensuite

 AAA Tourism
★★★★

Edenholme Grange, Settlers Cottage and The Coachhouse Apartments. Experience past times in this private Victorian mansion. set amongst secluded and substantial grounds, on the edge of the City and near the magnificent Cataract Gorge. There are uniquely themed rooms, furnished with antiques & some with spa baths. Close to the City yet secluded in the spacious grounds of the House are a self-contained rustic cottage, with modern amenities, including double spa bath and extra ensuite and 2 luxury apartments.

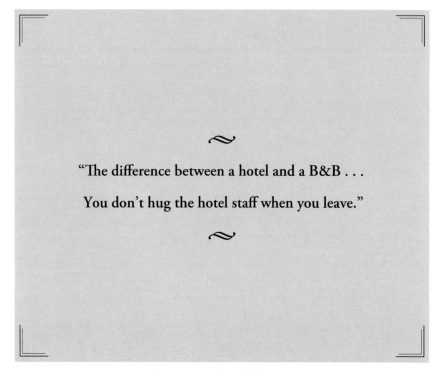

❧

"The difference between a hotel and a B&B . . .

You don't hug the hotel staff when you leave."

❧

Port Arthur - Taranna

Norfolk Bay Convict Station *10 km N of Port Arthur*
B&B & Homestay & Guest House
Lynton Brown & Lorella Matassini
5862 Arthur Highway
Taranna
Tas 7180

Tel (03) 6250 3487
Fax (03) 6250 3701
norfolkbay@convictstation.com
www.convictstation.com

Double $110-$180 Single $80-$120
Children Up to 12 yo $30
Continental breakfast
Dinner Nearby restaurants
Visa MC Eftpos accepted
2 Queen 2 Double 1 Twin 3 Single
(5 bdrm) All beds with electric blankets
Bathrooms: 3 Ensuite 2 Private
Private dedicated bathrooms but not connected to bedroom

S tay in living history and indulge yourself. Nature, adventure, history, culture, it's all here! Convict built in 1838 on this picturesque waterfront location, we are just minutes from Port Arthur, Eaglehawk Neck and all that the Tasman Peninsula has to offer. We offer warm, comfortable rooms, a guest sitting room with a log fire and a wonderful breakfast. This friendly B&B has history, charm and all the modern comforts. Enjoy a complimentary glass of Port, watch a DVD or explore our extensive library.

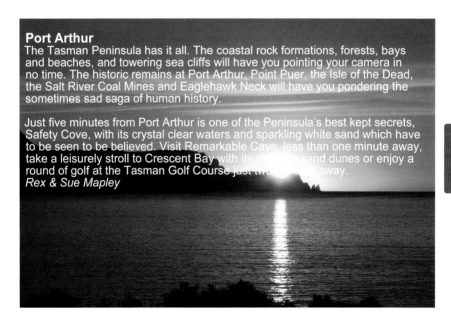

Port Arthur
The Tasman Peninsula has it all. The coastal rock formations, forests, bays and beaches, and towering sea cliffs will have you pointing your camera in no time. The historic remains at Port Arthur, Point Puer, the Isle of the Dead, the Salt River Coal Mines and Eaglehawk Neck will have you pondering the sometimes sad saga of human history.

Just five minutes from Port Arthur is one of the Peninsula's best kept secrets, Safety Cove, with its crystal clear waters and sparkling white sand which have to be seen to be believed. Visit Remarkable Cave, less than one minute away, take a leisurely stroll to Crescent Bay with its [...] sand dunes or enjoy a round of golf at the Tasman Golf Course just two [...] away.
Rex & Sue Mapley

Tasmania

Richmond

Mulberry Cottage B&B *In Richmond*
**B&B & Homestay & Self Contained
House**
Miriam Cooper
23a Franklin Street
Richmond
Tas 7025

Tel (03) 6260 2664 or 0407 473 015
miriam23@bigpond.net.au
www.mulberrycottage.com.au

Double $110-$160 Single $85-$110
Children b/a   Special breakfast
Dinner or platters b/a with Grannie
Seasonal Specials   Show included in
Grannie Rhodes Cottage
Visa MC accepted
1 King 3 Queen 1 Double 4 Twin 1 Single

(4 bdrm) Old English, French Boudoir, Attic
Bathrooms: 2 Ensuite 1 Guest share 1 Private can be shared or private

Charming, hosted B&B, in 'old worlde' cottage, built from the reclaimed wall of Hobart's Old Penitentiary. Self contained cottage on site 'Dobbin's Hole.' 'Excellent' Tourism Award Winning show included (Highly Commended, Cultural Heritage section). Valley views. Rustic gardens. Glass of wine on arrival. Cosy guest sitting room (pet free). Host lounge shared with greeting retrievers, cuddly cat. For the history & theatre lover; unique entertainment, by your hostess, a performance of 'Turn the Key of Time' about a cottage, a key and a convict in Grannie Rhodes' Cottage, on site 1830.

Richmond

Mrs Curries Bed and Breakfast *In Richmond*
B&B
Cheryl and Steven
4 Franklin Street
Richmond
Tas 7025

Tel (03) 6260 2766
Fax (03) 6260 2110
mrscurries@optusnet.com.au
www.mrscurrieshouse.com.au

Double $140
Single $100
No children under 10 years old
Full breakfast
Visa MC Diners Amex
Eftpos JCB accepted
1 Queen 3 Double 1 Single (4 bdrm)
Elegantly appointed
Bathrooms: 3 Ensuite 1 Private

   AAA Tourism ★★★★

Mrs Curries House, a lovely Georgian home built in the 1820's. Two storey with bedrooms upstairs and down. All have their own bathroom and their own charm. Tastefully decorated with antiques throughout. Open fires in the lounge and dining area. Complimentary port and sherry. Manicured gardens and lawns for all to enjoy. A great place to stay a while and wind down and enjoy the hospitality of Cheryl and Steve. We pride our selves on looking after you.

Swansea

Schouten House *0.5 km E of Swansea*
B&B
Cameron and Jodie Finlayson
1 Waterloo Road
Swansea
Tas 7190

Tel (03) 6257 8564
Fax (03) 6257 8767
enquiries@schoutenhouse.com
www.schoutenhouse.com.au

Double $150-$180 Single $130-$150
Children welcome,
additional charge applies
Full breakfast
Dinner by arrangement
Visa MC Eftpos accepted
5 Queen 1 Twin (6 bdrm)
Antique/Four Poster Queen Beds
Bathrooms: 6 Ensuite

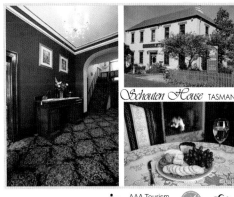

AAA Tourism
★★★★

Schouten House is c1844 Georgian Bed and Breakfast Accommodation. A landmark Heritage Listed property in the seaside town of Swansea, overlooking Great Oyster Bay and Freycinet Peninsula on the East Coast of Tasmania. Your hosts, Cameron and Jodie, welcome you to this gracious home. The house offers six suites, all with queen sized beds and private ensuites. Guests can enjoy two lounge areas, one with open fire, and a dining room where a generous continental and full cooked breakfast are served. Enquire about meals by arrangement.

~

Please tell your host,

"I found you in The Bed & Breakfast Book."

~

Victoria

Mildura

Swan Hill

Echuca

Sheppa

Horsham

Bendigo

Heat

Castlemair

Wartook

Halls Gap

Kyneton

Grampians

Daylesford

Sunbury

Ma

Ballarat

Ra

Hamilton

Yarra Va

Branxholme

Melbourne

Gembi

Port A

Geelong

Port Fairy

Allansford

Torquay

Rye

Warrnambool

Ventnor

Lorne

Princetown

Apollo Bay

Phill

Melbourne Airport

North Fitzroy • Fairfield
Melbourne
Richmond • • Blackburn
Williamstown • • Camberwell
• Yarra
Ranges

Dandenong Ranges

St Kilda

• Mornington

St Andrews • Sorrento
Beach

Cowes
Ventnor • • Rhyll

Phillip Island

Melbourne

0 Kilometres 15

0 Miles 9

NSW

CT

Rutherglen
Chiltern •   • Albury   • Cudgewa
• Corryong
Wodonga
ngaratta •   • Beechworth

• Benalla

roa

Bright •
• Mt Beauty

Mansfield

oie
Alexandra
Marysville

NSW

fras
• Dandenong Ranges   Sarsfield •
Neerim South   • Metung
• Nilma North   Bairnsdale •   Lakes
Nilma   Entrance
n
Warragul • Gippsland
• Mirboo North
Leongatha

• Foster

• Wilsons
Promontory

0 Kilometres 60

0   Miles   35

Victoria

- **Bed & Breakfasts**
- **Farmstays**
- **Guesthouses and Boutique Hotels**
- **Country Cottages**
- **Self Contained Accommodation**

Couples

Families

Groups

Pets Welcome

www.accommodationgetawaysvictoria.com.au
or call
1300 132 358

Victoria's Peak Industry Association
representing city and country quality accommodation

Victoria
Inn.House Bed and Breakfast Australia Inc

Throughout Melbourne and country Victoria, you'll find an Inn.House Bed & Breakfast property where you can depend on a warm welcome, excellent accommodation and friendly attention from your hosts.

Each member must meet the high standards set by Inn.House for hospitality, comfort and cleanliness.
Our high standards are your assurance of a quality bed and breakfast experience.

All members provide bed and breakfast and some offer other meals by arrangement. Your hosts are happy to assist with interesting and helpful local information. The properties are all different and individually owned, each having its own distinctive style and character, and comprise private homes, cottages and retreats located around Melbourne and Victoria.

Gift Vouchers Available (03) 5598 8169
or order on line at www.innhouse.com.au/giftvouchers.html

Full details on the Award Winning website www.innhouse.com.au

Alexandra
Idlewild Park Farm Accommodation *5 km N of Alexandra*
Farmstay & Self Contained Cottage
Elizabeth & Don Deelen
5545 Maroondah Highway
Alexandra
Vic 3714

Tel (03) 5772 1178
idlewild@virtual.net.au
www.idlewild.com.au

Double $140-$170
Single $100
Children $25
Full breakfast provisions
Egg collecting
1 King/Twin 1 Queen (2 bdrm)
Bathrooms: 1 Ensuite twin spa bath

 AAA Tourism
★★★★

Enjoy this 3,000 acre grazing property 128 km NE of Melbourne. The beautiful district offers horse riding, fishing, water and snow sports, bush walking, golf & adventure activities. Stay in a fully equipped two bedroom cottage with a double spa, wood heater, full kitchen air/con. Superb location with magnificent panoramic views. There is tennis, gas BBQ and a beautiful garden. Property has sheep, cattle, horses and poultry (also native animals and birds). Owners have four grown up children and one friendly Jack Russel.

Apollo Bay

Arcady Homestead *10 km W of Apollo Bay*
Homestay & Farmstay
Marcia & Ross Dawson
925 Barham River Road
Apollo Bay - Great Ocean Road
Vic 3233

Tel (03) 5237 6493
or 0408 376 493
Fax (03) 5237 6493
arcadyhomestead@fastmail.fm
www.bbbook.com.au/arcadyhomestead.
html

Double $110-$120 Single $75-$85
Children 50% discount
Full breakfast
Dinner B/A
2 Queen 1 Double 3 Single (4 bdrm)
Bathrooms: 1 Guest share

Set on sixty scenic acres, part farmland and part natural bush. Share breakfast with our Kookaburras, explore the Otway Forest trails, tree-fern and glow worm gullies and waterfalls, see some of the tallest trees in the world or visit Port Campbell National Park, which embraces Australia's most spectacular coastline. The Otway Ranges are a bushwalkers paradise. Bird-watchers? We have identified around thirty species in the garden alone! Many visit our kitchen window! Our home has wood fires & spring water. Our beds are cosy, our meals country-style, and our atmosphere relaxed and friendly.

Apollo Bay

Paradise Gardens *7.5 km W of Apollo Bay*
B&B & Self Contained Cottages
Jo and Jock Williamson
715 Barham River Road
Apollo Bay
Vic 3233

Tel (03) 5237 6939
or 0417 330 615
Fax (03) 5237 6105
paradisegardens@bigpond.com.au
www.paradisegardens.net.au

Double $120-$220
Full breakfast in B&B available
by request
Continental provisions provided in
cottages by request
Visa MC Eftpos accepted
1 King/Twin2 King 1 Queen (4 bdrm)
Bathrooms: 4 Ensuite All ensuite with spas

AAA Tourism
★★★★☆

Situated on 3 acres of landscaped gardens in a lush rainforest valley, our facility is only 10 minutes from Apollo Bay on a (sealed) scenic road. Our charming self-contained cottages (one and two bedroom) are built over a lake and feature wood fires, spas, bar-b-cues on the decking and air conditioning. Continental breakfast available by request. Laundry facilities. Our in-house B&B unit is comfortable with double spa and external entrance and includes continental breakfast. Enjoy walks, birdlife and glow-worms.

Apollo Bay

Point of View *1 km N of Apollo Bay*
Luxury B&B & Self Contained Apartment
Alan & Glenda Whelan
165 Tuxion Road
Apollo Bay
Vic 3233

Tel 0427 376 377
info@pointofview.com.au
www.pointofview.com.au

Double $250-$340
Continental provisions
2 night minimum stay ($580/620)
Visa MC Diners Eftpos accepted
5 King (5 bdrm)
Modern, open plan
Bathrooms: 5 Ensuite
Double shower and spa

B reathtaking views from every location in our architect designed luxury villas. Perfect retreat for couples for those special occasions.

Features wood fire, king beds, double shower, full kitchen, dishwasher, satellite tv, large therapeutic spa, DVD, electric heating, air conditioning, robes, toiletries, surround sound, spacious sundecks, BBQ, washing machine, dryer, fresh flowers, beach towels, hairdryer, continental breakfast supplies.

Ideal base to explore the 12 Apostles, Great Ocean Road or as a romantic, secluded getaway for you and your partner. Wine and chocolates on arrival. Spoil yourself.

Apollo Bay - Great Ocean Road

Glenoe Cottages *2 km N of Apollo Bay*
Luxury Self Contained Cottages
Dianne Beggs
235 Tuxion Road
Apollo Bay, Vic 3233

Tel (03) 5237 6555 or 0438 376 410
Fax (03) 5237 6555
dianne@glenoe-cottages.com
www.glenoe-cottages.com

Double $240-$300
Continental provisions
Exclusively for adults
2 night min stay
Visa MC Eftpos accepted
3 King (3 bdrm) 3 cottages
Bathrooms: 3 Private

Simply the best and none better for intimate classic relaxed romance. Only the ancient poets could find the words to give justice in describing these captivating cottages. The coastal views are absolutely entrancing.

Features wood fire, ducted central heating, TV/DVD stereo and surround sound. King size bed, large spa with rain shower, bath robes, toiletries, hairdryer and beach towels. Full kitchen with dishwasher, microwave oven, espresso coffee maker, washing machine and drier. Continental breakfast basket provided with complementary wine, chocolates and ice-cream. BBQ, surround veranda and undercover car park.

The limestone built cottages may be millions of years old but on entry you are introduced to a modern contemporary experience of space, comfort and quality. Ideal home base to explore the Great Ocean Road, Otway National park and 12 Apostles, or simply an intimate, romantic secluded escape for you and your partner.

Bairnsdale

Tara House *1.2 km W of town centre*
B&B
Phillip
37 Day Street
Bairnsdale
Vic 3875

Tel (03) 5153 2253
Fax (03) 5153 2426
enquiries@tarahouse.com.au
www.tarahouse.com.au

Double $160-$170 Single $130-$140
Children fold out bed in parents room,
extra $60
Full breakfast
Dinner by arrangement
Visa MC accepted
2 King/Twin 1 Queen (3 bdrm)
Traditionally decorated
Bathrooms: 3 Ensuite one ensuite with claw foot bath

Share a beautiful garden with a retired gardener. Be welcomed by the hostess, Tara, a seven year old Sydney Silky. A relaxing and refreshing time is assured. Sit on the verandah and watch the setting sun or have a glass of wine. Many areas to sit and forget your troubles. Come and smell the roses. Two hours to the snow, 20 minutes to lake, 30 minutes to sea. The perfect place to stay.

Bairnsdale - Sarsfield

Stringybark Cottages B&B *19 km N of Bairnsdale*
B&B & Self Contained B&B cottage
Lois & Neil Triggs
77 Howards Road
Sarsfield
Vic 3875

Tel (03) 5157 5245
or 0412 130 028
Fax (03) 5157 5639
neil@stringybarkcottages.com
stringybarkcottages.com

Double $160-$180 Single $100-$120
Children under 2 stay for free
Full breakfast provisions
Dinner is avaliable by prior
arrangement
Extra person: $35 per night
Visa MC Eftpos accepted
4 Queen 4 Single (6 bdrm) 2 Cottages have 2 bedrooms, 2 cottage have 1 bedroom
Bathrooms: 3 Private 1 cottage has double shower and bath

Experience that little piece of paradise, tranquil and delightfully different. Enjoy those cool evenings snuggled up in front of the wood fire, warmer nights spent relaxing on your verandah with a ceiling of millions of stars. Multi Award winning Stringybark Cottages are situated 19kms from Bairnsdale just off The Great Alpine Road. There are four cottages, accommodating from two to five people. Each cottage is fully self contained.

Victoria
Beechworth

Foxgloves *0.3 km N of PO*
Luxury B&B & Separate Suite
John & Sheila Rademan
21 Loch Street
Beechworth
Vic 3747

Tel (03) 5728 1224
Fax (03) 5728 1228
foxgloves1@westnet.com.au
www.foxgloves.com.au

Double $165-$205
Single $140-$205
Full breakfast
Twin share $185
Visa MC Eftpos accepted
2 Queen, 1 Queen/twin,
1 Queen private suite upstairs (4 bdrm)
Bathrooms: 4 Ensuite

W elcome to our tastefully restored Victorian cottage (c 1897) in the heart of historic Beechworth. We offer country hospitality in quietly elegant surrounds with all the delights of contemporary comforts. Our personal attention includes traditional cooked breakfast, homemade afternoon teas & complimentary port/sherry in our cosy lounge or on the plant-filled patio. All fully serviced bedrooms have heating/cooling, electric underblankets and quality linen. The guest lounge/dining room has TV/DVD, log fire in winter and cooling in summer for your comfort.

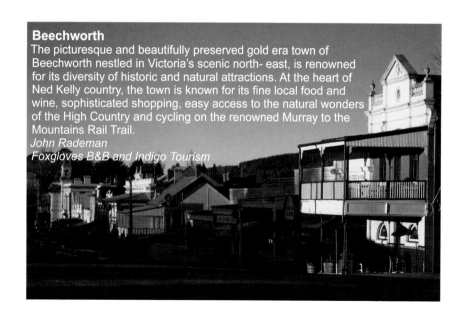

Beechworth
The picturesque and beautifully preserved gold era town of Beechworth nestled in Victoria's scenic north- east, is renowned for its diversity of historic and natural attractions. At the heart of Ned Kelly country, the town is known for its fine local food and wine, sophisticated shopping, easy access to the natural wonders of the High Country and cycling on the renowned Murray to the Mountains Rail Trail.
John Rademan
Foxgloves B&B and Indigo Tourism

Beechworth

Kinross Guest House *39 km S of Albury/Wodonga*
Luxury B&B
Terry and Gail Walsh
34 Loch Street
Beechworth
Vic 3747

Tel (03) 5728 2351
Fax (03) 5728 3333
contact@kinrossguesthouse.com.au
www.kinrossguesthouse.com.au

Double $165-$195
Single $130-$160
Full breakfast
Off-street parking
Visa MC Eftpos accepted
1 King/Twin 3 Queen (4 bdrm)
Bathrooms: 4 Ensuite (walk-in showers)

Experience the style, warmth and charm of Kinross, in the centre of Beechworth, close to excellent restaurants, specialty shops and historic precinct. Kinross (c1858) has four large fully-serviced guestrooms furnished with period pieces. Enjoy the luxury of your own ensuite, open fireplace, heating/cooling, TV/DVD, comfortable seating, tea/coffee making facility. Whether sitting with a book and glass of wine beside an open fire, or on the verandah enjoying the beauty of the cottage garden, you cannot help but feel the peace and quiet.

Beechworth

Freeman on Ford *In Beechworth*
Luxury B&B
Heidi Freeman & Jim Didolis
97 Ford Street
Beechworth
Vic 3747

Tel (03) 5728 2371
or (03) 5728 2055
or 0409 958 340
Fax (03) 5728 2504
freemanford@westnet.com.au
www.freemanonford.com

Double $195-$300
Single $195-$250
Full breakfast
Visa MC Diners Amex Eftpos accepted
1 King/Twin 3 Queen (4 bdrm)
Bathrooms: 4 Ensuite

The first and only 5 star in Beechworth. The hosts provide gourmet breakfast and afternoon tea and their mission statement is to make guests feel thoroughly spoilt. They have a love of history and have a wealth of information to offer about the historical and unique township of Beechworth. Gourmet Traveller magazine recommends the venue as 'excellent' (April May 2007). Onsite parking and AUSTAR channels, wide selection of DVDs, WiFi Internet, split systems, TVs in all bedrooms and all modern conveniences making it 5-star comfort.

Bright - Myrtleford

The Buckland - Studio Retreat *12 km SW of Bright*
Luxury Self Contained Chalets
Sabine Helsper & Eddie Dufrenne
116 McCormacks Lane
Buckland Valley
Vic 3740

Tel (03) 5756 2383 or 0419 133 318
Fax (03) 5755 2283
stay@thebuckland.com.au
www.thebuckland.com.au

Double $275-$340
Children only small babies travelling
with own port-a-cot or similar
Full breakfast
Visa MC Eftpos accepted
1 King (5 bdrm)
5 Luxury one bedroom chalets
Bathrooms: 5 Ensuite
Funky bathrooms with double rainwater showers

AAA Tourism
★★★★☆

The Buckland - Studio Retreat features luxury accommodation tucked away in the picturesque Buckland Valley close to Bright, Mt. Buffalo and the wineries of the Victorian High Country. Each of the 5 individual studios has an open plan lounge/kitchen area, king size bedroom and funky bathroom with double rainwater showers and private bush outlook. The décor is contemporary and stylish and creature comforts are well catered for: goosedown doonas, espresso coffee machine, seductive mood lighting, plush robes and L'Occitane aromatherapy products.

Bright

Bright is the town of four seasons and has something special to offer at anytime of year with miles of magnificent walking tracks along the banks of the gurgling Ovens River. The Autumn Festival, when the multitude of European trees change their colours, is known Australia wide.

It is located on the North East Gourmet Trail and the town and district abound in wineries and top class restaurants. The wineries of Rutherglen, Beechworth and Milawa are all just a day trip away.
Catherine Falcke

Castlemaine

Clevedon Manor *0.25 km N of Castlemaine*
B&B & Self Contained Spa Studio
Stuart Ryan & Phil Page
260 Barker Street
Castlemaine
Vic 3450

Tel (03) 5472 5212
or 0417 166 769
Fax (03) 5472 5212
clevedon@netcon.net.au
www.bbbook.com.au/clevedonmanor.html

Double $110-$150
Single $90
Full breakfast
Visa MC accepted
5 Queen 1 Double (6 bdrm)
Bathrooms: 3 Ensuite 3 Private
Spa in Self Contained Studio

  AAA Tourism ★★★★

This beautifully restored 19th century home offers elegant living set in half an acre 100 year old gardens. Clevedon offers guests a choice of spa room accommodation, ensuites and private facilities all with queen size beds. Private lounges and dining room with open fire, antique furnishings, central heating. Pool & BBQ. Clevedon is dedicated for guests only and is the perfect choice for either an intimate getaway or for groups wanting the complete package with meals. Clevedon is a 3 minute walk to central Castlemaine.

Chiltern

The Mulberry Tree B&B & Tea Rooms *In Chiltern*
B&B
Regina Welsh
28 Conness Street
Chiltern
Vic 3683

Tel (03) 5726 1277
www.mulberrytreechiltern.com.au

Double $160-$180
Single $130-$160
Special breakfast
Meals by arrangement
Tearooms next door
2 Queen (2 bdrm)
Bathrooms: 1 Ensuite 1 Private

Just 1 km off the highway. Indulge yourself in the heart of Country Victoria. At The Mulberry Tree you will find a haven to relax and enjoy delightful accommodation with gourmet breakfast. Choose from "The Bank Residence" with it's own lounge with open fire, private bathroom or "The Henry Handel Richardson Suite" with ensuite dining area. This delightful building was built in 1879 as "The Bank of Australasia" and is on the Historic Building Register. Be assured of a warm welcome with special attention to every detail. Situated in the centre of town. Come and see our beautiful cats, 'Paris' and 'Tina'.

Cudgewa - Corryong

Elmstead Cottages *12 km W of Corryong*

B&B & Farmstay & Self Contained Housc

Marja & Tony Jarvis
61 Ashstead Park Lane
Cudgewa
Vic 3705

Tel (02) 6077 4324
or 0427 774 324
Fax (02) 6077 4324
elmstead@corryongcec.net.au
www.bbbook.com.au/elmstead.html

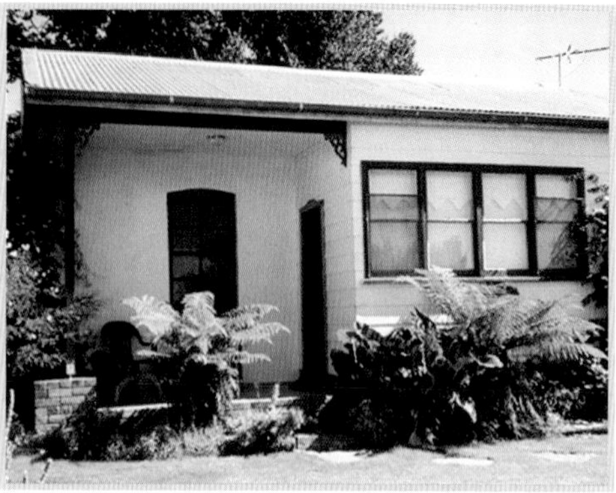

AAA Tourism ★★★☆

Double $80
Single $60
Children 12 and under $10
Breakfast by arrangement
Extra person $15
Eftpos accepted
2 Queen 4 Single (3 bdrm)
1 in Elmstead Cottage, 2 in Arthur's Cottage
Bathrooms: 2 Private

Elmstead Cottage: A one room cottage set amongst magnificent elm trees on a working farm, cute cosy and affordable. Arthur's Cottage: An eco-friendly, historic two bedroom cottage (circa 1887). Secluded location on the banks of the Cudgewa Creek where platypus and trout abound. Fully equipped kitchen, BYO linen.

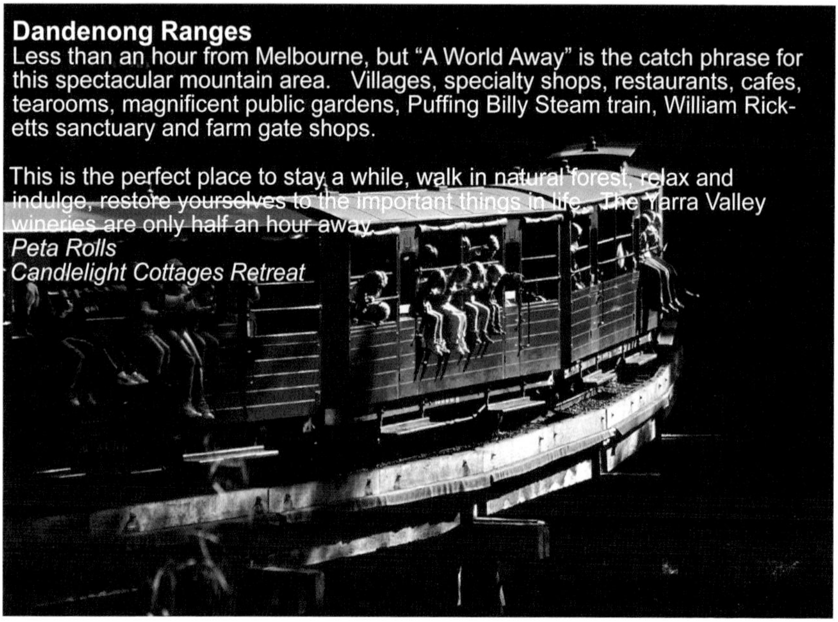
Dandenong Ranges
Less than an hour from Melbourne, but "A World Away" is the catch phrase for this spectacular mountain area. Villages, specialty shops, restaurants, cafes, tearooms, magnificent public gardens, Puffing Billy Steam train, William Ricketts sanctuary and farm gate shops.
This is the perfect place to stay a while, walk in natural forest, relax and indulge, restore yourselves to the important things in life. The Yarra Valley wineries are only half an hour away.
Peta Rolls
Candlelight Cottages Retreat

Dandenong Ranges

Candlelight Cottages Retreat *0.3 km N of Olinda*
B&B & Self Contained House & Self
Contained Cottages
Peta & Laurie Rolls
7-9 Monash Avenue
Olinda Village, Vic 3788

Tel (03) 9751 2464 or 1300 553 011
Fax (03) 9751 0552
stay@candlelightcottages.com.au
www.candlelightcottages.com.au

Double $215-$330 Single $210-$320
Children 0-3 yrs $10, 4-10 yrs $20p/n
Full breakfast provisions
Mini-bar dinner available
Extra couple $50 p/n
Woorich not suitable for children/pets
Visa MC Diners Amex Eftpos accepted
1 King/Twin 4 Queen 1 Double (6 bdrm)

Two 2 bedroom cottages, Two 1 bedroom
Bathrooms: 4 Ensuite 1 Guest share Two 2 bed/bath cottage; 2 2 bed/1bath cottage; 1 ensuite

Exquisite cottages in Olinda Village offering privacy, serenity. Spabath, luxurious beds, comfortable lounge, open-log fire, full kitchen, outdoor area - minutes stroll to restaurants, shops, cafes, galleries. Woolrich Retreat has 5 acres of historic gardens. Elegant, spacious with 2 bedrooms, 2 bathrooms, Jacuzzi spa, full kitchen, lounge, open fire, deck with BBQ overlooking gardens. New to the Collection is A Cottage in the Forest. Soak in the spa, lounge on your kingsize bed, sip wine by the open fire - hidden away on 1 acre.

Dandenong Ranges - Gembrook

Cherry Garden Cottages *7 km NW of Gembrook PO*
B&B & Self Contained Heritage
Style Cottages
Alison & Mark
200 Evans Road
Gembrook
Vic 3783

Tel (03) 5968 1944
alison@lovehopefaith.com.au
www.bbbook.com.au/
CherryGardenCottages.html

Double $185-$270
Full breakfast provisions
Anniversary packages incl.
cheese platter and bottle of wine
Massages available on request
Visa MC Eftpos accepted

AAA Tourism
★★★★

3 cottages - 2 cottages have four poster beds
Bathrooms: 3 Ensuite - all have double spas

Absolute seclusion with breathtaking views - where stress is forgotten. Luxurious self-contained heritage-style cottages, very romantic and tastefully decorated with antique furniture. Situated high on a mountain top the cottages have private balconies overlooking meadows, forests and mountains. Lay in bed watching the landscape change, have a relaxing spa, then cuddle up in front of your open fire. Cottages include two person spa, open fire, air conditioning, queen-size beds, fully equipped kitchen, TV/VCR and CD player.

Dandenong Ranges - Mount Dandenong

Observatory Cottages *2 km N of Mt Dandenong*
Luxury B&B & 4 Self Contained Cottages
Leeanne & Daniel Gazzola
8 Observatory Road
Mt Dandenong
Vic 3767

Tel (03) 9751 2436
Fax (03) 9751 2904
enquiries@observatorycottages.com.au
www.observatorycottages.com.au

Double $220-$320
Children $25 per child
Full breakfast provisions
$50 per extra person
Visa MC Amex Eftpos accepted
4 Queen (4 bdrm)
Open plan living
Bathrooms: 4 Ensuite

Sip wine by the twinkling night light views of the city skyline on a lazy summers evening. Slide into a deep hot bubbling spa with a good book or your true love. Curl up in an ultimately romantic four posted bed and watch the mountain mist roll in through the winter nights. Sleep late and enjoy a hearty breakfast to the serenade of the birds, the fragrance of the forest, and the tranquillity of a stunning garden paradise.

Dandenong Ranges - Sassafras

Clarendon Cottages *1 km S of Sassafras*
B&B & Self Contained Cottages
Pam & Ian Hankey
11 Clarkmont Road
Sassafras
Vic 3787

Tel (03) 9755 3288
or 0438 529 220
Fax (03) 9755 3288
pam@clarendoncottages.com
www.clarendoncottages.com

Double $140-$295 Single $140-$295
Children extra bedroom $50 per person
or foldout bed $30
Full breakfast provisions
Visa MC Eftpos accepted
3 Queen 1 Double (4 bdrm)
Bathrooms: 3 Private

Clarendon's boutique guest accommodation consists of three charming cottages in a secluded, peaceful and romantic setting. Two acres of English country gardens and meadow nestle amongst a huge variety of beautiful century old trees. The cottages are within easy walking distance of Sassafras Village and Sherbrooke Forest. Three cosy 1 & 2 bedroom cottages each with it's own individual charm are located separately on the two acre property. Log fires, spas, fully equipped kitchens, air conditioning and private decks are just some of the many features. TV, DVD & CD in all cottages. Full breakfast provisions are provided.

~

Dandenong Ranges - Yarra Ranges

The Villa Renaissance *Country House & Day Spa*
Leesa Stone
75 Underwood Road
Ferntree Gully
Vic 3156

Tel (03) 9758 0551 or (03) 9752 2169
or 0439 485 673
www.geocities.com/villa_r75
www.freewebs.com/thevilla

Double $200-$450 Single $150-$350
Special breakfast
Lunches, afternoon teas, dinners
available - bookings essential
Full Day Spa treatments and services
available by appointment
3 King 1 Queen (4 bdrm)
Large suites, include dining and living rooms with fireplaces
Bathrooms: 4 Ensuite Includes marble bathrooms and spas

Imagine driving 40 minutes east of Melbourne going off the usual route. Suddenly, seeing an old 200 feet long wall covered in ivy with huge ornate electric gates. "Shades of Sunset Boulevard". One of Melbourne's most private anti-aging, relaxation accommodation retreats and still a private 85 square home. Beautifully romantic for couples or people that need peace and tranquillity. Offering herbal baths, strong spa massages, mud wraps, unique body scrubs and more. Check-in at mid day and check-out at 2.00 pm. Personalised meals, late breakfast. Even a 2 hour visit is worth it to be pampered.

Daylesford - Hepburn Springs

Pendower House *0.1 km NW of Daylesford PO*
B&B
Renée Ludekens
10 Bridport Street
Daylesford
Vic 3460

Tel (03) 5348 1535
or 0438 103 460
Fax (03) 5348 1545
bookings@pendowerhouse.com.au
www.pendowerhouse.com.au

Double $150-$380
Single $105-$290
Children B/A
Full breakfast
Visa MC accepted
3 Queen 1 Twin (4 bdrm)
Bathrooms: 4 Ensuite

AAA Tourism
★★★★

P endower House, a beautifully restored Victorian House, situated in the heart of Australia's Spa Capital - Daylesford. RACV Rated 4 Pendower House offers first class amenities: fine linen, antique furnishings, big brass beds, loungeroom/library with open fire. Our luxurious Spa Suite, with corner spa, T.V/DVD & private courtyard is perfect for privacy, peace & pampering. Fantastic country breakfast, Muffins, hollandaise sauce drizzled on Eggs - more like brunch than breakfast! Easy walk to restaurants/galleries. Close to Spa resort. Massages & Spa packages or Gift Vouchers available.

Geelong

Ardara House *0.5 km S of Geelong*
B&B
Owen & Maureen Sharkey
4 Aberdeen Street
Geelong
Vic 3218

Tel (03) 5229 6024
Fax (03) 5229 6180
ardara@bigpond.net.au
www.ardarahouse.com.au

Double $130-$160
Single $80-$110
Children $20
Continental breakfast
1 Queen 2 Double 2 Single (5 bdrm)
Bathrooms: 4 Ensuite 1 Guest share

AAA Tourism
★★★★

B uilt in the Edwardian period (circa 1900) as a large family home, Ardara House offers the grace and homeliness of a bygone era. Guests can enjoy the relaxed and friendly atmosphere of fine Irish hospitality close to the heart of Geelong and on the beginning of the Great Ocean Road. Four spacious guest rooms feature luxurious beds and old world decor but with all the modern comforts and conveniences. Many of Geelong's finest restaurants, entertainment facilities as well as the shopping centre are only a stroll away.

Geelong

Baywoodbyne B&B *1.5 km N of Geelong*
B&B
Nola Haines
41 The Esplanade
Geelong
Vic 3215

Tel (03) 5278 2658
www.greatoceanroad.org

Double $120-$140
Single $110
Children Over 6 welcome
Full breakfast
Visa MC Eftpos accepted
2 Double 1 Twin (3 bdrm)
Bathrooms: 1 Ensuite 1 Private

Centrally located accommodation in a lovely 1921 California Bungalow style home. Superb view overlooking Corio Bay; a short stroll to city centre and colourful waterfront precinct. Warmth, comfort, convenience are yours, together with books and music. Offering: Ground floor, double bedroom with ensuite (extra bed available), sitting and dining room, open fire, picture window. First floor, two double bedrooms, sitting area and beautiful view. Tea/coffee making toaster, fridge. Off-street parking. Easy access to Melbourne, (train or car one hour) and the famous Great Ocean Road. Direct bus service to Geelong from Melbourne (Tullamarine and Avalon) airports. Local transport nearby to city, Lorne and Apollo Bay. Wildlife/birding tours can be arranged.

Geelong

Originally a port shipping gold and wool to the world, Geelong continues its rich transport history with Australia's newest commercial airport, Avalon Airport at Avalon, 15 kilometres north-east of Geelong. The airport is home to the Australian International Airshow, a popular and spectacular biennial event held in March.

The city's waterfront is a hive of activity, with cafes, restaurants, yacht club, marina, antique carousel, art- deco promenade and swimming pavilion. Visitors can also take a stroll along the waterfront to view the colourful Baywalk Bollards.
Nola Haines
Baywood B&B and Geelong Otway Tourism www.greatoceanroad.org.

Victoria

Gippsland - Nilma North

Springbank B&B *8 km E of Warragul*
B&B & Cottage
Kaye & Chris Greene
240 Williamsons Road
Nilma North
Vic 3821

Tel (03) 5627 8060
or 0437 350 243
Fax (03) 5627 8149
bookings@springbankbnb.com.au
www.springbankbnb.com.au

Double $165-$190
Single $130-$150
Full breakfast
Dinner & massage by arrangement
Res liquor license
Cottage: double $145-$165 single from $115
Visa MC Eftpos accepted
3 Queen (3 bdrm) 2 in House, 1 in Cottage
Bathrooms: 3 Ensuite Includes claw foot bath

AAA Tourism
★★★★☆

InnHouse

Springbank, a delightful 1890's Victorian Homestead offers luxury and boutique accommodation for a maximum of 3 couples set on 20 acres close to Warragul. Quiet, private & restful with extensive cottage gardens provides the perfect setting. Gourmet breakfasts, BBQ and outdoor cooking facilities, warm and friendly atmosphere. Open fires in the winter and reverse cycle airconditioning. Superb dining by arrangement.

Gippsland
Experience the four seasons and indulge the five senses. Enjoy lush pastures, magnificent forests, spectacular views and rolling hills, renowned cool climate wines, world famous cheeses and fabulous food.
Kaye Greene, Springbank Bed & Breakfast and James Walshe Photography

Grampians - Halls Gap

Mountain Grand Boutique Hotel *In Halls Gap*
Guest House
Kay & Don Calvert
Main Road Town Centre
Halls Gap
Vic 3381

Tel (03) 5356 4232
or 1800 192 110
don@hallsgap.net
www.mountaingrand.com

Full breakfast
Dinner, B&B $206-$248
Indulgence Getaway (all meals) $248-$295
Visa MC Eftpos accepted
3 King 3 Queen 7 Double (13 bdrm)
most rooms can become twin/triple
Bathrooms: 12 Ensuite
Spa Rooms available

The Mountain Grand is a boutique hotel/guest-house/conference centre set amongst the picturesque Grampians mountains. Rooms have ensuites some with spas, suiting the era of the guesthouse. Guests may serenely relax in three lounge areas with a book or DVD. An al fresco courtyard, upstairs balcony and a mezzanine sundeck offer alternative places to be served afternoon teas or enjoy fine wines & beers from the club bar. "The Balconies" Restaurant provides a Delightful Dining experience. Cool Jazz musicians feature Saturday nights.

Grampians - Wartook Valley

The Grelco Run *15 km W of Wartook*
Self Contained Luxury Cottages and Homestead B&B
Graeme & Liz McDonald
520 Schmidts Road
Brimpaen, Vic 3401

Tel (03) 5383 9221
Fax (03) 5383 9221
grelco@netconnect.com.au
www.grampiansgrelcorun.com

Double $143 Single $71.50
Children $27.50
Full breakfast provisions
Dinner $66
Homestead: Single $110, Double $220
includes full breakfast
Visa MC accepted
4 King/Twin 1 King 4 Queen 2 Twin 1 Single (5 bdrm)
Bathrooms: 4 Ensuite 2 Guest share

The Grelco Run offers 2 self contained cottages set apart in natural bush, sleeping 6 in each, and a luxuriously appointed homestead with 3 guest bedrooms each with an ensuite. By prior arrangement we serve elegant hosted dinners in a convivial atmosphere. Our son Cameron operates the renowned Grampians Horse Riding Centre with escorted tours from the property. As we are adjacent to the National Park there are superb opportunities for bushwalking, 4WD driving, fishing, viewing abundant wildlife and wild flowers and visiting all major scenic attractions and nearby wineries.

Grampians - Wartook

Wartook Gardens *29 km NW of Halls Gap*
B&B & Homestay
Royce & Jeanne Raleigh
2866 Northern Grampians Road
Wartook
Vic 3401

Tel (03) 5383 6200
Fax (03) 5383 6200
bookings@wartookgardens.com.au
www.grampiansnationalpark.com

Double $135-$160
Single $110-$120
Full breakfast
Dinner From $35
Visa MC accepted
1 King/Twin 2 Queen (3 bdrm)
Bathrooms: 1 Ensuite 2 Private

   AAA Tourism ★★★★

Just minutes from the Grampians National Park and set on 70 acres in the beautiful Wartook Valley famed for its mobs of kangaroos, Wartook Gardens offers elegant country living in a tranquil 5 acre garden of native and exotic plants and 118 bird species. Enjoy our delicious breakfast before visiting waterfalls, walks, wineries, lookouts, wildflower areas. Ceiling fans, air conditioning, saltwater pool, underfloor heating, wood heater, make your stay a very comfortable one - an all seasons destination. Enjoy friendly hospitality. Please phone.

Grampians

A spectacular area and one of the largest National Parks in Victoria, where you can see majestic waterfalls, rugged ranges and placid lakes and enjoy over 160 km of walking tracks.

There is a great diversity of vegetation - this is one of Australia's richest flora areas. The warmer northern and western sides of the Grampians are the best areas to view the wonderful wildflowers in the spring.

There are over 200 species of birds, large mobs of kangaroos. The area is also rich in Aboriginal culture including rock art sites.

Royce & Jeanne Raleigh
Wartook Gardens B&B

Heathcote
Once a gold mining region, Heathcote's new gold is Shiraz. Quickly becoming the Shiraz capital of Australia, winemakers and locals alike are keen to talk about the Cambrian soil and the big, beautiful red wines that come from grapes grown here.

Heathcote is surrounded by both National and State forests. Open-cut mining was popular in the 1850's, and its marks are still evident. Tread carefully through the forests and fossick if you like, as we're told there's still gold among the trees!
Leslye Thies
Emeu Inn B&B, Restaurant and Wine Centre

Heathcote - Goldfields

Emeu Inn Bed & Breakfast, Restaurant and Wine Centre *45 km SE of Bendigo*

Luxury B&B & Self Contained Cottage with mini kitchen
Fred & Leslye Thies
187 High Street
Heathcote, Vic 3523

Tel (03) 5433 2668
Fax (03) 5433 4022
info@emeuinn.com.au
www.emeuinn.com.au

Double $180-$270
Single $150-$220
Children $40
Continental breakfast
Dinner Two-courses $50 pp
Cottage $420/couple: two nights
Extra person $40/nt
Visa MC Diners Amex Eftpos JCB accepted

7 Queen (7 bdrm) Cottage sleeps four in queen-size bed and double sofa bed
Bathrooms: 6 Ensuite; Deluxe cottage with double spa and separate shower

Indulge yourself in luxury at the Award-winning Emeu Inn. Relax in the spacious suites with queen beds, private ensuites with spas or open fires and all the extras gourmet travellers expect. Dine in our Good Food Guide-recommended restaurant where international cuisine and local wines are standard fare. Our Wine Shop is stocked with local wines to take away! Enjoy some golf, Lake Eppalock, the forests, the shops or the wine! Part of the Goldfields, Heathcote's an easy weekend getaway!

Victoria

Heathcote - Goldfields

Hut on the Hill *120 km N of Melbourne*
Luxury Self Contained Rural Retreat
David & Astrid
720 Dairy Flat Road
Heathcote
Vic 3523

Tel (03) 5433 2329
bookings@hutonthehill.com
www.hutonthehill.com.au

Double $220-$250
Full breakfast provisions
You're the only guests in the property
Gift Vouchers available
Visa MC Diners Amex Eftpos accepted
1 King/Twin 1 Queen (2 bdrm)
Choice of King or Queen or both
Bathrooms: 1 Ensuite Spa bath
Separate shower & separate toilet

  AAA Tourism ★★★★☆

Enjoy MILLION DOLLAR VIEWS at HUT ON THE HILL from every room even the spabath, Heathcote's only 4 1/2 star luxury country farm stay self contained cottage. You're the ONLY guest, not another house in sight for miles on the horizon. Totally private, utterly unique, serenely beautiful. It's Heaven in Heathcote offering you secluded quiet. See eagles soar & kangaroos graze. Close to many wineries. Cosy fire in winter, Solar heated swimspa in summer. Deluxe packages available. Check website for more details.

Horsham

Orange Grove B&B *8 km NW of Horsham*
B&B & Self Contained Cottage
Graeme and Nola Hill
123 Keatings Road
Horsham
Vic 3401

Tel (03) 5382 0583
or 0427 536 346
Fax (03) 5382 7238
bookings@orangegrovebandb.com.au
www.orangegrovebandb.com.au

Double $150-$200
Single $100-$120
Full breakfast provisions
Pet-Friendly
Visa MC Amex Eftpos accepted
2 Queen 1 Twin (3 bdrm)
Bathrooms: 1 Private

Conveniently located approximately halfway between Melbourne and Adelaide, Orange Grove offers luxury accommodation in a restored historic mudbrick homestead (early 1900s) located on 25 acres just minutes drive from Horsham. Enjoy a relaxed friendly welcome to a spacious quiet country setting with renovated gardens for your pleasure. The whole cottage is available exclusively, and features an open living area with cooking facilities and lounge with open fire (air-conditioning in summer). There is also a private enclosed outdoor courtyard with BBQ facilities. Pets are welcome.

Lorne

La Perouse B&B *15 km W of Aireys Inlet*
Luxury B&B
Laurel & Sue
26A William Street
Lorne
Vic 3232

Tel 0418 534 422
email@laperouselorne.com.au
www.laperouselorne.com.au

Double $180-$250
Single $160-$225
Gourmet French breakfast
included in tariff
(we cater for gluten-free)
Visa MC Amex Eftpos accepted
1 King 3 Queen 2 Twin (4 bdrm)
Bathrooms: 4 Ensuite

AAA Tourism
★★★★

U nrivalled luxury in the heart of Lorne, La Perouse enjoys sensational views of the Great Ocean Road, known for its rugged coastline. All four suites host Victorian period features, whilst allowing you to enjoy modern day comforts including en-suite bathrooms. Breakfast is served Parisian style in our café. Discover the nearby restaurants, stroll along the beach or relax in front of the fire. Peaceful elegance, romance and attention to detail surround you. Let us pamper you with our own special brand of hospitality.

Lorne - Aireys Inlet

Lorneview B&B *14 km E of Lorne*
B&B & Separate Suite
Nola & Kevin Symes
677 Great Ocean Road
Eastern View
Vic 3231

Tel (03) 5289 6430
Fax (03) 5289 6735
lorneview@bigpond.com
www.lorneview.com.au

Double $130-$170
Single $120-$160
Continental breakfast
Visa MC accepted
2 Queen (2 bdrm)
Bathrooms: 2 Ensuite

AAA Tourism
★★★★☆

L orneview has two spacious guest rooms, separate from main house, one overlooking the ocean and the other overlooking the bush. Each room has QS bed, ensuite, TV, CD/DVD player, heating, air conditioning, refrigerator, iron, ironing board, tea and coffee facilities. Delicious breakfast of fresh fruit, homemade muesli, muffins and croissants is served in your room or on balcony overlooking beach. Dinner unavailable, but many excellent restaurants nearby. Barbecue and Games Room provided. Enjoy walks along the beach and go to sleep listening to the waves.

Lorne - Otway Ranges - Birregurra

Elliminook *38 km N of Lorne*
Luxury B&B & Heritage
Jill & Peter Falkiner
585 Warncoort Road
Birregurra
Vic 3242

Tel (03) 5236 2080
Fax (03) 5236 2423
enquiries@elliminook.com.au
www.elliminook.com.au

Double $160-$240
Single $140-$220
Full breakfast
Visa MC Diners Amex accepted
3 Queen 1 Double 3 Single (4 bdrm)
Bathrooms: 4 Ensuite
1 Spa Bathroom by arrangement

AAA Tourism
★★★★☆

InnHouse

Award winning Elliminook c1865 is a beautifully restored and decorated National Trust classified homestead providing a great relaxing getaway. Guests will enjoy the historic garden, croquet, boules, tennis court, open fires, liquor service, sumptuous cooked breakfast, fresh flowers in your room, and welcoming hospitality.

From Elliminook you can explore the Great Ocean Road, Twelve Apostles, Shipwreck Coast, Otway Fly Tree Top Walk, including Birregurra's historic walk, waterfalls and rain forest of the scenic Otway Ranges. For a unique accommodation experience be our welcome guest. "Guests enjoy the serenity of a flourishing garden and the grandeur or a magnificent historic home as seen in Australian House & Garden."

Macedon Ranges - Sunbury

Rupertswood Mansion *10 km N of Melbourne Airport*

Luxury B&B & Private Dinners, Functions, Conferences and Weddings
Margaret McLelland
3 Macedon Street
Sunbury, Vic 3429

Tel (03) 9740 5020
Fax (03) 9740 3686
info@rupertswood.com
www.rupertswood.com

Double $180-$495
Full breakfast
Dinner by arrangement
Visa MC Amex Eftpos accepted
11 Queen (11 bdrm)
Bathrooms: 11 Ensuite
Conferences, weedings and functions by arrangement

AAA Tourism
★★★★☆

Rupertswood is undoubtedly one of the most beautiful Victorian mansions in Australia. If you are a lover of heritage architecture then Rupertswood Mansion is something you must experience. The mansion offers exclusive accommodation in beautifully appointed rooms, all featuring exquisite antique furnishings, ensuites and heating/air conditioning. All accommodation tariffs include a Full Country Breakfast. Situated in Sunbury, the gateway to the Macedon Ranges, guests staying at Rupertswood will have the opportunity to explore the delights of the region by day and relax in the mansion at night.

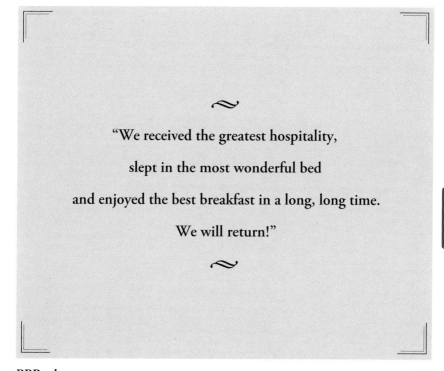

~

"We received the greatest hospitality,

slept in the most wonderful bed

and enjoyed the best breakfast in a long, long time.

We will return!"

~

Victoria

Villa Donati and CBD Apartment 401
2.5 km E of Melbourne CBD

B&B

Gayle Lamb & Trevor Finlayson
377 Church Street, Richmond, Vic 3121

AAA Tourism
★★★★☆

Tel (03) 9428 8104
or 0412 068 855
Fax (03) 9421 0956
email@villadonati.com
www.villadonati.com

Double $195-$225 Single $170 Full breakfast
CBD Apartment 401 from $220 per night
Visa MC Diners Amex Eftpos accepted
2 Queen 2 Double (4 bdrm)
Bathrooms: 4 Ensuite

Cool classic exterior, rich stylish interior - Villa Donati is a chic, inner city bed and breakfast. Previously home to distinguished architects, archbishops and the 'Moulin Rouge' massage parlour, Villa Donati has been restored to capture the essence of the European pensione. Today, this historic and charming property is a stunning mix of contemporary and antique design. Each of the en-suite bedrooms has its own unique style and furnishings - fine bed linen, imported toiletries, antiques and original art works. The guest sitting room offers city views and the café style breakfast room is the perfect place for indulgent breakfasts. Villa Donati is situated in cosmopolitan Richmond, only minutes from the CBD and Melbourne's main shopping, entertainment and sporting precincts.

From the Visitors' Book: Divine - everything!

Apartment 401 is a unique and stylish self contained Melbourne apartment enjoying a premier CBD location. Perfect for art lovers, foodies and shoppers, this stunning 1 bedroom apartment in the historic Majorca House Building is located right in the heart of Melbourne's bustling, bohemian arts precinct just one block from the Yarra river.

See it at www.apartment401.com.au

Melbourne - Brighton

Waratah Brighton Boutique B&B *12 km SW of Melbourne*
Luxury B&B
Brigitte & Harry Orth
70 Roslyn Street
Brighton
Vic 3186

Tel (03) 9592 0501
or 0419 596 300
Fax (03) 9592 0414
stay@waratahbrighton.com.au
www.waratahbrighton.com.au

Double $185-$275
Single $165-$195
Full breakfast
Visa MC accepted
3 Queen 1 Double (4 bdrm)
Bathrooms: 4 Ensuite

  AAA Tourism ★★★★☆   InnHouse

Waratah Brighton is a gracious relaxed 1880's period home set on a beautiful allotment with tranquil private garden, large swimming pool and Hydro Spa house. Facilities include a spacious formal guest sitting room with a large dining table, gas log fire place, high ceilings, chandeliers, decorated with a delightfully eclectic European Haute Bohemia style, lovingly created to provide a refreshingly out of the ordinary experience. An informal sitting room with open fire place, leather lounges and Foxtel TV leads to a sun shaded outdoor entertainment area. The centre of Waratah Brighton B&B is the open style kitchen where you can have a conversation with the hosts.

Melbourne - Camberwell

Springfields *9 km E of Melbourne*
B&B
Robyn & Phillip Jordan
4 Springfield Avenue
Camberwell
Vic 3124

Tel (03) 9809 1681
or 0434 353 750
Fax (03) 9809 1681
the.jordans@pacific.net.au
www.bbbook.com.au/springfields.html

Double $120
Single $80
Children welcome -
contact us for prices
Full breakfast
1 King/Twin 1 Twin (2 bdrm)
Bathrooms: 1 Guest share 1 Private
Guest bathroom is located between the two guest bedrooms

 AAA Tourism ★★★☆

"Springfields" is our attractive and spacious family home in a quiet avenue in one of Melbourne's finest suburbs. Guests comment on the quietness, and the fresh fruit salad at breakfast! Guests can enjoy the peace and privacy of their own lounge - or join us for a friendly chat. Public transport is nearby. Children are most welcome. Make our home your home when you next visit Melbourne.

Melbourne - Fairfield

Fairfield Guest House *5 km N of Melbourne*
B&B & Self Contained Apartment &
Guest House
Clare & Lindsay Nankivell
18 Station Street
Fairfield
Vic 3078

Tel (03) 9482 2959
or 0438 891 817
Fax (03) 9482 1956
fairfieldguesthouse@hotmail.com
www.babs.com.au/fairfield

Double $85-$180
Single $70-$160
Continental provisions
Visa MC Eftpos accepted
5 Queen 1 Twin 1 Single (7 bdrm)
Bathrooms: 3 Ensuite 2 Guest share
Double Spa in Self Contained Suite

 AAA Tourism ★★★★

Fairfield Guest House offers seven rooms ranging between rooms with shared bathroom facilities to rooms with private bathrooms and lovely self contained suite with double spa bath and all the comforts of home. We are only ten minutes from Melbourne CBD a short stroll to all public transport and the beautiful Fairfield Park Boathouse offering the best Devonshire Teas in Melbourne overlooking the Yarra River. We cater for all budgets and we are pet friendly for those that love travelling with their animals.

Melbourne - Richmond

Rotherwood *1.5 km E of Melbourne Central*
B&B & Self Contained Apartment
Flossie Sturzaker
13 Rotherwood Street
Richmond, Melbourne
Vic 3121

Tel (03) 9428 6758
Fax (03) 9428 6758
rotherwoodbb@bigpond.com
www.bbbook.com.au/rotherwood.html

Double $145-$185 Single $125-$175
Children additional
Special breakfast
S/C apt includes breakfast
Visa MC accepted
1 Queen (1 bdrm)
Separate Queen sized bedroom
Bathrooms: 1 Private

'On the Hill' in Richmond, 'Rotherwood' is at the heart of Melbourne's attractions. Walking distance of the MCG, Royal Botanic Gardens, National Tennis Centre, shops and cafés. 5 minute tram ride to City. Easy access to National Gallery, Concert Hall, Crown Casino, and Southbank. Private entrance to Victorian era apartment. Large sitting room leading to terraced garden. Bedroom, private bathroom, and separate dining room with cooking facilities. Special Breakfast provided. Extra fold-out bed. Airport transport available. TV and Wireless Internet. Short or long term stay.

Melbourne - St Kilda

Alrae Bed & Breakfast *5 km SE of Melbourne*
B&B
Vivienne Wheeler
7 Hughenden Road
St Kilda East, Vic 3183

Tel (03) 9527 2033
or 0409 174 132
Fax (03) 9527 2044
alrae2@bigpond.com
www.visitvictoria.com/alrae

Double $165-$205 Single $99-$121
Children $33 - $66
Special breakfast
Dinner $44 B/A
Spare sofa bed $66-$121
Visa MC Amex JCB accepted
1 Queen 1 Twin (2 bdrm) queen
bedroom. twin b/room
Bathrooms: 1 Ensuite 1 Private

Alrae, a well kept secret, is 5 km. from Melbourne CBD, handy public transport including daytime suburban airport shuttle bus, beach, shops, sports venues, restaurants and theatres. It features a Queen bedroom with ensuite, air-conditioning, fridge, private entrance. The Twin bedroom with a view has adjoining private bathroom with spa shower over bathtub, aircond. Air-conditioned guests' dining room cum lounge, specialty breakfasts and dietary variations. All rooms have TV/VCR, TV/DVD, clock radios, books etc. BBQ, OSP. Corporate, Seniors, Medical profession, Members Motor Organisations, Conditions apply.

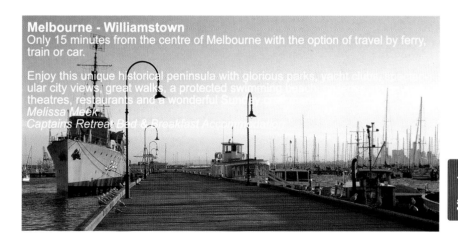

Melbourne - Williamstown
Only 15 minutes from the centre of Melbourne with the option of travel by ferry, train or car.

Enjoy this unique historical peninsula with glorious parks, yacht clubs, spectacular city views, great walks, a protected swimming beach, theatres, restaurants and a wonderful Sunday craft market.
Melissa Meek
Captains Retreat Bed & Breakfast Accommodation

Victoria

Melbourne - Williamstown

Captains Retreat B&B *In Williamstown*
Luxury B&B
Melissa Meek
2 Ferguson Street
Williamstown
Vic 3016

Tel (03) 9397 0352
or 0438 358 823
Fax (03) 9397 0352
captainsretreat@bigpond.com
www.captainsretreat.com.au

Double $145-$195
Full breakfast provisions
of cooked breakfast available
Elegant small functions by arrangement
Visa MC Diners Amex Eftpos accepted
1 King 4 Queen 1 Single (5 bdrm)
Bathrooms: 5 Ensuite 1 Private
3 ensuite with luxury double spa

Being just one door from the water, this
beautiful old recently refurbished,
Victorian, is in a fabulous location. This
charming house with it's somewhat chequered
history, including having been a nunnery and a
brothel!

Boasts very comfortable new beds and such
niceties as digital televisions in all rooms, and a
large guest lounge with fire and guest balcony.
Your choice of continental or cooked breakfasts
are served either in the downstairs kitchen or
up on the north facing rear deck. 'This is a
lovely place to just come and 'be'.

Mildura

Mildura's Linsley House *15 km E of Mildura at Trentham Cliffs*
B&B & Homestay
Colin & Desley Rankin
PO Box 959
Mildura
Vic 3502

Tel (03) 5024 8487
or 0417 593 483
Fax (03) 5024 8914
linsleybb@bigpond.com
www.innhouse.com/linsley.html

Double $110
Single $66
Full breakfast
Visa MC accepted
2 Queen 2 Single (3 bdrm)
Bathrooms: 2 Ensuite

Linsley House B&B has a magnificent river view. Colin and Desley Rankin take pleasure in welcoming you to their charming and tranquil home which is situated in a quiet rural setting and has panoramic views of the garden and Murray River from the bedrooms. The large lounge/dining area includes: full kitchen facilities, TV, fridge, woodfire, air-conditioning and comfortable antiques. Mildura is renown for its oranges, dried fruits, wineries and Mediterranean weather.

Mornington - Mount Eliza

Sartain's at Mornington *5 km SW of Mount Eliza & 5 km E of Mornington*
Luxury B&B & Self Contained
Cottage and Bungalow
Sally Sartain
75 Oakbank Road
Mount Eliza, Vic 3930

Tel (03) 5975 1014
Fax (03) 5975 1014
sally@sartains.com.au
www.sartains.com.au

Double $145-$190
Continental breakfast
Lunch & Dinner B/A
Cooked full breakfast $20 per couple
Double $145 Bungalow
Double $190 Cottage
Visa MC Eftpos accepted
2 Queen (2 bdrm)
1 Queen Cottage 1 Queen Bungalow
Bathrooms: 2 Private 1 Private The Cottage, 1 Private The Bungalow

AAA Tourism
★★★★

You are invited to share the Sartain's Experience. Stylishly renovated self-contained air-conditioned cottage and bungalow. First class facilities set in private gardens including tennis court with pavilion and excellent barbecue. Close to beaches, shops (5 minutes), golf and wineries. As much or as little as you would like to do. All set in a relaxing country atmosphere. Sartain's is licensed & can provide breakfast, lunch and evening meals. Prices from $145 per couple for bungalow or $190 per couple for cottage, per night.

BBBook.com.au

Victoria

Phillip Island - Cowes

Abaleigh on Lovers Walk *0.4 km E of Cowes PO*
Self Contained Apartment
Jenny & Robert Hudson
6 Roy Court
Cowes, Phillip Island,
Vic 3922

Tel (03) 5952 5649
Fax (03) 5952 2549
info@abaleigh.com
www.abaleigh.com

Double $180-$270
Single $170-$260
Full breakfast provisions
Apartment from $230 dble
Visa MC accepted
2 King/Twin1 King 2 Queen (5 bdrm)
Bathrooms: 5 Ensuite 5 Private spa

Abaleigh's FSC absolute beach frontage apartment and studios offer the finest accommodation. Featuring: spas, water views, Jetmaster log fires, double showers, breakfast-stocked kitchens, laundries, courtyards with barbecues for outdoor living, TV, DVD, stereo and more. Five minutes foreshore stroll to restaurants and central Cowes. Peaceful, private, ideal for couples or small groups of adults. Winner Best New Business, Best Hosted Accommodation Regional Tourism Awards. AAA ****1/2, "In one word perfect." J&M, Malvern.

Phillip Island - Cowes

Genesta House *0.3 km E of Post Office*
B&B & Guest House
18 Steele Street
Cowes
Vic 3922

Tel (03) 5952 3616
genesta@nex.net.au
genesta.com.au

Double $150-$160
Full breakfast
Visa MC Eftpos accepted
4 Queen (4 bdrm)
Own entrance and balcony
Bathrooms: 4 Ensuite

Historic guesthouse in the heart of Cowes, four houses from the beach and close to the main street with cafes and restaurants. Own entrance and balcony, outdoor spa, fully cooked English breakfast. Peaceful fountain and water feature in beautiful garden. Relax and unwind on the verandah.

Phillip Island - Cowes

Glen Isla House *0.15 km W of Cowes*
Luxury B&B & Hotel & Luxury
Country House B&B
Madeleine & Ian Baker
230-232 Church Street
Cowes, Vic 3922

Tel (03) 5952 1882 or (03) 5952 3000
Fax (03) 5952 5028
infobbb@glenisla.com
www.glenisla.com

Double $265-$395
Not suitable for children
Chef-prepared gourmet breakfast
Single Tariff POA
Visa MC Diners Amex Eftpos accepted
1 King 6 Queen 2 Twin (9 bdrm)
1 Heritage Suite 6 Glen Isla Rooms, 1 SC Cottage
Bathrooms: 7 Ensuite 1 Guest share Spa Bath in Anderson Suite

AAA Tourism ★★★★★ InnHouse

Set in the secluded heritage gardens of the historic Glen Isla homestead (c1870). Multi award- winning luxury country-house B&B offering elegant surroundings. Absolute privacy, 100 meters to the beach. "Arguably the island's best accommodation" - Melbourne Age. The historic Anderson Heritage Suite cottage with four-poster king bed, log fire, spa, period furnishings and HD TV+DVD system. Six purpose-architected Glen Isla "classic" rooms with walk-in robe/luggage room, private en-suite, LCD TV/DVD, superb garden vistas & separate entrances. Resident professional chefs, gourmet breakfast daily and private cellar.

Port Fairy

Cherry Plum Cottages B&B *2 km N of Port Fairy Central*
B&B & Self Contained Cottages
Ruth and Doug Maxwell
Albert Road
Port Fairy
Vic 3284

Tel (03) 5568 2595
Fax (03) 5568 2591
cherryplumcottages@bigpond.com
www.cherryplumcottages.com.au

Double $130-$280 Single $120-$160
Continental breakfast
Port Fairy has a good range of dining
choices for dinner
Visa MC accepted
2 Queen 1 Double (3 bdrm)
1 bedroom cottage and 2 bedroom cottage
Bathrooms: 1 Ensuite 1 Private bath

AAA Tourism ★★★★

On a quiet country lane in Port Fairy our cottages Cherry Plum and Arrondoon (c1862) are situated on four acres in a leafy garden amongst historic buildings. We deliver breakfast baskets to your cottage by request. Our accommodation features period furnishings, private entrance, guest sitting rooms, verandahs and off street parking. We are 3 mins by car (20 minutes walk) to the main street and well located to enjoy the town, restaurants, beaches, or trips to the 12 Apostles, regional wineries.

Princetown - Twelve Apostles

Arabella Country House *6 km E of Princetown*
Luxury B&B & Homestay
Lynne & Neil Boxshall
7219 Great Ocean Road
Princetown
Vic 3269

Tel (03) 5598 8169
Fax (03) 5598 8186
arabellacountryhse@bigpond.com
www.innhouse.com.au/arabella.html

Double $145-$160
Single $80
Children $25
Full breakfast
Dinner $15 - $30
Visa MC Eftpos accepted
3 Queen 1 Double 2 Single (4 bdrm)
Bathrooms: 4 Ensuite

   AAA Tourism ★★★★☆

A rabella Country House is situated within sight of 12 Apostles, Port Campbell N.P. and Otway N.P. All are must see attractions for visitors to Victoria. Our promise is that our superior B&B experience will add to our guests' adventure along the Great Ocean Road. With comfortable relaxing surroundings, quality fittings and the freshest food, plus local knowledge make special memories. Together with our dogs, we really enjoy our guests' visit and hope to see you soon.

Rutherglen

Ready Cottage *0.4 km N of PO*
B&B
Peter and Pauline Meade
92 High Street
Rutherglen
Vic 3685

Tel (02) 6032 7407
stay@readycottage.com.au
www.readycottage.com.au

Double $150-$165
Single $130-$145
Full breakfast
Visa MC accepted
3 Queen (3 bdrm)
Bathrooms: 3 Ensuite

AAA Tourism
★★★★

E nhance your visit to Rutherglen by staying at one of the town's original Victorian cottages. Ready Cottage blends stylish renovation with its old world charm and heritage. Enjoy traditional hosted Bed and Breakfast hospitality before setting out to explore the region's many attractions. After a day of wine tasting and touring, take time to relax in our private gardens before strolling to Main St to indulge yourself at the local restaurants, shops and hotels. All rooms include ensuites, queen size beds, TV and heating and cooling.

Rutherglen

Mount Ophir Estate *5 km SE of Rutherglen*
**B&B & Homestead and Self
Contained Cottages**
Ruth Hennessy
168 Stillards Lane
Rutherglen, Vic 3685

Tel (02) 6032 8920
mountophir@bigpond.com
www.mount-ophir.com.au

Double $190-$200
Special breakfast
Meals available on request
Rustic Function Centre
Accommodation only from $130 per couple
Visa MC accepted
6 Queen (6 bdrm)
Bathrooms: 4 Ensuite 1 Guest share

S tay a few days and enjoy your organic farm retreat at Mount Ophir Estate, a beautifully restored historic winery estate in the heart of Victoria's prime wine growing district. Choose B&B or Self Contained. The 1902 Homestead offers privacy, six comfortable bedrooms and a stunning country kitchen to indulge your cooking skills! The house is suitable for family groups and wedding parties as well as private retreats for couples. The self contained Gatehouse is a pleasant fully renovated 3 bathroom Victorian farm house accommodating up to 12. 'Muscat Place' accommodating 6 is also available. Mount Ophir Estate is a great place to view sunsets, stars while sipping a glass of Mount Ophir organic Shiraz!

Rutherglen
Rutherglen is known throughout Australia as a place with great soul and home to some of the world's greatest wines.

Rutherglen is also a place of country lanes, idyllic ancient River Red Gums and lush vineyards stretching. It's also a fantastic place for food and wine where the landscape and characters seem as one.
*Peter and Pauline Meade
Ready Cottage B&B*

Sorrento - Mornington Peninsula

Tamasha House *1 km E of Sorrento*
B&B
Naomi & Peter Nicholson
699 Melbourne Road
Sorrento
Vic 3943

Tel (03) 5984 2413
Fax (03) 5984 0452
tamasha@ozemail.com.au
www.peninsulapages.com/tamasha

Double $200
Single $120
Full breakfast
Dinner By arrangement
Visa MC Diners Amex JCB accepted
1 King/Twin 1 Double (2 bdrm)
Modern seaside decor with sittingroom
Bathrooms: 2 Ensuite

Tamasha House, set in a beautiful garden, is situated between Ocean and Bay beaches and is a short distance from historic Sorrento. An ideal place to stay while exploring the Mornington Peninsula. Take the ferry to Queenscliff or go swimming with the dolphins, visit the wineries or discover the galleries and restaurants, all within a short distance. Your caring hosts offer a warm welcome, fine food and local knowledge.

Swan Hill - Lake Boga

Burrabliss Farms B&B *2 km S of Murray Valley Highway*
B&B & Separate Suite
Tricia & Bruce Pollard
169 Lakeside Drive
Lake Boga, Vic 3584

Tel (03) 5037 2527
or 0427 346 942
info@burrabliss.com.au
www.burrabliss.com.au

Double $125-$180 Single $100-$150
Children $10
Country style breakfast included
Breakfast provisions in Villa
Dinner $40+
Visa MC Amex Eftpos JCB accepted
2 King/Twin1 King 2 Queen (5 bdrm)
1 suite, 1 villa, 2 traditional
Bathrooms: 3 Ensuite 1 Guest share

AAA Tourism
★★★★☆

After all you deserve it. Luxury accommodation at it's best - whether for your honeymoon, a romantic weekend or simply need to get away. Burrabliss is the idyllic location for a nature lover with 6 acres natural habitat. Suite Bliss offers stylish garden setting accommodation with king bed, spa, private lounge. Villa Bliss offers self contained. Traditional B&B also available. Enjoy yabbying, strolling through our country garden, exploring nearby wetlands with 68 bird species noted. Undercover BBQ facilities and car parking. Complimentary chocolates and wine. Burrabliss Farms offers complimentary guided tours of their Sharlea Ultra Fine Wool enterprise.

Torquay - Surf Coast

Ocean Manor B&B *17 km S of Geelong*
Luxury Self Contained Suite
Helen & Bob Bailey
3 Glengarry Drive
Torquay
Vic 3228

Tel (03) 5261 3441
or 0407 597 100
Fax (03) 5261 9140
oceanmanor@bigpond.com
www.bbbook.com.au/oceanmanorbb.html

Double $120-$180 Single $90-$100
Children $20
Extra adult $30
Continental breakfast
2 bedroom suite $130-$200
Visa MC Amex accepted
1 Queen 1 Twin (2 bdrm)
Bathrooms: 1 Ensuite 1 Guest share

AAA Tourism
★★★★☆

The 2 bedroom suite is situated upstairs to ensure privacy and take maximum advantage of the ocean view. The master bedroom features a queen sized bed, en suite bathroom. Adjoining is a combined lounge and dining area which leads onto a decked balcony with sweeping ocean views. The air conditioned lounge has Foxtel, TV and DVDs. The mini kitchen with fridge and microwave leads to a second bedroom with separate toilet facilities and 2 single beds. A continental breakfast is included.

Torquay
The Great Ocean Road is one of the major tourism icons in Australia. The Torquay Golf Club marks the official start of the Great Ocean Road and the Surf Coast region is home to some of the most spectacular scenery along this world renowned ocean drive including Bells Beach, the home of Australian surfing
Helen and Bob Bailey
Ocean Manor B&B

Victoria

Wangaratta

The Pelican *6 km E of Wangaratta*
B&B & Farmstay
Margaret & Bernie Blackshaw
606 Oxley Flats Road
Wangaratta
Vic 3678

Tel (03) 5727 3240
or 0413 082 758
pelicanblackshaw@hotmail.com
www.bbbook.com.au/thepelican.html

Double $120-$150 Single $75
Children $40
Full breakfast
Dinner $30 per person by arrangement
Extra person in double room $40
1 Queen 1 Twin 2 Single (3 bdrm)
Bathrooms: 1 Guest share 1 Private

AAA Tourism
★★★☆

The Pelican is a charming historic homestead set in parklike surroundings. Cattle and horses are raised on the 400 acres and early risers can go "trackside" to watch the harness horses at work. Guest rooms are in an upstairs wing of the home and have lovely country views where peacocks and pelicans are often spotted. The main bedroom has its own private balcony overlooking a lagoon fringed with giant red gums. Hearty breakfasts feature home grown produce and evening meals are available on request.

Warrnambool

Manor Gums *8 km NW of Warrnambool*
B&B & Separate Suite
Michael & Kittipat Esposito
170 Shadys Lane, Mailors Flat
Warrnambool
Vic 3275

Tel (03) 5565 4410
Fax (03) 5565 4409
Manorgums@bigpond.com
www.travel.to/manorgums

Double $135-$165 Single $120-$135
Children $20
Continental breakfast
Dinner $35+
Visa MC Eftpos accepted
3 Queen 1 Double (4 bdrm)
Bathrooms: 4 Ensuite
Ensuite with bath and spas available

AAA Tourism
★★★☆

Manor Gums is a quality and unique retreat surrounded by tall majestic gums and abundant birdlife. The distinctive architectural style and unique features offer couples luxury in private self contained suites, all designed to be different and capture the tranquillity of the bushland setting and views. Suites have fully equipped kitchenette, microwave, TV, VCR, CD player, climate control air conditioning. Some have a woodfire, balconies or large bath. A generous breakfast hamper is provided. Spa, sauna, gym and BBQ are available.

Warrnambool

Merton Manor Exclusive B&B *1 km N of Warrnambool PO*
Luxury B&B & Separate Suite
Pamela & Ivan Beechey
62 Ardlie Street
Warrnambool
Vic 3280

Tel (03) 5562 0720 or 0417 314 364
Fax (03) 5561 1220
merton@ansonic.com.au
members.datafast.net.au/merton

Double $150-$180
Single $130-$150
Full breakfast
Extra person $35
Visa MC Diners Amex
Eftpos JCB accepted
1 King/Twin 5 Queen 2 Single (6 bdrm)
Bathrooms: 6 Ensuite 6 double spas

AAA Tourism ★★★★☆ InnHouse

Merton Manor is a traditional B&B with mews style accommodation set within an historic Victorian villa. It features antiques, open fires, billiard and music rooms and grand dining room and is located mid way between Adelaide and Melbourne. All suites feature private entrances, climate control heating and air conditioning, private lounge rooms and ensuites with double spas. Merton Manor is situated close to the cultural attractions and restaurants of Warrnambool. The 12 Apostles, whale viewing, Tower Hill State Game Reserve and the Maritime Museum are all close by. AAAT 4 1/2 stars. Beach and Botanical Gardens nearby.

Warrnambool

Nestled in the heart of the rugged Great Ocean Road region and surrounded by a lush hinterland of rural landscapes, Warrnambool offers a delightful combination for the visitor. The city has an outstanding variety of accommodation, a large range of cafes and restaurants to tickle the tastebuds and an abundance of year round events and entertainment.

For more details pleasevisit www.warrnamboolinfo.com.au
Pamela Beechy
Merton Manor Exclusive B&B and Flagstaff Hill Maritime Village

Victoria

Warrnambool

Quamby Homestead *32 km N of Warrnambool*
B&B & Self Contained House
Julie & Karl Mischkulnig
3223 Caramut Road
Woolsthorpe
Vic 3276

Tel (03) 5569 2395
Fax (03) 5569 2244
quambyhomestead@bigpond.com
www.quambyhomestead.com.au

Double $140-$181.50 Single $121-$165
Children 3-12 $22, Baby cot provided FOC
Full breakfast
Dinner available by prior arrangement
Extra adult in Carriage House $33 each
Visa MC Diners Amex Eftpos JCB accepted
1 King 5 Queen 1 Twin 2 Single (8 bdrm)
Bathrooms: 7 Ensuite

Located just 20 mins inland from Great Ocean Road and Warrnambool, Quamby provides an ideal two night destination for exploring this fascinating region, which includes volcanic Tower Hill, historic Port Fairy and whale watching at Logan's Beach, Warrnambool, before travelling on to The Grampians, Ballarat Goldfields, Melbourne or Adelaide. Relax and enjoy local native wildlife (kangaroos, koalas, cockatoos, possums), watch cattle and horses graze in the paddocks, or take a stroll around the 2km property walk. Whatever your preference, come experience 'Quamby', Aboriginal for resting place.

Warrnambool - Allansford

Burnbrow Manor & Cottage *1 km N of Allansford*
B&B
Beverley & Robert Burns
1 Hopetoun Street
Allansford, Vic 3277

Tel (03) 5565 1380 or 0418 346 305
Fax (03) 5565 1380
stay@burnbrowmanor.com.au
www.burnbrowmanor.com.au

Double $130-$150 Single $110-$130
Children over the age of 5
Continental provisions
Dinner Vouchers for Allansford Hotel Bistro
Cottage 2-5 persons $130-$240
Extra person from $20 per night
Visa MC Eftpos accepted
2 Queen 1 Double 1 Twin 1 Single (4 bdrm)
Bathrooms: 2 Ensuite 1 Family share

Environmentally Friendly 4 Star Traditional Bed & Breakfast located at the western end of the Great Ocean Road (5 minutes east of Warrnambool). Upper floor dedicated to guests only, central guest lounge, kitchenette, dining area. All suites with en-suite or private bathroom facilities. 4 suites consist of: One queen suite with double spa, TV, DVD, Video. One queen suite with additional single bed, en-suite, large walk in robe, TV, DVD. Double Suite and Twin Suites, each with their own entrances with private bathroom facilities, also doubles as a Family Suite (maximum 4 persons).

Wilsons Promontory - Waratah North

Bayview House *16 km S of Foster*
B&B & Separate Suite
Ellen Fabel & Paul Greco
202 Soldiers Road
Waratah North
Vic 3959

Tel (03) 5687 1246
bayview@iprimus.com.au
www.bayviewhouse.com.au

Double $150-$190 Single $140-$180
Children under six months old free
Full breakfast
Extra person $30-$40
Specials for extended stays.
Visa MC Diners Amex
Eftpos JCB accepted
2 Queen 1 Double 1 Single (4 bdrm)
One 2 bedroom suite, two 1 bedroom suites
Bathrooms: 3 Ensuite

AAA Tourism
★★★★

B ayview House sits in three acres of gardens overlooking the magnificent Wilsons Promontory National Park, (one of the worlds oldest with its beaches, mountains and wilderness areas - only a fifteen minute drive away). We offer three private suites within our large house, 2 with kitchenettes, all with superb views and their own individual lounge areas. Breakfast is served in the main kitchen. Warm hospitality, pancakes, tranquillity, space, cleanliness, and good design have become our trademarks. We also speak Dutch, German, Swiss German and a little Cornish!

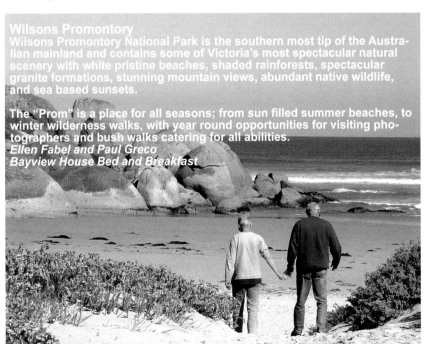

Wilsons Promontory
Wilsons Promontory National Park is the southern most tip of the Australian mainland and contains some of Victoria's most spectacular natural scenery with white pristine beaches, shaded rainforests, spectacular granite formations, stunning mountain views, abundant native wildlife, and sea based sunsets.

The "Prom" is a place for all seasons; from sun filled summer beaches, to winter wilderness walks, with year round opportunities for visiting photographers and bush walks catering for all abilities.
Ellen Fabel and Paul Greco
Bayview House Bed and Breakfast

Victoria

Yarra Valley - Dandenong Ranges

Holly Gate House Bed and Breakfast *5 km NE of Olinda*
Luxury B&B & Traditional
Loraine Potter
1308 Mt Dandenong Tourist Road
Kalorama
Vic 3766

Tel (03) 9728 3218
or 0415 192 690
Fax (03) 9728 3218
reception@hollygatehouse.com.au
www.hollygatehouse.com.au

Double $160-$225 Single $160-$185
Full breakfast included in price
Complimentary restaurant/function
venue transfer
Visa MC Eftpos accepted
3 Queen (3 bdrm)
Each room has a queen bed & private ensuite
Bathrooms: 3 Ensuite 1 ensuite with spa bath

  AAA Tourism ★★★★

Luxury adult retreat in the romantic Dandenong Ranges, the gateway to the Yarra Valley. Three beautifully appointed Queen bedrooms all with private ensuite (one with spa). Can accommodate up to six people. Package includes afternoon tea on arrival, fully cooked breakfast served in the guest's dining room. Sitting room with log fire. Outside pool in a pleasant garden setting. BBQ facilities. Complimentary transport to and from any local restaurant/function venue. Adult Retreat only/no pets. 45k from Melbourne. Melways Ref: Page52 J9.

Yarra Valley
Kalorama is set in the beautiful Dandenong Ranges near Olinda where you can visit all the local attractions the Dandenong Ranges has to offer, including art and craft markets, specialty gift and antique shops.

Wander through our picturesque walking trails and enjoy the wonderful surroundings such as, William Ricketts Sanctuary, Healesville Sanctuary, and Puffing Billy, plus various Yarra Valley Wineries. Indulge yourself with fine food and wine amongst the wide variety of local restaurants and cafes.
Loraine Potter

Yarra Valley - Healesville

AAA Tourism
★★★★☆

Myers Creek Cascades *4 km NE of Healesville*
Luxury Self-contained Cottages
Jan & James Allen
269 Myers Creek Road
Healesville
Vic 3777

Tel (03) 5962 3351 or 0407 960 678
jan@myerscreekcascades.com.au
www.myerscreekcascades.com.au

Double $265-$325
Continental provisions
4 luxury cottages
Visa MC Eftpos accepted
1 King (1 bdrm)
Stunning picture windows and French Doors
Bathrooms: 1 Ensuite

Welcome to Myers Creek Cascades . . . Your Special Place. Setting a new standard in self contained accommodation for couples. Luxury cottages in Healesville - the heart of the famous Yarra Valley. Step into your own private secluded hideaway and experience the ultimate bed & breakfast luxury as you start to unwind with a cup of plunger coffee or a herbal tea with our special nibblies provided for your enjoyment. If its chilly outside - don't worry, the cosy wood fire is set ready for you along with climate control airconditioning as a handy back up in your luxurious self contained bed & breakfast cottage! Enjoy panoramic views of breathtaking rainforest as you indulge yourselves in the deluxe oval spa, perfect for romantic couples. Awake to the sounds of the rainforest and enjoy a sumptuous gourmet breakfast hamper as you contemplate the many options that Healesville and the Yarra Valley have to offer... but the truth is, you'll want to stay in the luxury of your own romantic hideaway.

Yarra Valley - Yarra Glen

The Gatehouse at Villa Raedward *7 km S of Yarra Glen*

**Luxury B&B & Self Contained
Apartment & Self Contained Unit**
John & Sandra Annison
26 Melba Highway
Yering
Vic 3770

Tel (03) 9739 0822
or 0425 730 624
info@villaraedward.com.au
www.villaraedward.com.au

Double $210-$250
Single $210-$250
Full breakfast provisions
Visa MC Amex Eftpos accepted
1 Queen (2 bdrm)
Large, comfortable bedroom
Bathrooms: 2 Private
2 person spa, large shower in marble bathroom

AAA Tourism
★★★★☆

Two architect-designed fully self contained units with undercover parking and private entrance and patio looking out over the Yarra Valley. Marble bathroom with large shower and two person spa overlooking a private courtyard garden. Fully equipped kitchen, reverse cycle air conditioning, DVD/TV. Complimentary bottle of Yarra Valley Bubbly, slippers, bathrobes, port, fresh coffee, sumptuous 3 course breakfast provisions, DVD library.

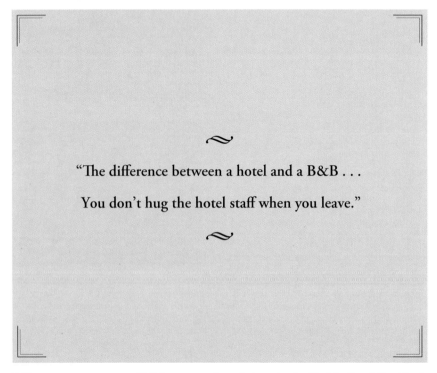

"The difference between a hotel and a B&B . . .

You don't hug the hotel staff when you leave."

Tell hosts you found them in the Bed & Breakfast Book

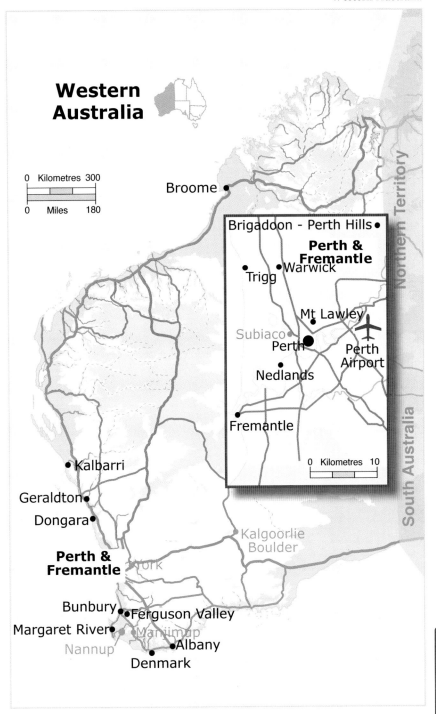

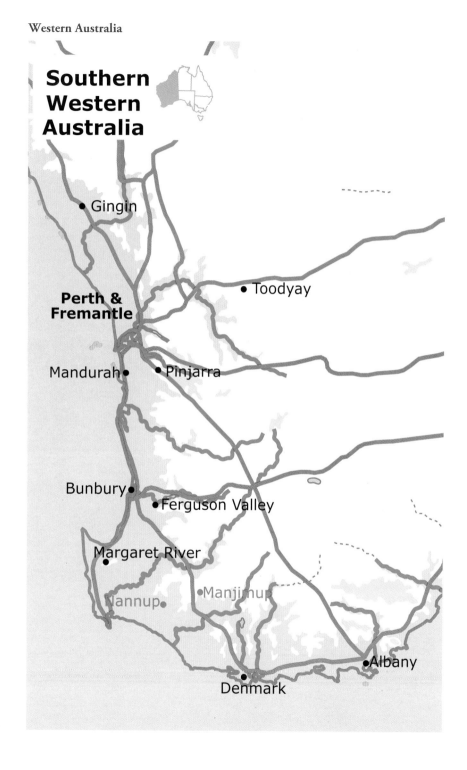

Southern Western Australia

Gingin

Toodyay

Perth & Fremantle

Mandurah • Pinjarra

Bunbury • Ferguson Valley

Margaret River

Nannup • Manjimup

Albany

Denmark

Albany

Albany View St Lodge B&B/Art Studio *1 km W of Town Hall*
B&B
Lew and Margaret Dowdell
35 View Street
Albany
WA 6330

Tel (08) 9842 8820
or 0427 428 820
Fax (08) 9842 8820
stay@albanyviewstbb.com.au
www.albanyviewstbb.com.au

Double $115-$130
Single $95-$105
Full breakfast
Discount for longer stays
Visa MC Eftpos accepted
3 Queen 1 Single (3 bdrm)
Suite 1 has a queen & single bed
Bathrooms: 3 Ensuite

AAA Tourism
★★★★

Lew & Margaret welcome you to our lovely B&B. Reception is part of Margaret's Art Studio & Gallery. We offer quality accommodation just a short walk to shops, restaurants etc. We have 3 suites (2 with kitchenette-no cooker), fridge, microwave, tea/coffee making, TV, DVD, quality linen, crockery etc. Relax & enjoy breakfast upstairs with beautiful views of the harbour. Lovely gardens at rear with covered patio and BBQ. Guests are welcome to use our laundry. Off street parking and separate guest entrance.

Albany

Situated on Princess Royal Harbour and King George Sound, Albany is Western Australia's oldest town. Albany's spectacular rugged coastline is unique in its own way. Located around Frenchman's Bay are the Natural Bridge and the Gap and Blow Holes.

You can see all the history of a bygone era and explore the Cheynes IV, one of the last whaling ships at the old Whaling Station, which is now a recognised whaling museum.

Historical old Albany Town has many Heritage listed buildings, like the old Goal and Courthouse. Just out of town is Mt Clarence, which features the Old Forts and the Light Horse Memorial to the soldiers and horses departing for Gallipolli. There are many local wineries, beautiful beaches and a scenic whale walk around King George sound which joins the Bibbulmun Track.

Betty Ramsell

Western Australia

Brigadoon-Perth Hills

Stocks Country Retreat *10 km N of Guildford/Midland*
Luxury B&B
Lyn & Gordon Straiton
26 Boulonnais Drive
Brigadoon
WA 6069

Tel (08) 9296 1945
Fax (08) 9296 1945
retreat2stocks@bigpond.com
www.stockscountryretreat.com

Double $175-$225
Full breakfast
Dinner A La Carte
Late check-out fee
Helipad landing fee
Visa MC Eftpos accepted
3 King (3 bdrm)
Bathrooms: 3 Ensuite, each has double spa & shower

Looking for somewhere special to take a break? Only 35mins from Perth City, this romantic 4½ star Tudor country house, former home of Hank B Marvin of the Shadows is sure to impress, with its king 4 poster beds & gourmet breakfasts. The property sits on the edge of the Darling Scarp surrounded by breathtaking views, overlooking the Swan Valley. Unwind in a double spa with a complimentary bottle of bubbly. Take a stroll to explore the beauty of Brigadoon with kangaroos grazing while eagles soar above.

Broome

BroomeTown B&B *In Broome*
Luxury B&B
Toni & Richard Bourne
15 Stewart Street
Broome
WA 6725

Tel (08) 9192 2006
or 0429 010 161
Fax (08) 9193 7626
info@broometown.com.au
www.broometown.com.au

Double $235-$350
Single $220-$330
Full breakfast
Visa MC Eftpos accepted
1 King/Twin 2 Queen (3 bdrm)
Bathrooms: 3 Ensuite Separate toilet

BroomeTown B&B has been built with your complete enjoyment in mind. Unwind and appreciate this unique Kimberley town from the comfort of this beautiful retreat situated close to 'Chinatown' and a short walk to many local attractions. We welcome you to enjoy warm hospitality, friendly service and touring advice in the appealing atmosphere of BroomeTown.

Bunbury

Colomberie B&B *7 km S of Bunbury*
B&B
Sandra & Edward Pigott
11 Duffield Place
Sleaford Park, Bunbury
WA 6230

Tel (08) 9795 7734 or 0417 913 398
Fax (08) 9795 7735
sp1@iinet.net.au
www.colomberie.com.au

Double $85-$110 Single $75-$85
Children on application by age
Continental provisions
Dinner by arrangement
Season rates apply Nov-Apr
1 Queen 1 Double 2 Single (2 bdrm)
Bathrooms: 2 Ensuite
Bath available by arrangement

AAA Tourism
★★★☆

Colomberie B&B is an ideal location between Perth and the south-west. Two ensuite bedrooms with extra fold-out beds available. Guests' kitchenette and living/dining. Within easy driving distance of Capes and Margaret River regions with wineries, olive, lavender and berry farms, and of course, the many Busselton and Bunbury attractions including golf and swimming with dolphins. Non-smoking, children welcome, but the property is not suitable for children under five years. House is on one acre in a cul-de-sac surrounded by bushland and a beautiful garden.

Dongara

Elaine Summers
Gracelyn B&B

Dongara - Geraldton

Gracelyn B&B *0.8 km NW of Dongara PO*
B&B
Elaine Summers
6 Delmage Street
Dongara
WA 6525

Tel (08) 9927 1938
or 0409 414 698
info@gracelynbedandbreakfast.com.au
www.gracelynbedandbreakfast.com.au

Double $80-$100
Single $70-$90
Children 50%
Continental breakfast
$10 extra pp for cooked breakfast
Stay 5 nights get the next 2 free
1 Queen 2 Twin (3 bdrm)
Bathrooms: 1 Guest share

Home away from Home at Gracelyn Bed & Breakfast. Enjoy the swimming pool and outdoor living with gas BBQ, wood fire & electric blankets. Your own full size fridge, tea & coffee facilities television and pool table. Laundry facilities. Walk to shops and beach or river trails to ocean. Good choice of restaurants to enjoy Dongara's famous Rock Lobsters. Try our 18 scenic hole golf links with grass greens to rival any. Ideal base for day trips to Geraldton or to view spring wild flowers.

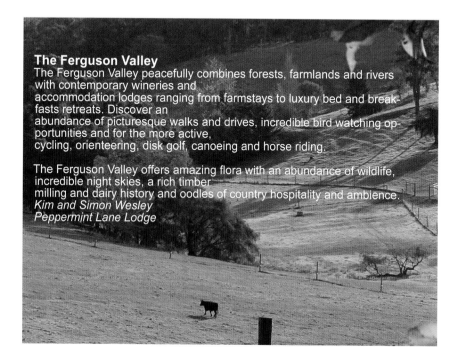

The Ferguson Valley
The Ferguson Valley peacefully combines forests, farmlands and rivers with contemporary wineries and
accommodation lodges ranging from farmstays to luxury bed and breakfasts retreats. Discover an
abundance of picturesque walks and drives, incredible bird watching opportunities and for the more active,
cycling, orienteering, disk golf, canoeing and horse riding.

The Ferguson Valley offers amazing flora with an abundance of wildlife, incredible night skies, a rich timber
milling and dairy history and oodles of country hospitality and ambience.
Kim and Simon Wesley
Peppermint Lane Lodge

Ferguson Valley - Bunbury

Peppermint Lane Lodge *20 km E of Bunbury*
Luxury B&B
Kim & Simon Wesley
351 Wellington Mill Road
Wellington Mill
WA 6236

Tel (08) 9728 3138
peppermintlanelodge@iinet.net.au
www.peppermintlanelodge.com.au

Double $240-$275
Single $180-$190
Full breakfast
Dinner $90 pp
Visa MC accepted
1 King/Twin 1 King
2 Queen 1 Single (4 bdrm)
Bathrooms: 4 Ensuite Spa

Secretly and superbly located, Peppermint Lane Lodge is the ideal place to spend some time away from city life. Our four suites offer wonderful well appointed accommodation. All rooms have ensuites with double doors opening to a terrace. Soak in the sunshine around the pool and spa or enjoy drinks and aperitifs around the pot belly on the cooler Valley evenings.

Ideally placed to explore the Ferguson Valley and Geographe wine region, close to beaches and only 2 hours from Perth. Fully licensed with an excellent cellar. Dinner is available on request.

Western Australia

Fremantle

Terrace Central B&B *12 km S of Perth*
B&B & Hotel
Barry White
79-85 South Terrace
Fremantle
WA 6160

Tel (08) 9335 6600
or 0428 969 859
Fax (08) 93367600
info@terracecentral.com.au
www.terracecentral.com.au

AAA Tourism
★★★★

Double $155-$165
Single $145-$165
Children $20
Continental breakfast
Saturday night only, extra $22
Visa MC Diners Amex Eftpos JCB accepted
10 Queen 6 Double 2 Twin 2 Single (18 bdrm)
Large Air-conditioned Ensuite
Bathrooms: 16 Ensuite

Heritage house in the city centre of Fremantle with 10 huge air-conditioned en-suite bedrooms and 4 apartments.

Close to rail and bus service. 3 minutes walk to Markets, shops. Close to all tourist attractions and ferry to Rottnest Island.

All rooms air-conditioned, en-suite bathroom. Free wireless broadband, TV & DVD Player, tea and coffee, fridge. Free parking.

Gingin - Muckenburra

Amirage Restaurant and B&B *20 km W of Gingin*

Luxury B&B
June Reith
1654 Gingin Brook Road
Gingin West
WA 6503

Tel (08) 9575 7646 or 0411 277 500
amiragerestbb@activ8.net.au
www.amiragerestaurantbb.com.au

Double $130 Single $115
Children $10
Full breakfast
Weekly stay negotiable
Visa MC Eftpos accepted
2 Queen (2 bdrm) Cosy bedrooms
Fold up bed available
Bathrooms: 1 Guest share

Only one hour north of Perth CBD there is Australian animal and birdlife a plenty to be experienced in 2.3 acres of wonderful gardens - from our relaxing 6 seater outdoor heated spa or from the windows of your cosy bedroom. Watch peacocks strutting about or pet and pat our animals, which are extremely friendly and therapeutic. Enjoy al fresco dining in our restaurant overlooking the gardens, which specialises in aged, grain-fed marbleised steak. Two comfortable rooms include electric blankets, television and DVD and use of a bar fridge. We are close to the Gravity Centre and The Chittering Valley Wine Trail.

Gingin
Gingin is a quaint historical township surrounded by picturesque farmland which is home to a veritable picnic hamper of fresh produce. In the Gingin town centre where you'll find a patch work of gardens, historical buildings and winding streets. This township is one of Western Australia's oldest and retains much of its historical charm, with heritage buildings, a character pub and a delightful rural atmosphere reminiscent of yesteryear.
Gingin Coast Tourism Association

Kalbarri

Gecko Lodge *0.3 km SW of Kalbarri*
Luxury B&B
Sharyn & Graham Geikie
9 Glass Street
Kalbarri
WA 6536

Tel (08) 9937 1900 or (08) 9937 1922
0439 968 305
Fax (08) 9937 1899
stay@geckolodgekalbarri.com.au
www.geckolodgekalbarri.com.au

Double $200-$250 Single $160
Full breakfast
Seasonal tariffs
Discounts for extended stays
Visa MC Eftpos accepted
1 King 3 Queen (4 bdrm)
Airconditioned with Ensuite
Bathrooms: 4 Ensuite 2 Spa Suites

Gecko Lodge is a luxury, romantically appointed purpose built Bed & Breakfast Lodge designed for couples. Located only a stone's throw from the beach, river mouth, shops and cafes, Gecko Lodge provides an ideal base from which to explore Kalbarri's attractions (yet benefits from total seclusion and privacy). Enjoy well appointed ensuite rooms (2 with spas, 2 with double showers), afternoon tea and evening Port and chocolates. Enjoy our high standards of service and comfort in this beautiful part of the world.

Mandurah - North Yunderup

Nautica Lodge *9 km E of Mandurah*
Luxury B&B
Glenda & Roger Lingard
203 Culeenup Road
North Yunderup
WA 6208

Tel (08) 9537 8000
or 0419 944 627
nautica@istnet.net.au
www.nauticalodge.com

Double $100-$150
Continental breakfast
Visa MC accepted
1 King/Twin1 King 1 Queen 3 Single
(2 bdrm) Luxury air-con suites with
LCD TV, en-suite and WIR
Bathrooms: 2 Ensuite

Situated in a unique and idyllic riverfront location on the beautiful Murray River 10 mins east of Mandurah. You can sit back on your terrace and appreciate an arm chair view of the river through the gum trees. It is an ideal place to relax while on holiday or unwind and/or entertain if on business. An exclusive guest lounge, dining, kitchenette and terrace overlook the river. The lounge has Internet, plasma HD TV, DVD, wine cellar, refrigerator, microwave, toaster and 24/7 tea & coffee.

Mandurah - Peel Region

Port Mandurah Canal B&B *1 km W of CBD*
Luxury B&B
Una Hird
3 Reverie Mews
Mandurah
WA 6210

Tel (08) 9535 2252
or 0438 444 707
uhird@iprimus.com.au
www.babs.com.au/portmandurah

Double $100-$170
Single $100-$140
Full breakfast
Long Stay Specials
2 Queen (2 bdrm)
Bathrooms: 2 Ensuite
Spa in Master Bedroom

Situated on the canals of Port Mandurah, Port Mandurah Canal Bed & Breakfast is the perfect place for a weekend get-away or that long hard earned break. Relax in a home away from home atmosphere and enjoy pure relaxation or hidden romance. Our luxury retreat offers twoair conditioned suites with private facilities, including lounge room and balcony in beautiful surroundings overlooking the waters of Mandurah's famous canals. Dolphins are regular visitors to the canals. Catch your crabs from your own jetty. Walk to beaches. Mandurah's stunning waterfront which is full of Restaurants and Cafes, is just minutes away. Will pick up from station.

Mandurah & Peel

The Peel region is so diverse, that it pleases even the most discerning visitor. There are water sports of all kinds, estuary & canal cruises, dolphin encounters, surfing, sailing, canoeing, boat & fishing charters and crabbing.

For the energetic there are walking and bike tracks, abseiling, sky diving, white water rafting, horse riding. For quieter activities there are tram rides, historic tours, golfing, wine tasting, live shows, theatre, animal parks, festivals, gardens & heritage tearooms, restaurants, aboriginal culture, arts & crafts and markets.
Una Hird
Port Mandurah Canal B&B

Margaret River

Rosewood Guesthouse *1 km W of*
Post Office
Luxury B&B & Separate Suite
Jane & Keith Purdie
54 Wallcliffe Road
Margaret River
WA 6285

Tel (08) 9757 2845 or 0427 772 911
Fax (08) 9757 3509
info@rosewoodguesthouse.com.au
www.rosewoodguesthouse.com.au

Double $189-$225 Single $179-$225
Special breakfast
Suite $220-$250 double
Extra guests from $49 Max 4
Visa MC Amex Eftpos accepted
2 King/Twin 4 King 1 Queen (6 bdrm)
5 B&B plus 1 spa suite
Bathrooms: 6 Ensuite
Suite has 2 person spa bath

 AAA Tourism ★★★★☆

Winner of 2007 WA Tourism Award for Hosted Accommodation - Rosewood Guesthouse maintains fabulous standards in providing a warm & friendly atmosphere, welcoming guests from all parts of the globe. Beautifully appointed en-suite rooms, log fire in the lounge with complimentary port, Rosewood breakfasts feature fantastic local produce. Just a 700 metre walk to the main street, 4 minute drive to wineries, Rosewood is the ideal base to explore the region and Jane & Keith will be happy to help plan your itinerary.

~

Please tell your hosts,

When making an enquiry or booking,

"We saw you in *The Bed & Breakfast Book*!"

~

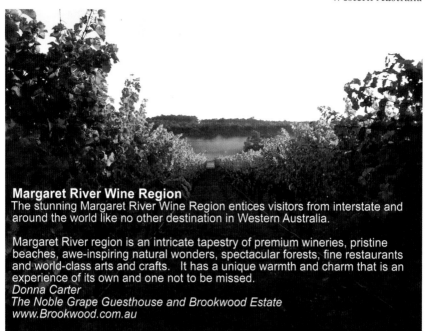

Margaret River Wine Region
The stunning Margaret River Wine Region entices visitors from interstate and around the world like no other destination in Western Australia.

Margaret River region is an intricate tapestry of premium wineries, pristine beaches, awe-inspiring natural wonders, spectacular forests, fine restaurants and world-class arts and crafts. It has a unique warmth and charm that is an experience of its own and one not to be missed.
Donna Carter
The Noble Grape Guesthouse and Brookwood Estate
www.Brookwood.com.au

Margaret River

The Noble Grape *12 km N of Margaret River*
Luxury B&B & Guest House
Rodney & Donna Carter
Lot 18, Bussell Highway
Cowaramup
WA 6284

Tel (08) 9755 5538
or 0418 931 721
Fax (08) 9755 5538
stay@noblegrape.com.au
www.noblegrape.com.au

Double $135-$180 Single $120-$150
Children $25
Continental breakfast
Extra adult $25
Visa MC Amex Eftpos accepted
1 King/Twin 2 King 4 Queen 2 Single (6 bdrm)
Bathrooms: 6 Ensuite

AAA Tourism
★★★★☆

The Noble Grape is an intimate Guesthouse in the heart of the Margaret River Wine Region. Colonial style charm with quaint antiques nestled in an English cottage garden. Vineyards, beaches, galleries, chocolate and cheese factories minutes away. Enjoy a leisurely breakfast in our dining room overlooking the garden while watching the native birdlife. Spacious country style rooms with ensuite & hairdryer, r.c. air-conditioning, TV, DVD, refrigerator, tea/coffee, comfortable arm chairs and private courtyard. Guest barbecue. Wireless Internet Access. Room with universal access. Smoking outside only.

Perth

Pension of Perth *1 km N of Perth*
B&B
Hoon & Steve Hall
3 Throssell Street
Perth
WA 6000

Tel (08) 9228 9049
or 0421 739 443
Fax (08) 9228 9290
stay@pensionperth.com.au
www.pensionperth.com.au

Double $150
Single $120
Children by arrangement
Full breakfast
Extra person $30
Discounts for long stays
Visa MC Eftpos accepted
2 King 2 Queen (5 bdrm) 1 family room
Bathrooms: 4 Ensuite 1 Private

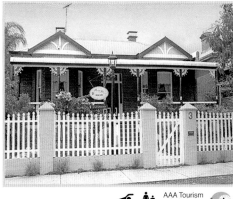

AAA Tourism
★★★★

The Pension of Perth is the perfect choice for couples looking for a special place to stay or business travellers wanting somewhere that is value for money, sophisticated, homely and private. It has the amenities of a fine hotel. The luxurious refurbishment reflects the elegance and comfort of its origins in 1897. It overlooks Hyde Park. Within walking distance from the centre of Perth. Our A-la-carte breakfast menu will make your stay memorable.

Perth - Mt Lawley

Durack House Bed and Breakfast *3 km N of Perth*
Luxury B&B
Sandra and Bill Durack
7 Almondbury Road
Mt Lawley Perth
WA 6050

Tel (08) 9370 4305
Fax (08) 9371 2508
durackhouse@westnet.com.au
www.durackhouse.com.au

Double $150-$180
Single $130-$150
Special breakfast
Visa MC accepted
1 King/Twin 2 Queen (3 bdrm)
Bathrooms: 3 Ensuite

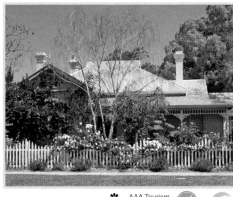

AAA Tourism
★★★★

Durack House is an Edwardian home in quiet, leafy suburb, only 300m from bus/train and 3km from City. R/C air-conditioning, TVs, DVDs, electric blankets, hairdryers, comfortable beds and a cosy sitting room exclusive to guests. Relax in lush gardens after a busy day. Enjoy a complimentary drink each evening in the open courtyard. Sightseeing, shopping, beautiful Swan River and Kings Park within easy reach. The vibrant café strip on Beaufort Street is within walking distance, with an excellent selection of fine dining and affordable restaurants.

Perth - Nedlands

Caesia House Nedlands *5 km W of Perth Central City*
B&B & Homestay & Self Contained Apartment
Jane & David Tucker
32 Thomas Street
Nedlands, Perth
WA 6009

Tel (08) 9389 8174
or 1800 008 206
Fax (08) 9389 8173
tuckers@iinet.net.au
www.caesiahouse.com

Double $145-$180 Single $140-$175
Breakfast by arrangement
Visa MC accepted
1 King/Twin1 King (1 bdrm)
Relax in your room overlooking the garden
Bathrooms: 1 Ensuite

A quiet serene oasis in the city, only 7 minutes from Perth city centre and Kings Park, within walking distance to numerous cafes, or wonderful riverside BBQ/picnic spots. Close to UWA, Sir Charles Gardiner and Hollywood Hospitals bus to historic Fremantle, and beaches or Perth City centre. Convenient base for tours to scenic Rottnest Island, savour those wines in the Swan Valley or wildflowers in Hills. Offstreet parking, groundfloor apartment including spacious ensuite bedroom with garden outlook, lounge area and dining/kitchen. BBQ and outdoor area.

Perth
Perth, the capital of the West, embraced by tree clad hills and golden beaches.

Take a ferry down the Swan River to Fremantle, our historic port. Continue to Rottnest Island and enjoy a swim in a magnificent peaceful bay; watch for whales, dolphins or cycle around the island and meet the quokkas. Visit the Swan Valley vineyards for wines, cheeses and other fresh products or wander into the hills to experience the wildflowers.
Jane Tucker
Caesia House.

Western Australia

Perth - Trigg - Scarborough - North Beach

Trigg Retreat Bed and Breakfast *15 km N of Perth*
B&B
Sue Stein
59 Kitchener Street
Trigg
WA 6029

Tel (08) 9447 6726
or 0417 911 048
Fax (08) 9447 6525
sue@triggretreat.com
www.triggretreat.com

Double $150-$180
Single $130-$160
Gourmet continental breakfast
Visa MC Eftpos accepted
1 King/Twin 3 Queen (4 bdrm)
Bathrooms: 4 Ensuite

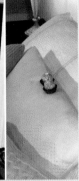

AAA Tourism
★★★★☆

An affordable indulgence! 4¹/₂ star tastefully furnished two-storey home. Four bedrooms with ensuite, A/C, luxurious queen or twin beds, TV, DVD, fridge, tea/coffee, free broadband wireless access, bedside treats. A gourmet, continental breakfast, served in guest dining room or garden courtyard. Optional hot selection available from enticing menu. A computer and unlimited access to the internet provided free. 'Stroll to the beach', exquisite WA coastline, walking, riding paths and cafes. Airport - 30 min direct route. Guest and owners facilities are separate. Prepare to be pampered!

Pinjarra – Peel Region
Located 86 km south of Perth on the banks of the Murray River, in the Peel Region. Pinjarra is a small historic town which lies only a few kilometres from the substantial coastal centres of Mandurah and Rockingham. Established in 1834, Pinjarra is one of the oldest towns in Western Australia and has many interesting historic sights to see.
Liz Nicholas
Lazy River Boutique B&B and Pinjarra Visitor Centre

Pinjarra - Peel Region

Lazy River Boutique Bed & Breakfast *1 km W of Pinjarra*
Luxury B&B
Liz and Steve Nicholas
34 Wilson Road
Pinjarra
WA 6208

Tel (08) 9531 4550
or 0417 922 457
unwind@lazyriver.com.au
www.lazyriver.com.au

Double up to $350
Single up to $300
Full breakfast
Visa MC Eftpos accepted
1 King/Twin 3 Queen (4 bdrm)
Luxury suites opening onto big
verandahs with great views
Bathrooms: 4 Ensuite

    AAA Tourism ★★★★☆

Lazy River is a hideaway luxury boutique hotel in Pinjarra, just one hour South of Perth. This 4.5 star gourmet paradise, which is set apart from the hosts homestead, offers 4 spacious spa suites with big verandahs. We emphasise exquisite cuisine, with dinners prepared by Steve, a Swiss trained chef, and served in your suite. All this set in 5 acres of landscaped gardens on the Murray River. Activities include tennis, fishing, kayaking and croquet. Massages can be arranged by appointment.

Toodyay - Avon Valley

Pecan Hill B&B *4 km W of Toodyay*
B&B
Craig & Suzanne Lomax
Lot 59 Beaufort Street
Toodyay
WA 6566

Tel (08) 9574 2636 or 1300 766 721
Fax (08) 9574 2367
info@pecanhill.com.au
www.pecanhill.com.au

Double $105-$115
Continental breakfast
Dinner $25 pp by arrangement
Full breakfast additional $12 pp
1 King/Twin 3 Queen (4 bdrm)
Bathrooms: 4 Ensuite
Visa MC Diners Amex Eftpos JCB accepted

 AAA Tourism ★★★★

Pecan Hill offers a true country experience with peace and tranquillity. Four tastefully furnished rooms with ensuites look out into natural woodland filled with native birds, Alpacas and Sheep. All have glass sliding doors that access the wide verandah, carpet, reverse cycle air-conditioning, overhead fan, electric blankets and tea/coffee making facilities. The large comfortable guest lounge has TV/VCR/DVD, piano, library, log fire and air-conditioning. The pool is surrounded by gardens, paved areas and a pergola. As an adults retreat we do not cater for children or pets. Your hosts Craig and Suzanne Lomax (and Buster the cat) look forward to the pleasure of your company soon.

Index by Location

Index by Name of Accomodation

M

N

O

P

Q

R

21st Edition 2009